WARREN BUFFETT

INSIDE THE ULTIMATE
MONEY MIND

ROBERT G. HAGSTROM

WILEY

Published by John Wiley & Sons, Inc., Hoboken, New Jersey.
Published simultaneously in Canada.

For general information on our other products and services or for technical support, please
contact our Customer Care Department within the United States at (800) 762-2974, outside the
United States at (317) 572-3993 or fax (317) 572-4002.

Wiley also publishes its books in a variety of electronic formats. Some content that appears in print
may not be available in electronic formats. For more information about Wiley products, visit our
web site at www.wiley.com.

Library of Congress Cataloging-in-Publication Data

Names: Hagstrom, Robert G., 1956- author. | John Wiley & Sons, Ltd.,
  publisher.
Title: Warren Buffett : inside the ultimate money mind / Robert G.
  Hagstrom.
Description: Hoboken, New Jersey : Wiley, [2023] | Includes index.
Identifiers: LCCN 2020055833 (print) | LCCN 2020055834 (ebook) | ISBN
  9781119714590 (hardback) | ISBN 9781394168446 (paperback) | ISBN
  9781119714637 (adobe pdf) | ISBN 9781119714644 (epub)
Subjects: LCSH: Buffett, Warren–Philosophy. | Buffett, Warren–Anecdotes.
  | Investments.
Classification: LCC HG172.B84 H34 2021 (print) | LCC HG172.B84 (ebook) |
  DDC 332.6–dc23
LC record available at https://lccn.loc.gov/2020055833
LC ebook record available at https://lccn.loc.gov/2020055834

Cover Design: Wiley
Cover Image: Kevin West

SKY10038853_112222

Contents

Prologue

Omaha, Nebraska. May 6, 2017.

It's the first Saturday in May, and for those who follow Warren Buffett, that means just one thing: the annual Berkshire Hathaway shareholder meeting. In the investment world, there is nothing quite like it.

For five straight hours (not counting a one-hour lunch break), Warren, and Charlie Munger, chairman and vice chairman of Berkshire Hathaway, answer questions from shareholders in the audience, from finance journalists on behalf of their readers and viewers, and from securities analysts. No attempt is made to vet the questions ahead of time, and every one is answered fully and with candor, warmth, and the gentle wit that is the trademark of both men. There is nothing on the head table but water glasses, cans of Coke, See's candy and peanut brittle, and two microphones; no notes, no briefing books, just two men happy to answer questions and talk about their ideas. Some 30,000 people hang on their every word. I am one of them.

Earlier that morning I had driven from my hotel to the Century Link Center in downtown Omaha, site of the event. The parking lot was nearly full. The 20,000-seat arena was already filled with Berkshire Hathaway shareholders, with thousands more filing into the overflow ballrooms that surround the arena. Many had been in line since 4:00 a.m., waiting for the doors to open at 7:00. Once inside, many of them dash directly for the line of chairs set up at the 11 microphone stations scattered around the arena and the surrounding ballrooms; with any luck, the people sitting in those chairs will get a chance to ask their question.

There was a time I would have been in that early line with them. But I had stopped getting up at dawn years ago, and I was certainly too old to race down the grand hall, up the escalator then hop down the steps into the arena to grab one of the coveted seats. My routine was now more relaxed.

Once inside, I took my time meandering around the giant exhibition hall, with its booths displaying all the businesses Berkshire owns. It's like an indoor shopping mall. You can stock up on snacks like See's Candies, Dairy Queen ice cream, and Coke. You can browse modular homes, boats and recreational vehicles. You can check out the new colors of Benjamin Moore paint and the latest style of Kirby vacuum cleaners. You can even sign up for GEICO insurance.

Near 8:30 a.m., I head up to the second floor and walk into Grand Ballroom B, where I customarily take my seat. Several thousand chairs in the ballroom are divided into two sections, each with a massive television screen that will soon be showing the traditional Berkshire Hathaway movie before live streaming Warren and Charlie answering questions in the arena next door. I settle into the last row on the right-hand side, stretch out comfortably, and smile.

So far, everything seems exactly normal. There is no hint that at today's meeting, something remarkable will happen.

The format for the question and answer period is well established. On one side of the main table, where Warren and Charlie sit, there is a station for the three journalists—Carol Loomis of *Fortune*, Becky Quick of CNBC, and Andrew Ross Sorkin of the *New York Times*. They will present questions from their readers and viewers. On the other side is a station for the equity analysts: Jonathan Brandt, research analyst at Ruane, Cunniff & Goldfarb; Jay Gelb of Barclay's; and Gregg Warren, senior analyst at Morningstar. And at those 11 stations, dozens of eager shareholders sit nervously in their chairs, mentally rehearsing their questions.

Warren serves as master of ceremonies, calling first on one of the journalists, then one of the analysts, then one of the audience stations, in numerical order; then back to the journalists for the next cycle.

The morning session begins as usual. There's a question about driverless trucks and the threat it may pose to BNSF Railway or GEICO. Another question about Berkshire's reinsurance deal with American International Group. A discussion about technology stocks including IBM, Apple, Google, and Amazon. Warren was asked about the competitive nature of the airline industry, his thoughts on Coca-Cola, and the continuing struggle with Kraft Heinz.

Then, toward the end of the morning session, a shareholder at station 9 asked the 28th question, addressed to both Warren and Charlie. "The two of you have largely avoided the capital allocation mistakes by bouncing ideas off of one another. Will this continue long into Berkshire's future?" Although on the surface the question is about capital allocation, its focus is clearly on succession and who will be making capital allocation decisions in the future.

Warren responds first. "Any successor that's put in at Berkshire, capital allocation abilities and proven capital allocation abilities are certain to be the uppermost in the board's mind." He points out that CEOs of a great many companies get to the top from a variety of backgrounds, including sales, legal, or manufacturing. But once in a leadership role, the CEO has to be able to make the decisions on allocating capital. "Berkshire would not do well if somebody was put in who had a lot of skills in other areas but really did not have an ability to allocate capital."

What he said next made me sit upright in my chair.

Warren begins, "I've talked about it as being something I call a Money Mind. People can have 120 IQs or 140 IQs or whatever it may be, and some of them have minds that are good at one kind of thing and some of them another. They can do all kinds of other things that most mortals can't do. But I have also known very bright people who do not have Money Minds and they can make very unintelligent decisions. That skill [capital allocation] isn't the way their wiring works. So we do want somebody and hopefully they've got a lot of talent. But we certainly do not want somebody if they lack a Money Mind."

A Money Mind. I had never heard Warren say those words before. At that moment I knew that after all those years of studying Warren Buffett, I was only half right.

■ ■ ■

My first exposure to Warren Buffett was in July 1984. I was training to be a stockbroker with a Mid-Atlantic brokerage firm. Part of my training included reading a Berkshire Hathaway annual report. Like so many, I was instantly impressed with the clarity of Warren's writing. Most importantly, I was struck with how sensibly he laid out the idea that owning a stock was equivalent to owning a business. As a liberal arts major in college, I didn't study finance or accounting, so trying to understand stocks using rows of numbers in balance sheets and income statements did not come easy to me. But when Warren explained that stocks should be thought of as companies run by managers who sell products to consumers, suddenly everything made sense.

When I earned my broker stripes and went into production I knew exactly what I was going to do. I was going to invest my clients' money in Berkshire Hathaway and in the stocks Berkshire bought for its own portfolio. I wrote to the Securities and Exchange Commission for all the past Berkshire Hathaway annual reports and the annual reports of the public companies Berkshire owned. Over the years, I collected all the newspaper and magazine articles written about Warren and Berkshire. I was like a kid following a ballplayer.

I have never met anyone who disagrees with Warren's investment principles. These principles became the investment tenets in *The Warren Buffett Way*. And when I asked a client if they would like to invest in the same way, the answer was almost always yes, definitely! But as time passed, I discovered some investors who had chosen to invest like Warren were struggling. The gap between knowing why you own a stock and having the emotional wherewithal to withstand the push and pull of the market was, for many, too wide. I came to understand there was a big difference between knowing the path and walking the path.

But on that Saturday 30-some years later, I finally realized what was needed to help people invest successfully had less to do with the investment tenets and much more to do with the right mindset. Although both Ben Graham and Warren had for years written about the importance of temperament, I had pushed aside that idea in favor of sharpening my pencil to figure out what a stock was worth. The harder it became for people to invest in the stock market, the more I sharpened my pencil. Then, on that Saturday morning I finally realized I had discounted the most important advice.

■ ■ ■

What does it mean to have a Money Mind? Exploring that question, and all its ramifications, is the goal of this book. We will accomplish this by starting at the beginning, where we find some early influencers that may surprise you. Example: Almost a decade before he first read *The Intelligent Investor*, 11-year-old Warren was intrigued by a book he found in the local public library. F. C. Minaker's *One Thousand Ways to Make $1000* helped form his earliest ideas of a Money Mind. Example: The role and influence of Warren's father in shaping the underpinnings for Warren's investment philosophy has not often been addressed in writings about Warren. Example: We know that young Warren studied everything about finance and investing he could get his hands on, but he also began to incorporate the principles of rationalism and pragmatism, two precepts crucial to a true Money Mind.

Then, once he had acquired the basic building blocks of a Money Mind, how did Warren employ that mindset to successfully navigate the investment landscape these past 65 years? We will explore the ways others might incorporate those building blocks into their own mental framework, so that they ultimately become a person we can now call a Money Mind. And most importantly, we will show how such a person can best manage their portfolio in this new, fast-paced, media-frenzied world. Finally, armed with this knowledge, we will make the argument that those investors who work toward achieving a Money Mind will stand a much better chance of becoming successful.

Let me be clear. This is an entirely new book. It is not a new edition of *The Warren Buffett Way*. It is not an update of the second edition that 10 years later combined the *Investment Strategies of the World's Greatest Investor* with the portfolio management approach outlined in *The Warren Buffett Portfolio: Mastering the Power of the Focus Investment Strategy*. Neither is it similar to the third edition, which added an eight-chapter investment workbook of questions, answers, and explanations meant to assess an understanding of the investment approach outlined by Warren Buffett. This is not a method book. It is a thinking book.

■ ■ ■

"Money Mind." In his usual precise way, Warren gave us a memorable name for a complex notion. That easy-to-remember phrase describes, at one level, a way of thinking about major financial issues such as capital allocation. At another level, it summarizes an overall mindset for the modern business world. It identifies a person who has made a commitment to learning and stretching and facing down irrelevant noise. At a still deeper level, the profound philosophical and ethical constructs at its core tell us a great deal about the person we call a Money Mind, a person who is quite likely to be successful in many aspects of life—including investing. This Money Mind thing is a powerful idea. We should learn more about it.

The Young Warren Buffett

Legends tend to accumulate around people who have accomplished something extraordinary in their lives. In particular, we seem to be fascinated with tidbits about their earliest years, wondering whether, if we look carefully, we could spot clues on how they became successful.

There are many popular stories that swirl around Warren Buffett, universally described as the world's greatest investor. You probably know most of them.

How at age six he set up a sidewalk table selling candy, gum, and soda pop. He bought a six-pack of Coca-Cola from his grandfather's grocery store for 25 cents and sold individual bottles for a nickel—a 20 percent return. The next year, he asked Santa Claus for a book about bonds. The year after that, he wanted more, so he began reading his father's books on the stock market. At age 11, he bought his first shares of stock. At age 17, he and a friend bought a used pinball machine for $25 and set it up in a neighborhood barber shop. With the proceeds, they bought two more machines. A year later, they sold the business for $1,200.

But there's one story you may not know, and it is quite possibly the most significant of all.

In 1941, 11-year-old Warren, browsing in the Benson branch of the Omaha Public Library, came across a distinguished-looking book with a shiny silver cover—*One Thousand Ways to Make $1000: Practical Suggestions, Based on Actual Experience, for Starting a Business of Your Own and Making Money in Your Spare Time* by F.C. Minaker, published by the Dartnell Corporation in 1936. In the fashion of the time, Frances Mary Cowan Minaker used initials to disguise her gender.

Think about a young boy living in Omaha, Nebraska, in the 1940s. There were no televisions, no video games, no personal computers, no smartphones. Yes, there were radio programs and a rare Saturday afternoon movie at the downtown cinema. But for most people, including Warren, entertainment was reading—newspapers, magazines, and books.

Now imagine young Warren running home from the library, tightly clutching his new treasure, bursting into the house, plopping down in a chair, opening the book to page 1 and diving into a new world of how to make money—a world he had not yet fully understood or appreciated.

Minaker's book is long (408 pages) and comprehensive. In addition to hundreds of specific suggestions for new businesses, it offers clear, straightforward lessons on good salesmanship, advertising, merchandising, customer relations, and much more. It is filled with stories of people who turned a good idea into a good business, sometimes with stunning success.

Some of the names are familiar today.

There is the stirring story of James C. Penney, whose first job paid him a measly $2.27 a month. Penney combined his small grubstake with two other partners and opened the first J.C. Penney on April 14, 1902. That first year, store sales amounted to $28,891. James' share of the profits was a tad over $1,000.

Warren flipped another page and read the story of 23-year-old John Wanamaker, who persuaded his brother-in-law, Nathan Brown, to combine their piddling savings and open a gentleman's clothing store in their home town, Philadelphia. Before them lay the prospects of a national civil war. Behind them were the remnants of the 1857 banking depression that caused massive unemployment and the almost complete ruination of manufacturers and wholesalers.

Undeterre...
later ...
Unite...
    Wit...
    When...
a huge gri...
something t...
more than five
service business...
pool tables in loc...
spective, we can see...
ball business six years...

    In that same Cha...
another story, one that h...
thinking. Here's what happ...

    In 1933, a man named ...
drugstore when someone (w...
him how much he weighed. ...
coin-operated scale; he put in hi...
then moved over to the cigar coun...
waited in line, seven other custome...
scale. That caught Harry's attention, a...
The store owner explained that the n...
that his 25 percent share of the profits ...
(approximately $384 in today's dollars)—lea...
company that owned the scale.

    That, Harry told Minaker, was the start of ...
$175 from savings, bought three machines, and w...
monthly profit of $98. "Pretty good return on the...
wryly noted. But it was what Harry did next that intr...
"I bought 70 machines altogether. . . . The other 67 w...
of the pennies taken from the first three. . . . I've earned...

interest is the eighth wo...
it, earns it; he who doe...
cept is broader and m...
profits. Harry Larson...
Warren Buffett.
    Many years later...
describe his thinkin...
stand," he said. "I c...
buy more weighing...
machines, and ev...
I thought—that'...
what could be ...
that formed th...
Berkshire Hath...
    And so we...
found influe...
$1000 lives...
new-busine...
in our hig...
    But for u...
tal princ...
teacher...
particu...
tial te...
goals,...
ing ...
War...
wr...
li...

nder of the world, He who understands
sn't, pays it." But at its the core the con-
ore powerful: use profits to make further
instinctively understood it; so did a young

Warren used the penny-weight machines to
g. "The weighing machine was easy to under-
buy a weighing machine and use the profits to
machines. Pretty soon I'd have twenty weighing
rybody would weigh themselves fifty times a day.
where the money is. The compounding of it—
etter than that?"[2] It was that exact mental model
outline, the architecture, of what would become
away.

come back full circle to Minaker's book and its pro-
nce on Warren Buffett. *One Thousand Ways to Make*
up to the spirit, if not the letter, of its title: I count 476
s suggestions. Many would qualify as buggy-whip ideas
h-tech world, but many others are remarkably prescient.
today, the real value of the book lies in the fundamen-
ples it offers. Minaker, in her no-nonsense, listen-to-your-
style, lays down important basic concepts about money. In
ar, she wants readers to understand the mindset, the essen-
nperament they would need in order to reach their dollar
Taken together, those passages about the essence of mak-
honey are some of the key building blocks that helped form
en's Money Mind.

"The first step in starting a business of your own," Minaker
tes, "is to know something about it. . . . So read everything pub-
hed about the business you intend to start, to get the combined
xperience of others, and begin your plans where they left off."
hat means, she insists, learning all you can from both sides of
he question: how to succeed *and* how not to fail. Reading about
business, she says, is like sitting down with a businessman in his
parlor and talking about your problems. "Only those who think
hey know all there is to be known—and more besides—consider

such an exchange of ideas foolish," she writes. What's really foolish, she points out, is spending hundreds of dollars (in today's dollars, probably hundreds of thousands, even millions) to discover that your idea won't work, when someone else who has already tried it and wrote about it can tell you "exactly *why* it is not a good idea."[3]

To give her readers a boost with their research, Minaker includes a 35-page appendix that lists books, magazines, periodicals, pamphlets, and government publications related to how to start and operate a business. In all, there are 859 different citations on how to succeed at your chosen business.

The lesson was not lost on Warren. At Berkshire Hathaway's headquarters in Omaha, the largest room on the executive floor is not Warren's office but the reference library down the hall. It is lined with row upon row of filing cabinets, all filled with the stories of businesses. These cabinets contain every annual report, past and present, of all the major publicly traded companies. Warren has read them all. From these he has learned not only what worked and was profitable but, more important, what business strategies failed and lost money.

The second step in developing a Money Mind is simple enough to articulate but hard for most people to do. It can be encapsulated in two words: Take action. Or, as Minaker so compellingly puts it, "The way to begin making money, is to begin."[4] Hundreds of thousands of people have dreamed about starting their own business, she notes, but never did because they were stuck. Waiting for business forecasts to improve, or perhaps waiting for their own prospects to get better, or just simply waiting for the right moment. They often delay getting started, Minaker writes, "because they cannot see clearly ahead." The caution here is to be aware that the perfect moment is never known beforehand, and waiting for it is simply a way to hide in the safety of doing nothing.

Another manifestation of this phenomenon, Minaker points out, is people who become frozen because they spend too much time seeking counsel from others. "If you ask the advice of enough people," she warns, "you are sure to almost end up doing nothing."[5] On the surface that might seem to contradict the first dictum (learn everything you can) but it is really a question of common sense and balance. Finding the right balance between educating yourself and then knowing when to take action is, in fact, a key element of a Money Mind.

Those who have studied Warren Buffett easily recognize Minaker's counsel. Yes, Warren discusses big ideas with his longtime business partner, Charlie Munger. But it is also true that if Warren believes Berkshire is in line to make a good purchase he won't spend all day talking on the phone. He never pauses to make a final decision because the stock market is up or down, or the economy is growing or contracting, or the forecast for interest rates is rising or falling. If it is a good business at a good price, Warren takes action.

Along with her advice, Minaker also delivers compelling inspiration. "Leaving the harbor [with your new business] is like the captain of a ship at sea; you rely on your own judgment and ability," she writes. She calls it the most satisfying part of a business life.[6]

It's easy to imagine the young Warren recognizing the truth of that. From the time he started selling candy and soda pop at age six, Warren was his own boss. He was steadfastly confident and loved his independence. By the time he graduated high school he was already the richest 16-year-old in Omaha. He may very well have been the world's richest self-made teenager. But he was not yet the millionaire he had once bragged about becoming. That required him to stay in school.

■ ■ ■

In 1947, Warren enrolled at the Wharton School of Finance and Commerce at the University of Pennsylvania. Despite his father urging him toward higher education, Warren was not easily motivated. He figured he was already doing well and that college would be a waste of time. Anyway, he had already read over a hundred books on business and investing. What could college teach him?

Warren was right. After two unrewarding years at Wharton it was clear he knew more than his professors about accounting and business. Warren was spending more time at Philadelphia brokerages studying the stock market than studying for class. When the fall semester began in 1949, Warren was nowhere to be found.

Back in Omaha, Warren enrolled at the University of Nebraska, and earned a bachelor's degree in one year taking 14 courses over two semesters. All that year, and even after graduating, most days Warren could be found in the library absorbing every book he could find on business and investing.[7]

Sometime in that summer of 1950 he found a copy of a newly published book by Benjamin Graham—*The Intelligent Investor*. More than any of the hundreds of books he had read, he regards this one as the book that changed his life.

It led him to start researching business schools, and later that same summer he discovered that Benjamin Graham and David Dodd, coauthors of the seminal work *Security Analysis*, were listed as professors at Columbia University. "I figured they were long since dead," he said.[8] So he quickly submitted an application to Columbia and was accepted. By September 1950 he was 1,200 miles away from Omaha, walking onto the New York City campus.

Warren's first class was Finance 111-112, Investment Management and Security Analysis, taught by David Dodd.[9] Before heading to New York, Warren had grabbed a copy of *Security Analysis*; by the time he got to Columbia, he had practically memorized it. "The truth was that I knew the book. At that time, literally, almost in those seven or eight hundred pages, I knew every example. I just sopped it up," he said.[10]

When the spring semester began in 1951, Warren could hardly contain himself. His next class was taught by Benjamin Graham, a seminar that combined the teachings in *Security Analysis* and the lessons from *The Intelligent Investor* linked to actual stocks that were then trading in the market.

Graham's message was simple to understand but revolutionary in practice. Before *Security Analysis*, the common Wall Street approach to picking stocks was to begin with some overall opinion about a stock—do you like it or not—then to try to figure what other people might do with that stock—buy or sell it. The financial facts were largely overlooked. Ben Graham backed up the train.

Before you throw money at a stock based upon nothing more than prevailing opinions, he argued, why not first figure out what it might be worth.

In the beginning, Graham's method was simple: Add up the company's current assets (account receivables, cash and securities), then subtract all its liabilities. That gives you the company's net worth. Then, and only then, look at the stock price. If the price was below the net assets, it was a worthwhile and potentially profitable purchase. But if the stock price was higher than the company's net worth, it wasn't worth investing. This approach fit comfortably into Warren's sense of numbers. Ben Graham had given him what he had been seeking for years—a systematic approach for investing: buy a dollar's worth of securities for 50 cents.

It has been said that for Warren, attending Columbia University was very much like the experience of someone emerging from a cave where he had lived all his life, stepping outside, blinking at the sunlight, perceiving truth and reality for the first time.[11] Warren relished every moment of the experience. When not in class, he could be found in the Columbia library reading old newspapers about the stock market going back 20 years. He never stopped, seven days a week from early in the morning to late in the evening. Most wondered if he ever slept. At the end of the semester, Warren received an A+, the first time Graham had ever awarded that grade in his 22 years at Columbia University.

When school was over, Warren asked Graham about working at Graham-Newman, the investment partnership Graham managed while teaching at Columbia. Graham turned him down. Warren offered to work for free. Again, a polite no thank you. So Warren returned to Omaha, determined to see what he could do on his own.

He was just turning 21 years old.

It Begins

When Warren arrived in Omaha the summer of 1951, his mind and energy were singularly focused on investing. He was no longer interested in part-time jobs to make extra money. First Graham then Warren's father cautioned him that now was not the time to invest in the stock market. A correction was long overdue, both men warned. Warren heard only Minaker: "The way to begin making money is to begin."

Warren was offered a job at the Omaha National Bank but he turned it down, preferring the familiarity of his father's firm, Buffett-Falk & Company. A friend of Howard Buffett's asked if the name would soon become Buffett & Son; Warren replied, "Maybe Buffett & Father."[12]

Warren threw his heart and soul into Buffett-Falk & Company. He enrolled in the Dale Carnegie course for public speaking and was soon teaching "Investment Principles" at the University of Omaha; the lectures were based on Graham's book *The Intelligent Investor*. He wrote a column for *The Commercial and Financial Chronicle* under the headline "The Security I Like Best." In it he touted one of Graham's favorite investments, a little-known insurance company called Government Employees Insurance Co. (GEICO). Throughout this period, Warren maintained his relationship with Ben Graham and sent him stock ideas from time to time.

Then one day, in 1954, Graham called his former student with a job offer. Warren was on the next plane back to New York.

The two years Warren spent at Graham-Newman were exhilarating but also frustrating. One of six employees, Warren shared an office with the legendary investors Walter Schloss and Tom Knapp. They spent their days pouring over the Standard & Poor's *Stock Guide* and pitching ideas for the Graham-Newman mutual fund.

Graham and his partner Jerry Newman batted down most of their recommendations. When the Dow Jones Industrial Average hit 420 in 1955, the Graham Mutual Fund was sitting on $4 million in cash. No matter how compelling were Warren's stock picks, the door for investing at Graham-Newman was closed. The only place for Warren's ideas was his own portfolio. The following year, 1956, Graham had enough. He retired and moved to Beverly Hills, California, where he continued to write and teach, this time at UCLA, until his death at the age of 82.

So Warren returned to Omaha for the second time, far different from the young graduate five years earlier. He was now older, more experienced, certainly wiser about investing, and definitely a lot richer. And he knew one thing for sure. He would never work for someone else again. He was ready to be his own captain.

Chapter Ten of *One Thousand Ways to Make $1000* is titled "Selling Your Services." The chapter begins by asking the reader to take a personal inventory. Figure out what you're good at, Minaker instructed, what you do better than anyone else. Then figure out who needs help with that and how best to reach them.

Through his teaching at the University of Omaha and his popular column on investing, Warren had already begun to build his reputation in Omaha; the time at Graham-Newman only added to his credibility. So no sooner did he arrive in Omaha than family and friends pounced, asking him to manage their money. His sister Doris and her husband, his loving Aunt Alice, his father-in-law, his ex-roommate Chuck Peterson, and local Omaha attorney Dan Monen—all wanted in. Collectively, in the spring of 1956 they gave Warren $105,000 to invest. Thus was born the investment partnership Buffett Associates, with Warren as general partner.

When everyone gathered for the kickoff meeting at a local Omaha dinner club, Warren set the tone. He handed each person the formal partnership agreement, assuring them there was nothing nefarious about the legalistic look of the agreement. Then with complete disclosure he set the ground rules for the partnership.[13]

First, the financial terms. Limited partners would receive annually the first 6 percent return of the investment partnership. Thereafter, they would receive 75 percent of the profits, with the balance going to Warren. Any annual deficiencies in performance goals would be rolled over to the next year. In other words, if the limited partners didn't get their 6 percent return in any one year, it would be extended into the next year. Warren would not receive his performance bonus until his partners were made whole.

Warren told his partners he could not promise results, but he did promise that the investments he made for the partnership would be based on the value principles he learned from Ben Graham. He went on to describe how they should think about yearly gains or losses. They should ignore the daily, weekly, and monthly gyrations of the stock market—which, in any event, were beyond his control. He suggested they not even put overly much emphasis on how well or poorly the investments performed in any one year. Better, he thought, to judge results over at least three years. Five years was even better.

Lastly, Warren told his partners he was not in the business of forecasting the stock market or economic cycles. That meant he would not discuss or disclose what the partnership was buying, selling, or holding.

At dinner that night, everyone signed up for the partnership. Over the years, as more partners were added, they were given the same ground rules. Lest anyone forgot, Warren included the ground rules with the performance results sent every year to each partner.

In addition to the annual 6 percent performance bogey, Warren also believed it was helpful for the partners to judge how well he was doing compared to a broader stock index, the Dow Jones Industrial Average. Over the first five years, the results were impressive. From 1957 to 1961, the partnership achieved a cumulative return of 251 percent compared to the Dow's 74 percent.

Hearing about Warren's success, more investors joined in. By 1961, the Buffett Partnership had $7.2 million in capital—more than Graham-Newman managed at its peak. By the end of the year, $1 million of the Buffett Partnership belonged to Warren. He had just turned 31.

Warren was applying Graham's investment playbook for the Buffett Partnership, with stunning success. He continued to soundly beat the Dow Jones Industrial Average. After 10 years, the Buffett Partnership's assets had grown to over $53 million. Warren's share was near $10 million. In 1968, the Buffett Partnership returned 59 percent compared to the Dow's 8 percent. It was the single best performance year of the partnership. Ever the realist, Warren wrote to his partners that the results "should be treated as a freak—like picking up thirteen spades in a bridge game."[14]

Despite the partnership's heroic performance returns, difficulties were mounting. Scouring the market, Warren was having great difficulty finding value. Bereft of investment ideas and more than a little fatigued with the performance derby he had been running for the past 12 years, in 1969 Warren announced that he was closing down the partnership. In a letter to his partners, Warren confessed he was out of step with the current market environment. "On one point, however, I am clear," he said. "I will not abandon a previous approach whose logic I understand, although I find it difficult to apply, even though it may mean forgoing large and apparently easy profits to embrace an approach which I don't fully understand, have not practiced carefully and which possibly could lead to substantial permanent capital loss."[15]

In 1957, Warren had set a goal to beat the Dow Jones Industrial Average by 10 percentage points each year. Over its 13-year period, 1957–1969, the average annual compounded rate of return for the Buffett Partnership was 29.5 percent (23.8 percent net to partners); the Dow return was 7.4 percent. In the end, Warren beat the Dow not by 10 percentage points per year but by 22! From its initial asset base of $105,000, the partnership had grown to $104 million in assets under management. For this, Warren earned $25 million.

In shutting down the Buffett Partnership, Warren took extra care to ensure all the partners clearly understood the next steps. He outlined three different options. For those who wished to remain in the stock market, Warren recommended Bill Ruane, a former Columbia classmate. Twenty million dollars in Buffett Partnership assets were transferred to Ruane, Cunniff, & Stires and thus was born the famous Sequoia Mutual Fund.

A second option for partners was to invest in municipal bonds. To Warren's mind, the 10-year outlook for stocks was approximately the same as for the less risky, tax-free municipal bonds. The consummate educator, Warren sent each partner a 100-page manifesto on the mechanics of buying tax-free bonds.[16] As a third option, partners could also allocate their assets to one of the partnership's major holdings—the common shares of Berkshire Hathaway.

Warren was, as always, upfront and plainspoken. He told his partners he was going to move his personal investment in the Buffett Partnership to Berkshire Hathaway. As Doc Angel, one of the early Buffett Partnership loyalists, said, "That's all anybody had to hear if they had any brains."[17]

From Investment Partnership to a Compounding Conglomerate

Early in the Buffett Partnership timeline, Warren bought shares in a New England textile manufacturer, a merged enterprise of Berkshire Cotton Manufacturing and Hathaway Manufacturing. It was a classic Ben Graham purchase. The stock was selling for $7.50 per share with working capital of $10.25 and a hard book value of $20.20.

Warren was well aware of the difficulties US textile manufacturers faced in competing against much cheaper foreign imports. Even so, he couldn't resist the attractiveness of "picking up a discarded cigar butt that had one puff remaining in it."[18] The "cigar-butt" theory is the name given to Graham's emphasis on buying hard assets on the cheap even though those assets had little economic vitality. With the cash and securities on the balance sheet along with even a limited potential for business profits going forward, Warren figured there was not much downside to Berkshire Hathaway and a reasonable likelihood of making money.

By 1965, the Buffett Partnership owned 39 percent of the Berkshire Hathaway common shares outstanding. Warren was then locked in a proxy battle with the board of directors to take over the company, fire the inept management, and replace them with better capital allocators. When the dust settled, Warren won the fight but in doing so found he had allocated 25 percent of the Buffett Partnership's assets to an economically sinking ship with no exit strategy. "I became the dog who caught the car," he said.[19]

The journey from managing one of the greatest investment partnerships in history to then parlaying his net worth into owning a dying manufacturing business had all the makings of a Greek tragedy. What was Warren thinking?

It's clear what he was *not* thinking. He had no grand plan to engineer a complete turnaround. And even though he had Ben Graham whispering in his ear, he never intended to sell the company to a greater fool. Who would have wanted to buy a 75-year-old, low-margin, capital-intensive, labor-dependent, nineteenth-century

New England maker of fabric liners for men's suits? No, Warren was guided by a stronger principle, a principle that in fact lies at the heart of his investing philosophy—long-term compounding.

From an early age, Warren was taught the benefits of compound interest. More important, he experienced the benefits of a compounding machine firsthand when he took the earnings from his various jobs and plowed them back into his little business enterprise. If one paper route was a good job for making money, then having two paper routes meant more money. If owning one pinball machine added to his savings, then owning three was even better. Even as a kid, Warren was not geared to spend the money he had earned.

In many ways, Warren's childhood enterprises were like a conglomerate, allowing him to transfer money unimpaired from one business to another or, better yet, plowing more money back into the best business. And 20 years later, a conglomerate is what he had with Berkshire Hathaway, although few recognized it.

Most thought that Warren had rolled the dice on a beaten-down textile business, but what they missed is that in one bold step he now owned a corporate entity called Berkshire Hathaway that in turn owned a textile company. Warren figured all he had to do was to wring out whatever cash was left from Berkshire Hathaway manufacturing and reallocate it to a better business. Fortunately, the textile group of manufacturers under the Berkshire name did generate enough capital to allow Warren to buy other businesses, which, as we will see, is a much brighter story. It wasn't long before the metamorphosis of Berkshire Hathaway was complete, from a single-line textile manufacturer to a conglomerate that owned a portfolio of diversified business interests.

In the 2014 Berkshire Hathaway Annual Report, Warren gave shareholders a short tutorial on the advantages of owning a conglomerate. "If the conglomerate form is used judiciously, it is an ideal structure for maximizing long-term capital." A conglomerate is perfectly positioned to allocate capital rationally and at a minimal cost, he explained. Furthermore, a conglomerate that owns different businesses is in an ideal position: "Without incurring taxes or much in the way of other costs [it can] move huge sums from businesses that have limited opportunities for incremental investment to other sectors with greater promise."[20]

You have probably noticed that with his decisions about Berkshire Hathaway, Warren had pulled away from the teachings of Ben Graham. Maximizing long-term capital gain was not a Ben Graham strategy. His approach to buying stocks was to keenly focus on cheap, hard-asset-based stocks with limited downside price risk. Once the stock price reset back to fair value, Graham would quickly sell the stock and move on to the next investment. The idea of compounding an existing stock position over several years was not part of Graham's calculation. In fact, the word *compound* appears nowhere in *Security Analysis* or *The Intelligent Investor*.

In contrast, even in the earliest years of the partnership Warren was writing about the "Joys of Compounding." In the 1963 Buffett Partnership letter to his partners, Warren relayed the story of Queen Isabella underwriting the voyage of Christopher Columbus for $30,000. He pointed out that if that investment compounded at 4 percent, it would have been worth $2 trillion five hundred years later. Year after year, Warren would school his partners on the wonders of compounded interest. A $100,000 investment compounded at 4 percent rate becomes $224,000 in 30 years, he explained, but can become $8,484,940 when compounded at 16 percent. His advice: live a long life and compound money at a high rate.

However, we should not forget that the partnership years, and Graham's influence thereon, are critical to the story of Warren Buffett. He grew the Buffett partnership assets by perfectly executing Ben Graham's core methodology. Its success helped to build Warren's net worth, and the yearly performance bonus added to his financial security. That allowed him to provide a solid foundation for his family. But once their financial future was secured, the question became, what next?

One option was to continue the partnership—keep on buying and selling stocks each year, paying commissions and taxes along the way, always having to navigate the rocky shores of overpriced markets. The other was to change vessels and chart a new course.

To date, Berkshire Hathaway is the sixth largest company in the world. The original A-shares, which Warren purchased in 1962 at $7.50, today trade for $334,000. What is spectacular about this achievement is that Berkshire reached this milestone not by inventing a blockbuster drug or new technology but rather from perfecting an older miracle—the seventeenth-century idea of financial compounding.

CHAPTER 2

Developing an Investment Philosophy

Investing is a thinking game. It is not a physical challenge. It doesn't matter how strong you are or how fast and far you can run. But it does matter—a lot—how you conceptualize the world and your role in it.

Another name for that is your worldview. It is a complex, fascinating mix of your innate temperament, the experiences of your life to this point and your reaction to them, and the ideas you absorbed along the way—from formal education, from reading, from significant people in your life. All these elements go into shaping a mental mosaic that is your personal philosophy of life, something so fundamental it is revealed in countless ways at every turn. But here we are concerned specifically with just one dimension: your philosophy of investing and how it influences your decisions and then in turn is affected by them.

A good working definition of an investment philosophy is "a set of beliefs and insights about how financial markets work and what it takes to exploit those workings in the service of an investment objective."[1] Like all good definitions, it is compact and succinct; to get its full meaning, we need to break it open and look closely at its parts.

First, let's explore "a set of beliefs and insights." It asks, What is your personal set of beliefs, your overall view of how the financial markets operate? And where did it come from? What have you learned that shaped your view? For his part, Warren tells us the stock market is frequently efficient, but not always. This is his *view* of financial markets.

Second, "what it takes to exploit the market." This is a more complex question, for it involves two separate considerations: methods and personal traits. Here, too, Warren gives us guidance. He believes we should run a concentrated, low-turnover portfolio comprising stocks based on business-driven principles and valuing companies using the discounted present value of future free cash flow. This is his process, the *methods* he uses to beat the market. For the second aspect, personal traits, Warren speaks of the importance of what he calls the "temperament" of an investor.

All these separate components—your view of the market, your methods, and your temperament as an investor—reflect the totality of your philosophy of investing. When all three are working in harmony, we might even say we're looking at a person who displays a Money Mind.

A fortunate thing about humans is our capacity to learn. If your set of beliefs about the market has not served you as well as you would like, it is within your power to change that, to try out new concepts and sharpen your own Money Mind. And I can think of no better model than Warren Buffett, the ultimate Money Mind.

We have no shortage of information to draw from. But I believe that most of the time, we have focused too much on analyzing Warren's methods and too little on appreciating the philosophical underpinnings, acquired over the years, that enabled him to successfully apply those methods. The goal of this chapter is to help you better conceptualize the investment world in the same way as Warren Buffett.

We'll do that with a deep look at the significant influences that played a role in shaping his investment philosophy, starting with one influencer I believe has not been fully recognized—his father. Once we understand just how much his father's influence impacted Warren, then we begin to better appreciate the roots of Warren's philosophy—a philosophy that has guided not only his personal life but his approach in the investment world as well.

Howard Homan Buffett

Warren is not shy about reminding everyone that a good deal of his success can be attributed to having been born at the right time and in the right place. He calls it the Ovarian Lottery. "I've had it so good in this world," he says. "The odds were fifty-to-one against me being born in the United States in 1930. I won the lottery the day I emerged from the womb by being in the United States instead of in some other country where my chances would have been way different."[2] To which I would add, he also won the Powerball by being born in Omaha, Nebraska, as a member of the Buffett clan.

We can trace the Buffetts all the way back to John Buffett, who married Hannah Titus on the north shore of Long Island, New York, in 1696.[3] Fast-forward to 1867, when Sidney Homan Buffett, hearing the call of the West, left New York and took a job driving a stagecoach to Omaha. Once there, he decided to stay, and in 1869 he opened the S.H. Buffett grocery, setting into motion the Buffett business dynasty that remains in Omaha today.

It was an opportune time to start a business. The town was bustling. A scant 15 years earlier, land speculators from nearby Council Bluffs, Iowa, had crossed the Missouri River at the Lone Tree Ferry (the exact spot where the Lewis and Clark Expedition had passed in 1804) to homestead the land, the beginnings of what we now recognize as Omaha's pioneer period. After a series of 26 separate treaties with the Native Americans, the land was ceded into what is today east-central Nebraska. Then, in 1862, President Abraham Lincoln designated Omaha as the eastern terminal of the Union Pacific Railroad connecting with the Trans-Continental Railway. In short order, the city became the new economic center for the continuing western expansion of the United States.

Most of us know the basic outlines of this phase of American history, but for our purposes in this chapter, we should take a minute to think about what life was like for these pioneers. Without pay or promise of employment, they left their homes for the unknown. Along the way they endured scorching heat, lashing rains, mud pits, and drownings. They lost loved ones in ferocious attacks from bears, wolf packs, and rattlesnakes. Countless numbers of pioneers succumbed to diseases for which there was no treatment. All were constantly on guard against Indian attacks.

Why did they do it? What drove them ever westward? Freedom, in all its facets, and, not least of those, the freedom to pursue their own business opportunities to better provide a secure financial future for their family.[4]

According to the National Bureau of Economic Research, the United States had 15 recessions between 1854 and 1913. That's one economic downturn about every four years, many of them severe, including the 1873 recession that lasted until 1879. There was no shortage of explanations and plenty of blame to go around—the weather; uncertainty over how to plan for the future; innovations of a modern society; construction of new industrial equipment that displaced workers; the cyclicality of built-up savings then massive overproduction; the failure of banks and the unethical behavior of corporate titans.[5] But all of these excuses collapsed into one singular blame—the political establishment. Washington, DC, and by connection New York City, had for years mismanaged the American economy. The pioneers who headed west wanted a new start, unchained by the bad decisions of a government they desperately wanted to leave behind.

By 1900, Omaha was sprinkled with tall buildings and cable cars. Its population had swelled to 140,000. Sidney Buffett expanded his grocery business. Soon his two sons joined him. The youngest, Ernest, left his father's bigger downtown location and established in the suburbs a new grocery store he grandly called Ernest Buffett, Grocer and Master Merchant. Ernest had four sons, one of whom—Howard—became the father of Warren Buffett.

But Howard Buffett had little interest in the grocery business. He dreamed of becoming a journalist and at the University of Nebraska became editor of the school newspaper, the *Daily Nebraskan*. Then, in his senior year a chance meeting with Leila Stahl, soon to be Mrs. Howard Buffett, changed his future. To win Leila's heart and her father's approval, Howard forsook a career in the news business and instead took a more dependable job selling insurance. He later parlayed that sales experience into a new job as a securities salesman, and that led to the formation of a new brokerage firm, Buffett, Skelincka & Company.

. Howard Buffett worked hard for his family and was successful at business, but he was not driven to make more and more money. Instead, his passions were politics and religion. He served on the Omaha School Board and taught adult Sunday School classes. He was a man of unquestionable integrity and forthrightness. He did not drink or smoke. And when an investment turned out poorly for a customer he often felt so bad he repurchased it for his own account. He reminded all his children—Warren and his two sisters, Doris and Bertie—that they had a duty not only to God but to the community. "You are not required to carry the whole burden," he said. "Nor are you permitted to put down your share."[6]

In 1942, Howard Buffett was the Republican candidate for Nebraska's second Congressional district. His political slogan was "Do you want your children to be FREE?" In newspaper ads featuring pictures of his wife and children, he promised, "If you're tired of the way selfish politicians are messing up our government—if you want to see politics removed from our war effort . . . then let's get together on it. You and I, as dyed-in-the-wool Americans, have it in our power to keep America free for our children."[7] Howard Buffett was considered an underdog but he was popular and his message of freedom resonated with Omaha's pioneer spirit. He won the 1942 election and was re-elected in 1944, 1946, and 1950.

Today, Howard Buffett is politically remembered as a libertarian, an "Old Right" member of the GOP. The Old Right was an informal designation of a branch of American conservatism that included both Republicans and Democrats united in their opposition to military intervention overseas, to the removal of the gold standard as a backstop for paper currency, and most especially to President Roosevelt's New Deal coalition. It was Howard Buffett's profound belief that government, particularly the policies of the Roosevelt administration, had shackled human ingenuity and were leading the country to ruin. Howard was also a close friend of Murray Rothbard, an American economist who supported the development of modern libertarianism under the belief that all government services could be more efficiently provided by the private sector.

As a politician, Howard Buffett resurrected his dreams of being a journalist and became a prolific political writer. In one noted article written in 1944 for the *Omaha World-Herald* titled "Government Puts Handcuffs on Use of Human Energy," Howard pointed out it was "human energy that discovered electricity, invented the automobile, and created the sulfa drugs and penicillin and all other good things we enjoy today." He goes on to say, "Human history goes back about six thousand years. For over 5,800 of those years, governments blocked the free use of energy. Then came the American Revolution and human energy was turned loose for the first time in history. As a result, the day laborer has conveniences and comforts unknown to even a king one hundred years ago."

Libertarianism is a political philosophy that at its core upholds liberty—not only political freedom but freedom of choice. At the heart of libertarianism is the celebration of "self"—the individual over the state, whose authority is met with skepticism. Here in the United States we can trace libertarianism to John Locke, whose 1689 *An Essay Concerning Human Understanding* established the basis of liberal political theory. Thomas Paine espoused libertarian ideals in his political pamphlet *Common Sense* (1776), calling for the independence of the colonies. The poet and naturalist Henry David Thoreau was also an early influencer of libertarian ideals, reflected in his book *Walden* (1854), which advocated simple living and self-sufficiency. But there is no greater voice for the idea of libertarianism than the American philosopher, essayist, and poet Ralph Waldo Emerson. According to Harold Bloom, the famed literary critic, "the mind of Emerson is the mind of America."[8]

It was Roger Lowenstein in his thoughtful and well-written book, *Buffett: The Making of an American Capitalist*, who first made the connection between Ralph Waldo Emerson and Howard Buffett, and thence to Warren. "Buffett's trademark self-reliance," Lowenstein writes, was connected to the "sweetness of Emersonian independence which Buffett had learned from his father."[9]

Emerson was a champion of individualism and a critic of society's countervailing forces against individual thought. "Self-Reliance," first published in 1841, is considered his most famous essay. In it he presents three major themes. First is *solitude and community*. Emerson warns us the community is a distraction to self-growth; he believes more time should be spent in quiet reflection. Second is the sense of *nonconformity*. "Whoso would be a man," he writes, "must be a nonconformist." He argues that an individual must do what is right no matter what others think. Lastly, the theme of *spirituality* is especially important. Emerson tells us truth is within oneself and warns that relying on institutional thought hinders an individual's ability to mentally grow.

Those who have read "Self-Reliance" can easily spot the connections between Emerson's philosophy and Warren's investment behavior. Can we describe Warren as nonconformist? Put his widely known approach to investing side by side with the standard practices of Modern Portfolio Theory, which dominates today's money management industry, and you have your answer. Giving us another link, Emerson writes, "What I do is all that concerns me, not what the people think." Warren has always been puzzled why people desperately seek conversations about the stock market. It is not that Warren doesn't think about investing and the markets, but the need to be in constant communication with others baffles him. "I don't want to hear what a lot of other people think. I just want a lot of facts. I mean, in the end, I'm not handing my money over to anybody else."[10]

Emerson is careful to warn us that operating in solitude is a challenge. "It is harder because you will always find those who think they know what is your duty better than you know it. It is easy in the world to live after the world's opinion; it is easy in solitude to live after your own; but the great man is he who in the midst of the crowd keeps with perfect sweetness the independence of solitude."

One of the more difficult challenges investors face is how to maintain a level of independent solitude in a media environment that is constantly grabbing your attention. But the Money Mind recognizes how important it is to protect and maintain the "sweet independence" of solitary thinking.

However, this solitary thinking has a cost. The solitary man, by definition, is often the nonconformist. And as Emerson reminds us, "society everywhere is in conspiracy against the manhood of every one of its members," particularly the nonconformist. Emerson writes, "Society is a joint-stock company, in which the members agree, for the better securing of his bread to each shareholder, to surrender the liberty and culture to the eater." Lest there be any confusion, Emerson plainly states, "The virtue in most request is conformity" and "self-reliance is its aversion."

I ask you to consider that self-reliance is a robust trait of the Money Mind, and that it requires twin incubators of solitude and reflection. But that's not all. A Money Mind also needs the mental strength to overcome the disdain the greater whole has for those who are independent in thought and action. "For non-conformity, the world whips you with its displeasure," writes Emerson. "And therefore a man must know how to estimate a sour face." And at that moment of weakness the Money Mind is strengthened remembering Emerson's most famous quote: "A foolish consistency is the hobgoblin of little minds. To be great is to be misunderstood."

Before executing an order to buy or sell a security, investors are alone with their final decision. Make no mistake, successful investing is about self-reliance. It lies at the core of the Money Mind. Those who have self-reliance do well. Those who don't, suffer. Emerson sympathizes. "We must go alone," he says. "Isolation must precede true society." Emerson then reflects on how he always liked the "silent church before the service begins, better than the preaching." Looking around the sanctuary, Emerson asks, "Why should we assume the faults of our friends because they have the same blood? All men have my blood and I have all men's. Not for that will I adopt their petulance or folly, even at the extent of being ashamed." In many ways, Berkshire Hathaway headquarters in Omaha, 1,200 miles away from New York City, is a peaceful and quiet sanctuary far away from the bombastic sermons preached on Wall Street.

Emerson goes further: "Our isolation must not be mechanical, but spiritual, that is, must be elevation. At times the whole world seems in conspiracy to importune you with emphatic trifles, all knock at once at thy closet door and say 'come unto us.'" But he pleads, "Do not spill thy soul, do not at all descend; keep thy state; stay at home in thine own heaven; come not for a moment into their facts, into their hubbub of conflicting appearances." Thus Emerson travels through Howard Buffett onto Warren.

■ ■ ■

The close bond between Warren and his father is well known. During Warren's childhood, father and son were inseparable. Howard called his little boy "fireball," and Warren wanted nothing more than to imitate his dad. Years later he confessed that if his father had been a shoe salesman "I might be a shoe salesman right now."[11]

Warren has often said his dad was the number one teacher in his life, the person who introduced him to his love of books. We all know Warren spends the greatest amount of his time each day reading and learning in quiet solitude. I believe Emerson would approve.

Now take a moment and reflect on what it was like for Warren growing up in Omaha in a home with a father he adored. Day after day he listened to his dad discuss current issues, always from the libertarian point of view. In the evenings, conversation at the dinner table often turned to politics, and the calculus was always "will this add to, or subtract from, human liberty."[12]

Without doubt, Warren inherited his sense of patriotism from his father. But he also learned the primacy of honesty, integrity, and virtuous behavior. Warren once said, "The best advice I've ever been given is by my father who told me it took 20 years to build a reputation and 20 minutes to lose it. And if you remember that you'll do things differently."[13]

Congressman Howard H. Buffett died April 30, 1964. His last will and testament records an estate value of $563,292, of which $335,000 was invested in the Buffett Partnership. A trust was established for his wife Leila and daughters Doris and Bertie; Warren was named trustee. Aside from a few personal items of sentimental value, no bequeath was made to Warren. Howard explained his reasoning: "I make no further provisions for my son, Warren, not out of any lack of love for him, but because he has a substantial estate in his own right and for the further reason that he has advised me that I not make any further provision for him."[14]

Yet though the tangible inheritance items were small, there can be no doubt that the intangibles Warren received from his father were far more valuable. "Nothing can bring you peace but yourself," wrote Emerson. "Nothing can bring you peace but the triumph of principles." That was a father's ultimate gift to his son.

Warren was once asked whom he would choose if he could go back and speak to anyone in history. He didn't hesitate. "My father."[15]

Benjamin Graham

Benjamin Graham was born in London in 1894 to a Jewish family of merchants who imported china and bric-a-brac from Austria and Germany. In 1895, Graham's father moved his family to New York to open an American branch of the business. Soon after, Ben's father died at the young age of 35, leaving his mother to raise him and his two brothers.

Despite the financial setback, Graham's mother held the family together. Ben Graham attended the prestigious Boys High School in Brooklyn, then enrolled at Columbia University. A brilliant scholar, Graham mastered the teachings of mathematics and philosophy all the while consuming the major classical works in Greek and Latin. His long-time friend Irving Kahn said that Graham's "speed of thought was so great that most people were puzzled at how he could resolve a complicated question directly after having heard it." Graham, Kahn continued, "had another extraordinary characteristic in the breadth and depth of his memory." He could read Greek, Latin, German, and Spanish. Without ever formally studying the language, Graham once translated "a Spanish novel into literary English so professionally that it was accepted by an American publisher."[16]

Graham graduated Columbia University second in his class and was immediately offered teaching jobs by the philosophy, mathematics, and English departments. But Graham, concerned about the low starting salaries in academia, asked Columbia's dean, Frederick Keppel, for advice. Dean Keppel must have known his man, for he steered Graham to Wall Street, and in 1914, Benjamin Graham joined Newburger, Henderson & Loeb as an assistant in the bond department. His salary: $12 per week.

Ben Graham would become one of history's greatest investment thinkers. In 1934, with the publication of *Security Analysis,* cowritten with David Dodd, he became the undisputed father of financial analysis. Fifteen years later, Graham wrote *The Intelligent Investor,* the seminal book that Warren Buffett discovered in 1950 and that he later described as "by far the best book about investing ever written." According to Jason Zweig, the well-known financial journalist who edited the revised edition, *The Intelligent Investor* "was the first book ever to describe, for individual investors, the emotional framework and the analytical tools that are essential to financial success."[17] In Chapter 3, "The Evolution of Value Investing," we will further explore the analytical tools Graham used to identify value. But here, we remain focused on Graham's philosophical construct and how it contributed to the "temperament" of an investor and the formation of the Money Mind.

It was Roger Lowenstein, you may recall, who first connected Howard Buffett's Emersonian philosophy to Warren's investment approach. He also showed us how clearly Emerson's philosophy can be found in Graham. At the conclusion of *The Intelligent Investor,* Graham tells us, "Have the courage of your knowledge and experience. If you have formed a conclusion from the facts and if you know your judgment is sound, act on it—even though others may hesitate or differ. You are neither right nor wrong because the crowd disagrees with you. You are right because your data and reasoning are right."[18] Classic Emerson.

Little wonder, then, that when Warren was asked what particular aspects of Graham's teachings were the most conducive to successful investing he replied, "Graham was not swayed by what other people thought or how the world was feeling that day or anything of that sort."[19]

The close bond between Warren Buffett and Ben Graham is well known. But usually we think about their relationship in business terms, particularly how their investment methods dovetail. Now, if we look closely at the set of beliefs and values they share from the perspective of underlying philosophy, we see a clear linkage. Emerson to Howard Buffett to Warren Buffett, and simultaneously Emerson to Graham.

Warren's philosophical foundation had already been formed by his father, but now he had the natural connection to combine what he had learned from his father to Graham's writings. Lowenstein explains: "Ben Graham opened the door, and in a way that spoke to Buffett personally. He gave Buffett the tools to explore the market's manifold possibilities and also an approach that fit his student's temper." As a result, Lowenstein writes, "Armed with Graham's techniques . . . and steeled by the example of Graham's character, Buffett would be able to work with his trademark self-reliance."[20] But Warren's relationship with Graham went deeper than this. Although Warren readily took in Graham's investment methods he "saw Graham in idealized terms—as a 'hero,' like his father." Indeed, Warren once said that "Ben Graham was far more than an author or a teacher. More than any other man except my father, he influenced my life."[21]

■ ■ ■

Today, when Warren talks about Graham and investing he urges us to "pay special attention to the invaluable advice" in two chapters of *The Intelligent Investor:* Chapter 8, "The Investor and Market Fluctuations" and Chapter 20, "Margin of Safety as the Central Concept of Investment." Both chapters contain philosophical pearls of wisdom. Warren reminds us, "To invest successfully over a lifetime does not require a stratospheric IQ. What is needed is a sound intellectual framework for making decisions and the ability to keep emotions from corroding that framework."[22] An investment method combined with the proper philosophical architecture is what is required to be successful.

As we have seen, that philosophical architecture rests on a foundation of Emersonian ideas and ideals, a foundation shared by Howard Buffett and Benjamin Graham. But we cannot leave our discussion of Graham's way of looking at the world without noting another important philosophical insight we can glean from him, something that may come as a surprise. Although Ben Graham's reputation centers on his contributions to finance and investing, little attention has been paid to his other passion—the study of the Greek and Roman classics.

The classical age is generally described as spanning from the time of Homer to the decline of the Roman Empire—that is, from the eighth century BC to the sixth century AD. Those years saw an astonishing depth and breadth of intellectual pursuit, producing what most historians consider the foundation of Western civilization. The great minds of ancient Greece and Rome articulated concepts in art, architecture, literature, philosophy, science, mathematics, law, and warfare that we still rely on.

In a thousand different ways, our society rests solidly on a foundation of the ideas and principles expressed by those writers many centuries ago. With their insights about the universal nature of the human experience, these ancient works remain vital to this day, and are considered by many to be the cornerstone of a well-rounded education. Today, thoughtful men and women are rereading the writings of those ancient scholars, and in both the clarity of ideas and the beauty of the language are finding inspiration for navigating rough times and living a meaningful life.

Ben Graham certainly felt this way. He read all the major classic works of literature, many in their original language, seeking heroes and role models. He particularly admired, we are told, the Roman emperor Marcus Aurelius.

Marcus, who governed the empire from 161 until his death in 180, was the last emperor of the Pax Romana, an age when Romans lived in peace, stability, and prosperity. He is considered one of the Five Good Emperors. And he was the only emperor who was also a philosopher. Today, Marcus Aurelius is best known for his book *Meditations*, widely acknowledged as one of the great texts of philosophy.

When he was quite young, Marcus was introduced to the philosophy of Stoicism by his teachers, and found there the fundamental principles that would guide his life. A natural scholar, he very early on began writing down his thoughts on how best to apply those principles to daily challenges. He continued that practice all his life, writing himself reminders on how a Stoic should live. Those writings, which were always intended for himself alone and not for wider publication, became the text now known as *Meditations*.

Ben Graham, with his love of the classics, was especially attracted to *Meditations* and incorporated many of its ideas into his own personal philosophy—particularly, as we will see, the embrace of Stoicism.

The original precepts of Stoicism were first articulated in the third century BC by the Greek philosopher Zeno of Citium; in the twenty-first century AD, those precepts are often mischaracterized. Today, when we describe a person as "stoic," we likely mean that they respond to any kind of pain or bad news by not responding at all. They silently absorb the blows of misfortune, sometimes seeming almost like zombies in their apparent lack of emotion. That is a far cry from the original principle, which stressed the importance of recognizing those events in life that are out of our control and not allowing emotional reactions to those events to overwhelm good judgment.

In ancient times those who called themselves Stoics came to understand that a life plagued with negative emotions would never bring happiness. Hence, the virtuous goal was to develop techniques that would work to prevent the onset of these negative emotions and instead allow one to achieve a steady, favorable state of mind. It was called *ataraxia*, a Greek term that is generally translated as "unperturbedness" or "tranquility."[23] The Stoics characterized ataraxia as being in a state of robust equanimity free from distress and worry, and a deliberate indifference to those aspects of life over which we have no control.

Can we say that Ben Graham was a Stoic? It was Janet Lowe in her book *Benjamin Graham on Value Investing* who noted that he "embraced stoicism as his personal philosophy."[24] Although he himself never used that term, as far as we know, it's clear that the fundamental principles of Stoicism suited his natural temperament, and profoundly influenced both his personal and professional life.

How does the Stoic Ben Graham think about investing? There is no better way to illustrate this than the parable of Mr. Market.[25] Graham asks us to imagine we own a private business with a partner he calls Mr. Market. Mr. Market is very accommodating. He shows up each day with an offer to either buy your shares in the business or sell you his shares for the same price. But Mr. Market has acute emotional problems. On certain days, he is wildly excited and names you a very high price. Other days, he is deeply depressed, seeing nothing but trouble ahead, and quotes a very low price.

Mr. Market is, of course, the stock market, and it is exactly that wild manic-depressive behavior that causes so many investors to make bad decisions. Unable to distinguish between price and value, they look at rising prices with greed and envy and falling prices with fear and anxiety—the exact emotions the Stoics seek to avoid.

Ben Graham often reminded us that investors' worst enemy is themselves. When investors cannot detach themselves from the market's emotional rollercoaster, they inevitably succumb to its negative forces, and that ultimately penalizes their portfolios. Warren Buffett continues his teacher's parable of Mr. Market with his own. He writes, "Like Cinderella at the ball, you must heed one warning or everything will turn to pumpkins. It is his [Mr. Market's] pocketbook, not his wisdom, that you will find useful. If he shows up some day in a particularly foolish mood, you are free to ignore him or take advantage of him, but it will be disastrous if you fall under his influence." The Stoics would tell investors to react with tranquility to Mr. Market. But it is what Warren said next that makes us better appreciate the connections in developing an investment philosophy.

"If you aren't certain that you understand and can value your business far better than Mr. Market, you don't belong in the game. And as they say in poker, if you've been in the game 30 minutes and you don't know who the patsy is, *you're* the patsy"[26]—extremely important words that every investor needs to understand. If you have done the work to determine the value of a company, the stock you own, then you will look upon the stock market prices with a large degree of disinterest. It is no longer the primary indicator of how well you are progressing in your investments. The economic returns of your investment determine your financial well-being. The stock market's manic attitude thus becomes a secondary indicator that may or may not benefit you in deciding to add or sell shares. Once you reach this level in your investment thinking, it is easy to maintain a Stoic indifference to the stock market's inherent price volatility.

Indeed, we can clearly see Warren's Stoic attitude when it comes to investing. He is largely ambivalent about what goes on in the stock market, at least in the short run. "In my opinion, investment success will not be produced by arcane formulae, computer programs or signals flashed by the price behavior of stocks and markets," he wrote. "Rather an investor will succeed by coupling good business judgment with an ability to insulate his thoughts and behavior from the super-contagious emotions that swirl about the marketplace. In my own efforts to stay insulated, I have found it highly useful to keep Ben's Mr. Market concept firmly in my mind."[27]

Charles Thomas Munger

Charlie Munger has been by Warren's side far longer than the time Warren shared with his father, Howard Buffett, or his teacher, Ben Graham. Warren and Charlie met in 1959 and became instant friends. When Charlie started his own investment partnership, Wheeler, Munger & Co, in 1962, they became investment buddies. And in 1978, when Charlie became vice chairman of Berkshire Hathaway, they cemented a business partnership that has lasted to this day. The two have a 61-year friendship, with a passion for investing that has lasted for 58 years, and over the last 42 years they have perfected a "pilot–copilot" relationship that has steered Berkshire into becoming one of the largest and most respected companies in the world. In all, over half of Warren's and Charlie's lives have been spent in the company of each other.

In the category of "it's a small world," Charlie Munger was born in Omaha, Nebraska, on January 1, 1924. He grew up only 200 yards from where Warren lives today. He even worked in Ernest Buffett's grocery store, although he and Warren never met as kids. Charlie left Omaha and attended the University of Michigan and the California Institute of Technology but World War II interrupted his education; he served as a meteorological officer in the Air Force. After the war, despite the lack of an undergraduate degree, Charlie was admitted to Harvard Law School and graduated in 1948.

When Warren and Charlie finally met in 1959, introduced by Omaha friends, Charlie was settling his father's estate. Warren was already in the early innings of managing the Buffett Limited Partnership and suggested to Charlie the road to riches was not the law but investing.

It has been said that Warren's first attraction to Charlie was largely based on how much Charlie reminded him of Ben Graham. Both men fostered a belief in independent thought. Both were known for their "integrity and dedication to objectivity and realism."[28] And both were voracious readers with deep interests in history, literature, and science. Graham's preferences, as we have seen, leaned more to the classical writings, whereas Charlie devoured hundreds and hundreds of biographies, one after another. Graham and Munger were also admirers of Benjamin Franklin and both absorbed Franklin's message of lifelong learning.

Charlie is a polymath. The scope of his knowledge is staggering; there appears to be little he doesn't know. And like Graham, his ability to reach conclusions with lightning speed is mesmerizing. "Charlie has the best 30-second mind in the world," said Warren. "He goes from A to Z in one move. He sees the essence of everything before you finish the sentence."[29] With all that Charlie has accomplished, he deserves his own book. Thankfully we have several: *Poor Charlie's Almanack: The Wit and Wisdom of Charles T. Munger* and other fine books have captured the magnificence of Charlie's mind.[30]

If we were to investigate the deep well that is Charlie's knowledge, we would pull up three distinct buckets: the *pursuit of worldly wisdom*; the *study of failure*; and the *moral imperative to embrace rationality*.

In April 1994, Charlie Munger's wellspring of knowledge burst onto the scene in a remarkable lecture he gave to Dr. Guilford Babcock's Student Investment Seminar at the Marshall School of Business at the University of Southern California. The students were primed to hear Charlie's thoughts about the stock market and perhaps pick up a few investment tips. Instead, Charlie announced he was going to play a little joke on them. Rather than talking about investing directly, he was going to talk about "stock picking as a subdivision of the art of achieving worldly wisdom." For the next hour and a half, he challenged the students to think of the market, finance, and economics not as individual topics but as a larger collection of studies that would also include physics, biology, social studies, mathematics, philosophy, and psychology.

It was straight out of the playbook of one of Charlie's heroes.

In 1749, Benjamin Franklin, who identified himself as B. Franklin, Printer, published a pamphlet entitled *Proposals Relating to the Education of Youth in Pensilvania*. In it, he laid out his views on the fundamental purpose of higher education and proposed establishing an academy built on those ideas. It was astonishingly radical. At the time, institutions of higher education were meant to prepare people for the ministry; Franklin's vision was much broader. He believed it was vital to educate young people for leadership in business and government, and that to do so they should be exposed to many disciplines. He also firmly believed that such education should be available to students from the working class as well as the upper classes that then dominated most campuses. To make his vision a reality, he carefully nurtured the support of some of Philadelphia's leading citizens, and in 1751 the Academy and Charitable School in the Province of Pennsylvania (which we know today as the University of Pennsylvania) opened its doors.

It's almost impossible to overstate how groundbreaking Franklin's ideas were. Dr. Richard Beeman, former dean of Penn's College of Arts and Sciences, calls Benjamin Franklin the originator of the liberal arts education. Franklin believed that after students mastered the basic skills of reading, writing, arithmetic, physical education, and public speaking, they should turn their attention to discovering the connections that exist among the wider bodies of knowledge. Dr. Beeman describes this as Franklin cultivating certain habits of mind.

We can see a straight line from Ben Franklin's *habits of mind* to Charlie Munger's focus on achieving *worldly wisdom.* According to Charlie, we do not need to become an expert in every discipline in order to reach worldly wisdom; all we need is a basic understanding of the major mental models within each discipline. We would then have, in effect, a liberal arts education in investing, and we would be well on the way to enjoying what Charlie calls "the lollapalooza impact" of worldly wisdom.

But what exactly would a liberal arts education in investing look like?[31]

In physics, we would certainly study Isaac Newton. In *Principia Mathematica* Newton outlines the three laws of motion, the second of which—for every action there is an equal and opposite reaction— connects directly to established principles of economics, primarily the principles of supply and demand. When they are in balance, we say the economy is in equilibrium. But if this equilibrium becomes displaced by accidents of production or consumption, then the economy will react with countervailing forces of compara- ble strength that will restore equilibrium balance. Disequilibrium cannot long survive. Studying Newton helps us absorb this immu- table truth.

However, there are many who do not see an economy and a stock market from a physics point of view. Perhaps they are more naturally drawn to biology, in which case I would say, read Charles Darwin, who taught us that living systems learn, evolve, adapt, and can change unexpectedly. There is no doubt markets are living, breathing systems. That makes them the exact opposite of atomic physical systems, which are highly predictable and can repeat the same actions thousands of times with near precision. They act most often in perfect equilibrium. Biological systems, in contrast, exhibit non-equilibrium traits whereby small effects can some- times have large consequences, while large effects can have small consequences. In physics, negative feedbacks push the system predictably back to equilibrium. But in biology, we observe positive feedback loops that can push the system into new and unforeseen directions—just like the stock market.

Studying sociology gives us another mental model: the most optimal and efficient societal body is one that is most diverse. But once diversity collapses, when the agents become of one mindset, the system becomes unstable, leading to booms and busts—again, just like the stock market.

From mathematics we learn about probability theory, formulated by Blaise Pascal and Pierre de Fermat. We take additional note of the eighteenth-century Presbyterian minister Thomas Bayes, whose theorem gave us a mathematical procedure for updating our original beliefs and thus changing the relevant odds. Taken together, Pascal, Fermat, and Bayes give us an outline to properly estimate the future free cash flows of companies, which in turn makes it possible to determine the intrinsic value of our investments.

In philosophy we would no doubt study both the ancient Stoics and modern philosophers such as René Descartes, Francis Bacon, David Hume, and Immanuel Kant (we will meet them again later in this chapter). We would read Ludwig Wittgenstein, the Austrian-born philosopher whose field of study included logic, mathematics, and the philosophy of language. From Wittgenstein we learn that when we speak of "meaning," we are referring to the words we use to create a description that ultimately leads to our explanation of events. And that when we fail to explain outcomes it is often because we did not form the proper description.

Our studies of philosophy would be incomplete without reading Ralph Waldo Emerson and William James. We made the acquaintance of Mr. Emerson earlier in this chapter, and we will learn more about James shortly. He is considered one of the founders of the unique American philosophy called pragmatism, which we analyze in some detail later in this chapter. And, as we will see in the next chapter, being a pragmatist is what made possible Warren's shift from Graham's asset-centric valuation techniques to the future free cash flow estimates of better businesses articulated by Charlie.

But no liberal arts study of investing is complete without a deep dive into psychology. And doing so takes us immediately into the study of failure, Charlie's second bucket of knowledge. In Charlie's mind, while it is important to study what works, it is absolutely imperative to study what doesn't work. And getting to the root of failure starts with psychology, for almost without exception our failures, our mistakes, start with errors in thinking that are embedded in psychological missteps.

German-born philosopher Dietrich Dörner describes these damaging patterns of thought that bedevil modern society in his highly regarded book, *The Logic of Failure: Recognizing and Avoiding Error in Complex Situations.* He shows us that in the modern world we are asked to plan, act carefully, and solve systems that are complex, obscure, and dynamical while lacking a complete and correct understanding of the overall system. That sounds daunting; it's almost a guarantee of failure. However, Dörner believes that failure is not inherently inevitable but rather the result of bad habits, by which he means bad mental habits. Rather than one giant mistake, he argues, we humans are more likely to fail in increments, with a small mistake here, a bad decision there, until it suddenly adds up. "Failure does not strike like a bolt from the blue," he writes; "rather it develops gradually from its own logic."[32] Or, as Charlie might say, from its own illogic.

For his part, Charlie says that he has "always been interested in standard thinking errors." Even as a young college student, he wanted to understand the psychology of decision making, but found little help from his formal curriculum. So, soon after receiving his law degree in 1948, Charlie began what he calls "a long struggle to get rid of the most dysfunctional part of my idea of *x.*"[33]

Note the year—1948. It is important to appreciate that Charlie's quest to understand the psychology of decision-making occurred during a period when little was published about the link between psychology and investing. What today is popularly known as behavioral finance did not exist as a field of study in the 1950s, '60s, or '70s. The first serious work—*Judgment Under Uncertainty: Heuristics and Biases,* by Daniel Kahneman and Amos Tversky—did not appear until

1982 and even then it was buried deep in academia. The next year produced *Influence: The Psychology of Persuasion* by Robert Cialdini; it became one of Charlie's favorite books. Almost 40 years later, we still struggle with understanding mental errors, a journey Charlie began some *70* years ago. In short, Charlie drew his own roadmap on how to avoid cognitive failures long before the rest of the world had named the problem.

It should come as no surprise that Charlie took control of his "struggle to get rid of psychological ignorance" by building his own roadmap for improving decision-making. Soon after the lecture at the Marshall School of Business in the 1994, Charlie gave two back-to-back talks at the Cambridge Center for Behavioral Studies, one in the fall of 1994, the other in the spring of 1995. Under the title "The Psychology of Human Misjudgment," Charlie offered a list of what he called "psychology-based tendencies that often mislead along with some antidotes to errors."[34] Charlie outlined 25 tendencies, from "Reward and Punishment/Super-response Tendency" to "Lollapalooza Tendency—The Tendency to Get Extreme Consequences from Confluences of Psychological Tendencies Acting in Favor of a Particular Outcome." With each one, he provided a detailed description of the thinking errors, followed by antidotes on how to avoid future missteps. All 25 tendencies and their antidotes can be found in *Poor Charlie's Almanack.*

Here's an example: number 15 is called "Social-Proof Tendency." It describes the very common and very human tendency to adopt the beliefs and behaviors of people around us, without considering their worth. Essentially, it's about self-confidence. A person's behavior becomes oversimplified, Charlie warns, when he "automatically thinks and does what he observes to be thought and done around him." So by the actions of others we risk being pulled into misguided action. Or, which is equally dangerous, we are lulled into inaction at times when action is precisely what is needed. The antidote is simple: "Learn how to ignore the examples from others when they are wrong. Few skills are more worth having."[35] Pure Charlie.

With all that has been written about decision-making and the psychology of investing over the past 40 years, you would think investors have fine-tuned their thinking skills. But we know that is not the case. Dietrich Dörncr tells us the problem lies with people who take mental shortcuts; he calls it economizing our thinking. "Instead of clarifying the complex interrelationships among the variables in the system," he says we tend to select only one variable. This is mentally economical, because it frees us from a great deal of additional work.[36] But it is exactly this cutting-corners-type thinking that causes problems.

When Charlie defined the tendencies in "The Psychology of Human Misjudgment" he didn't just name one or two, he wrote 25. And in writing the 25 antidotes he challenged us to continually reassess our positioning. "In the practical world," Charlie asks, "what good is the thought system laid out in this list of tendencies?" He answers his own question: "The psychological thought system described, when properly used, enables the spread of wisdom and good conduct and facilitates the avoidance of disaster."[37] Here, in one tidy sentence, Charlie sums up his main themes—developing worldly wisdom, learning to avoid failure, and conducting oneself intelligently. He calls that last one "good conduct" and it gives us a natural lead-in to investigating his third bucket: the *embrace of rationality*.

Roger Lowenstein, Warren's biographer, says that Warren's "genius was largely a genius of character—of patience, discipline and rationality."[38] Without question, the same can be said of Charlie. Indeed, if there is but one word that permeates throughout Berkshire Hathaway, it is rationality. It was Charlie who said, "Berkshire is sort of a temple to rationality."[39] But for Charlie rationality is not just a passing definition; it is the moral compass that guides everything. For him, being rational is the highest calling one can answer. That makes it the most important mental bucket in the formation of Charlie's thinking, and compels us to parse its full meaning.

Rationalism is one of those words that have developed a slippery coating over the years. In its purest sense, the philosophical construct named rationalism refers to a theory about how we gain knowledge. In this theory (simplified here), rationalists learn by thinking and analyzing—that is, through deductive reasoning and the power of their mind. This is referred to as *a priori* knowledge. The antithesis is known as empiricism, which holds that the only way we gain knowledge is through direct observation of our own sense experiences (*a posteriori*). To empiricists, nothing is true unless they can see it, hear it, taste it, and so on. Of course, in real life people can, and generally do, use both approaches according to the circumstances at hand. It's not an either/or game.

However, in casual conversation we often use the word *rational* much more loosely. When we hear someone say, "You're not being rational," they usually mean not being logical or sensible, not thinking straight.

Both Warren and Charlie refer often to this concept of rationality. As we will soon see, they tend to value it over all other mental models. So when they talk about the importance of being rational, it behooves us to listen. But do we know for sure what they mean? Are they using the term in its more casual sense of being logical, sensible? Maybe. Or are they two men who relish serious reading, thinking of the classic arguments between two academic schools of thought? Maybe that too.

What is more likely, I suspect, is an amalgam of the two. Warren and Charlie have spent years reading and thinking about important concepts and sculpting their own sense of truth from many sources. We would be wise, I think, to take the time to explore the various philosophical threads that have led to this uniquely Berkshirist approach to rationality.

■ ■ ■

Two important figures in modern philosophy—Francis Bacon and René Descartes—illustrate the two opposite views. The two men were contemporaries, from the late sixteenth to mid-seventeenth centuries, and both rejected the teachings of medieval universities they inherited but disagreed on what should come next. Francis Bacon, an empiricist, argued all knowledge must either originate with or be testable by actual experience. He believed in the value of practical knowledge, like that acquired by builders, carpenters, farmers, sailors, and scientists with their telescopes and microscopes. They were, in his view, united in their philosophical inquiry by how things are, not by how we imagine things may be. Descartes, a rationalist, epitomizes the opposite camp, wherein true knowledge can only be achieved by reason, by the inference of first principles or self-evident truths. The tension between empiricists and rationalists was quite real, and offered little guidance for those attempting to define a personal philosophy to help navigate life's challenges.

A century later, during the Age of Enlightenment, a new voice emerged. Immanuel Kant, one of history's great philosophical minds, is credited with bridging the impasse between the rationalists and the empiricists by synthesizing their concepts.

Starting in 1755 and continuing for the next four decades, Kant taught at the University of Köninsberg, in what was then known as East Prussia, where he himself had been a student years earlier. His lectures reflected an astonishingly wide range of interests, including physics, astronomy, mathematics, geography, anthropology, and psychology (does that remind you of anyone?). But today we remember him primarily for his contributions to the field of philosophy, crystallized in several seminal works, particularly *Critique of Pure Reason* (1781), which secured his position as one of the great philosophers.

In his struggles to resolve the dispute between rationalists and empiricists, Kant turned to David Hume, the Scottish philosopher, economist, and historian. Hume eschewed the debate; he was much more interested in understanding just how the mind works. Hume's major philosophical work was *A Treatise of Human Nature* (1739). Years later he rewrote his masterpiece, dividing the *Treatise* into two books, *An Enquiry Concerning Human Understanding* (1748) and *An Enquiry Concerning the Principles of Morals* (1751). In *Human Understanding* he argues that we form "mental habits of connecting ideas together" such that whenever we think of *X* our mind automatically and immediately goes to thinking of *Y* with such inevitability that we assume the two ideas must be connected.

Hume's idea of how the mind works was the insight Kant needed to develop a metatheory that would combine both the rationalists' and empiricists' approaches to knowledge. In Kant's new perspective, later referred to as Kantianism, both are right, and both are wrong. A.C. Grayling, British philosopher and philosophy historian, summarizes it this way: "The empiricists are right to insist that there cannot be knowledge without sensory experience but they are wrong to say the mind is a blank slate. The rationalists are right to insist that there are *a priori* concepts supplied by our mind, but they are wrong to say *a priori* concepts are sufficient by themselves for knowledge of the world."[40]

Now let's consider the various theories from the point of view of a few familiar individuals. We can look upon Ben Graham as a rationalist, firmly in René Descartes' camp. Graham's knowledge is built through a series of simple mental steps, each connected and then carefully reviewed until the chain is complete. His approach is mathematical, relying on self-evident truths. His estimation of value, for example, is built upon *a priori* reasoning, not the actual experience of running the companies he bought. Thus, Graham tended toward cheap "cigar butt" stocks with low profit margins, high capital intensity needs that generated little cash—in other words, data that can be collected through research rather than through hands-on sensory experience

Charlie sits in the Francis Bacon camp. For Charlie, truth is based on observable facts and personal experiences that provide evidence toward knowledge. When Charlie began his investment partnership in 1962 he was aware of Graham's teachings but not fully convinced. For his own investment approach, Charlie favored identifying good businesses through a process of observing and analyzing the full scope of the company's operation, not simply a bargain price.

Charlie's experience helped move Warren away from Graham's reasoning. "It took Charlie Munger to break my cigar-butt habits (buying cheap stocks—bad businesses) and set the course for building a business that could combine huge size with satisfactory profits," said Warren. "From my perspective, Charlie's most important architectural feat was the design of today's Berkshire. The blueprint he gave me was simple. Forget about buying fair businesses at wonderful prices; instead buy wonderful businesses at fair prices."[41]

Examining Warren's investment philosophy, we can see Immanuel Kant at work. On one hand, Warren is a rationalist. He pledges allegiance to Graham's method of buying stocks only when its low price, lower than the company's intrinsic value, provides a margin of safety. "I still think those are the three right words," he says. But he also appreciates the lessons learned from the experiences of owning companies, and from that we can say he is an empiricist. Hands-on experiences that come from actually owning a business have added mightily to Warren's understanding of investing. We appreciate the philosophical bridge that Charlie built for Warren when Warren says, "I am a better investor because I am a businessman and a better businessman because I am an investor."[42]

At a dinner one night, Charlie was asked what one quality accounts for his success "I'm rational," he replied. "That's the answer. I am rational."[43] He added, "People who say they are rational should know how things work, what works, and what doesn't, and why."[44] It's not a passing idea; it's fundamental to him. As Charlie has often said, "It's a moral duty to be as rational as you can make yourself."[45]

The good news is, rationality can be learned. "An increase in rationality is not just something you choose or don't choose," Charlie says.[46] The implication is clear: you have to work at it. "Becoming more rational is a long process. It's something you get slowly, with a variable result. But there's hardly anything more important."[47]

■ ■ ■

At the 2010 Berkshire Annual Meeting, a shareholder asked Warren and Charlie to describe their theory of life. The answer, I thought, had to be rationality but Charlie surprised me. He quickly grabbed the microphone and announced, "Pragmatism!" I sat up straight in my seat and leaned forward to listen. "Pragmatism. Do what suits your temperament. Do what works and keep doing it," said Charlie. "That's the fundamental algorithm of life—repeat what works."[48] This was the first time I had heard Warren or Charlie use the word *pragmatism*, and I knew it was worth learning more.

What is pragmatism exactly, and where does it fit? We know rationalism is what's needed to be successful in investing, but my reading led me to conclude that pragmatism is what's required to be *continually* successful.

Unlike the other philosophical models we have examined in this chapter, American pragmatism is relatively new. It was introduced by William James in an 1898 lecture at the University of California, Berkeley; he named it "Philosophical Conceptions and Practical Results." During the lecture, James introduced what he called the "principle of Peirce, the principal of pragmatism." It was an homage to his friend and fellow philosopher Charles Sanders Peirce. Twenty years earlier, James had been profoundly influenced by Peirce's publication "How to Make Our Ideas Clear." In it he wrote, "The whole function of philosophy is to produce habits of action."[49] Indeed, the word *pragmatism* is derived from the same Greek word *pragma*, meaning *action*, from which the words *practice* and *practical* originate. It was Peirce's contention that our beliefs are really rules for taking action.

William James did not begin as a philosopher. He earned his medical degree in 1869 but never practiced medicine. Instead his interests were fixed on psychology, studying what he called "soul-sickness." James meticulously studied the Roman Stoic Marcus Aurelius, the same philosopher so influential to Ben Graham, and compiled his thoughts in a diary that he shared with friends who were suffering bouts of ill mental health. In 1890, James published his monumental book *The Principles of Psychology*, a 1,200-page two-volume work that took 12 years to write. He became instantly recognized as one of the leading thinkers in psychology.

How is it, then, that today we think of James as a philosopher rather than a psychologist? In truth, the distance between the two is not great. Both involve studying the mind. Psychology examines mental defection, while philosophy seeks ways to improve thoughtful reflection as a means to better decision-making. James' philosophy was crafted into "what he called healthy-mindedness" and what nowadays we call pragmatism.[50]

William James' father, Henry Sr., was an American theologian. In his studies he met and befriended Ralph Waldo Emerson, who in turn became William James' intellectual godparent. In 1837, Emerson wrote "The American Scholar," which "heralded the coming of a new type of thinker." Little did he know then that he was talking about his future godson.[51] It was William James who would assume from Emerson the mantle of the leader of American philosophy.

Pragmatism has been called a uniquely American philosophy, but at its core it is not a philosophy as much as it is a way of doing philosophy. Pragmatists rely not on absolute standards and abstract ideas but rather on results—those things that are actually working and that help you reach your goals. Indeed, James believed philosophers had wasted far too much time debating abstract principles trying to prove or disprove metaphysical issues. Instead, he argued, they should ask what practical effects come from holding one philosophical view over another. More bluntly, James asks, in his famous statement, "what is the cash-value" of a particular belief in terms of a person's practical experience? How do we get from old philosophical beliefs to new ones? According to James, the process is the same as that followed by any scientist. In his essay titled "Pragmatism: Conception of Truth," he explains:

> An individual has a stock of old opinions already, but he meets a new experience that puts them to strain. Somebody contradicts them; or in a reflective moment he discovers they contradict each other; or he hears of facts with which they are incompatible; or desires arise in him which they cease to satisfy. The result is inward trouble to which his mind till then had been a stranger and from which he seeks to escape by modifying his previous mass of opinions. He saves as many of them as he can, for in this matter of belief we are all extreme conservatives. So he tries to change first that opinion and then that (for they resist change very variously), until at last some idea comes up that he can graft upon the ancient stock with a minimum of disturbances of the latter, some idea that mediates between the stock and the new experience and runs them into most felicitously.[52]

Those with a pragmatic orientation can readily adopt a new idea while preserving the older truths with as little disruption as possible. The new truths are simply go-betweens, transition-smoothers that help us get from one point to the next. "Our thoughts become true," says James, "as they successfully exert their go-between function."[53] A belief is true and has "cash-value" if it helps us get from one place to another. Truth becomes a verb, not a noun.

So, we can say pragmatism is a process that allows people to navigate an uncertain world without becoming stranded on the desert island of absolutes. Pragmatism has no prejudices, dogmas, or rigid canons. It will entertain any hypothesis and consider any evidence. If you need facts, take the facts. "In short, pragmatism widens the field of search for God," says James. "Her only test of probable truth is what works best in leading us."[54]

How do we link the philosophy of pragmatism with Charlie's moral imperative to act rationally? As it happens, William James wrestled with the same question. According to John Kaag, professor of philosophy at the University of Massachusetts at Lowell, James' pragmatism worked to bridge not only the differences between empiricism and rationalism but also the relationship between rationalism itself with pragmatism.

Kaag tells us that the American philosophy of pragmatism "represents a philosophical middle ground, aiming to mediate between competing theoretical schools, between the thinkers who focused on the trees and those who saw only the forests."[55] And James, he believes, wanted to see both. Kaag compares James to Immanuel Kant, who, you may recall, spent the last years of his life synthesizing the ideas of two competing schools of thought, in his case rationalists and empiricists. For his part, James called rationalists "the tender-minded" and empiricists "the tough minded" and worried that neither seemed to recognize that the experiences of others, whether they be ethical or scientific, are central to forming one's own understanding.

So James' pragmatism was a form of Kantianism that helped provide a bridge between the tough-minded scientist and the tender-minded idealist. In this sense, James, according to Kaag, "picked up where Kant left off."[56]

Bill Miller, founder and chief investment officer of Miller Value Partners and the former portfolio manager of the Legg Mason Value Trust, has thought long and hard about rationality and pragmatism. We will meet Miller again in the next chapter, "The Evolution of Value Investing." He acknowledges that, in a strict definitional sense, it is possible to be rational without being a pragmatist and to be pragmatic without necessarily being rational. But he firmly believes that in practice the two philosophical approaches are inextricably linked. "To do what works, to be pragmatic, is to be rational," he explains. "Rational does not entail being wed to an abstract theory of what reason demands, but to what works in the real world."[57]

As we discuss in the next chapter, the "cash value" of an idea, which is the hallmark of pragmatism, is what helped Warren move from Stage One of value investing to Stage Two, and then on to Stage Three. A philosophical perspective that blends pragmatism with a Kantian approach to rationalism has proved to be a powerful foundation for his 65 years of successful investing. In an industry where the tenure of an all-star portfolio manager rarely exceeds a decade, that record of success calls us to read, study, and embrace the philosophical lessons outlined in this chapter.

In Closing . . .

To appreciate the intricacies of a Money Mind, it is critical that we fully embrace the investment methods we would need to define, purchase, and manage value-creating businesses. In Chapter 4, "Business-Driven Investing," we will explore these core competencies. But that is not the whole story, for as we have also learned in this chapter, a philosophical foundation is equally critical to our understanding the world of investing.

What, then, can we say about a Money Mind?

We can say a Money Mind is self-reliant, as defined by Ralph Waldo Emerson. A Money Mind knows what it owns and why, which not only strengthens self-confidence but also reinforces a Stoic attitude toward the stock market's negative emotions of fear and greed. A Money Mind seeks to build worldly wisdom, as outlined by Charlie Munger, through studying the major mental models in different disciplines. Just as important, the Money Mind studies failure to avoid making the mistakes of others. The Money Mind is a rational mind, but rational in the sense that it appreciates both *a priori* knowledge and *a posteriori* experiences, knowing full well the greatest benefit comes from combining both. Lastly, the Money Mind is pragmatic: it appreciates knowledge but is humbled by what there is left to learn.

3

The Evolution of Value Investing

S oon after joining Newburger, Henderson & Loeb in 1914, Ben Graham grew restless. He had started his new job as a clerk, but in short order he was moved into the bond department and trained to be a salesman. But what he really wanted to do was write, not sell bonds. Despite lacking any formal training in economics or accounting, Graham began researching railroad companies, specifically railroad bonds, on his own and writing research reports.[1]

One of his reports, on the Missouri Pacific Railroad, caught the eye of a partner at J.S. Bache and Company, a respectable NYSE firm. He was quickly offered a job as a statistician with a 50 percent increase in salary. Graham let Newburger know that although he felt a sense of loyalty to the firm, he was not motivated to be a salesman. Newburger countered with its own pay raise. It was not quite 50 percent but it included a sweetener: the opportunity for Graham to start his own statistical department. He decided to stay and pursue his writing at the same time.

At that time, serious investment capital was limited to buying bonds. Common stock investing was thought to be a speculative game played not on the basis of financial data but insider information. Nonetheless, Graham began writing articles for *The Magazine of Wall Street*, a newsletter with investment tips for stocks as well as bonds. He soon developed a following. He next published a pamphlet titled

"Lessons for Investors." In it he argued "If the market value of a stock is substantially less than its intrinsic value, it should also have excellent prospects for an advance in price." It was the first time the words *intrinsic value* appeared.[2]

Graham left Newburger in 1923 to start his own investment firm. Two years later he hired Jerome Newman and formed the Graham-Newman Corporation, which lasted until 1956. Graham's early investment results were promising. Much of his portfolio was hedged or in arbitrage situations, which dampened the steep losses of the 1929 stock market crash. But in 1930, Graham tiptoed back into the stock market—this time unhedged—believing stocks had bottomed. When the market dropped again, Graham, for the second time in his life, was near financial ruin.

But all was not lost. In 1927, before the crash, Graham had begun teaching a night class on investing at his alma mater. The Columbia University catalog promised that a Wall Street investment professional would be teaching Advanced Security Analysis on Monday evenings in Room 305 of Schermerhorn Hall. The class description read "Investment Theories subjected to practical market tests. Origin and detection of discrepancies between price and value." It was in this class that Graham coined the term *security analysis* and replaced the Wall Street job title of statistician with a new name—security analyst.[3]

Graham had but one stipulation in agreeing to teach the class: someone had to be assigned to take detailed notes. David Dodd, a young finance professor with recent degrees from the University of Pennsylvania (BS) and Columbia University (MS), volunteered. Dodd's notes formed the substance for their seminal book, *Security Analysis*. When it appeared in 1934, Louis Rich of *The New York Times* wrote, "It is a full-bodied, mature, meticulous and wholly meritorious outgrowth of scholarly probing and practical sagacity. If this influence should ever exert itself, it will come about by causing the mind of the investor to dwell upon securities rather than upon the market."[4]

Although Ben Graham and David Dodd will be forever connected to each other through *Security Analysis*, they never taught a class together. In Columbia's fall semester, David Dodd taught Investment

Management and Strategy for first-year graduate students based on *Security Analysis*. In the spring, Graham taught a smaller, more intimate investment seminar for only 20 students. For his seminar, Graham also took the lessons from *Security Analysis* but with the added benefit of connecting them to stocks currently being traded. When Warren Buffett enrolled at Columbia University in 1951, he first took Dodd's class, then the next semester he sat for Graham's seminar.

Stage One: Classic Value Investing

What did Warren learn about value investing from *Security Analysis* and from David Dodd's and Ben Graham's classes? To begin at the beginning, the first line of the book is "Analysis connotes the careful study of available facts with the attempt to draw conclusions therefrom based on established principles and logic."[5] Graham and Dodd believed securities analysis was a scientific method in much the same way as law and medicine. But just like law and medicine, securities analysis is not an exact science. No analysis is perfectly predictable, said Graham, but if the analyst follows established, quantifiable facts and methods, the probabilities of success are greatly enhanced.

The facts Graham looked for in both stocks and bonds were those that were easily measurable and current. The methodology outlined in *Security Analysis* placed greater emphasis on the here and now while discounting the uncertainty of what can happen tomorrow. That which cannot be easily measured, in Graham's mind, can be badly measured and whatever is badly measured brings with it increased risk and the propensity for loss. Graham became anxious when too much emphasis was placed on the future; "speculation," he wrote, "in its etymology, meant looking forward." He was much more comfortable with the traditional definition of investment "allied to vested interests, to property rights and values taking root in the past."[6]

In *Security Analysis*, Graham included a table to help distinguish between the forces of speculation and investment. He described the "*market factors* including technical, manipulative, and psychological" as speculative. At the opposite end, he aligned investment with *intrinsic value factors* including earnings, dividends, assets, and capital structure. Stuck in the middle, straddling both investment and speculation, Graham identified *future value factors*: management reputation, competitive conditions and prospects for the company, including changes to sales, prices, and costs.[7]

Clearly, we cannot totally separate intrinsic value factors from future value factors. Even so, Graham's preference for calculating value emphasized intrinsic value factors over future factors. Indeed, analysts that worked at Graham-Newman were dissuaded from visiting and questioning management about the future prospects of their business for fear these insights would tilt too much in favor of the future factors over the intrinsic value factors. Graham even refused to look at a picture of a CEO, worrying that might prejudice his analysis if he didn't like the photo.[8]

The essence of Graham and Dodd's value investing methodology is to pay low prices in relation to current earnings, current dividends, and current assets. To the degree you purchase only companies with low prices relative to these factors, you have built a margin of safety into your purchase. Interestingly, the term *margin of safety* did not originate with Graham. He found it in Moody's *Manual of Investments* prior to 1930. "Authorities used the expression 'margin of safety' to mean the ratio of the balance after interest to the earnings available for interest."[9] Indeed, when Graham called for a margin of safety in the analysis of stocks, he applied the same methodology he used in analyzing bonds. There is a "close similarity between the techniques of investing in common stocks and that of investing in bonds," he wrote, "The common-stock investor also [wants] a stable business and one showing an adequate margin of earnings over dividend requirement."[10]

Graham reasoned the larger the margin of safety, the less downside risk the investor would face in the event of a market sell-off or deteriorating future prospects. He believed the greatest danger for investors was paying too high a price for earnings, dividends, and assets. He cautioned investors to look beyond the obvious. The danger of overpaying can be found not only with good companies but also with low-quality companies that were priced high because business conditions were currently favorable but not permanent.

■ ■ ■

At the heart of value investing stand two golden rules. Rule number one is *Don't lose.* Rule number two is *Don't forget rule number one.* Graham's rule: A large margin of safety—the difference between a company's current prospects and its stock price—is critical to avoiding the financial damage he himself experienced in the stock market.

In *Security Analysis,* Graham drew a difference between market analysis and security analysis. "Security analysis has several advantages over market analysis, which are likely to make the former a more successful field of activity for those with training and intelligence." Graham believed market analysis was "essentially a battle of wits" played against other like-minded investors all trying to guess what the stock market is going to do over the short term. In this game, there is no hedge. "In market analysis, there is no margin of safety; you are either right or wrong, and if you are wrong you lose money."[11]

The margin of safety concept is unquestionably a smart strategy. It is almost the perfect hedge to investing. Buying a common stock at a large discount to your calculation of intrinsic value can give you a handsome return if all works out well but also limits your losses if the future turns out unexpectedly. But that's not all. In addition to providing positive returns, the margin of safety is also an intellectual psychological investment, an investment in temperament that makes achieving profitable returns possible.

The additional benefit of using the margin of safety is that it strengthens an investor's resolve to hold steadfast against the market's inherent short-term volatility. In Chapter 2 we pointed out how important it is for investors to remain indifferent to the market's emotional whirlwinds. Knowing the value of your investment, knowing you have the cushion of a large margin of safety, strengthens your fortitude. Operating with a margin of safety emboldens investors to act with the Stoic attitude they need to protect themselves while riding the emotional roller-coaster that is the stock market.

A few paragraphs ago I described the margin of safety as almost the perfect hedge. That means it is not *always* the perfect hedge. Graham believed if glamorous projections for future growth went unfulfilled it was far better to focus on current assets, even if they were not generating much of an economic return, because someone, somewhere, somehow would squeeze out a decent return even from a poorly operating business. As a last resort, the assets could be liquidated. Of course, this presupposed that someone would always stand ready to buy the book value of bad companies.

A few years later, Warren Buffett learned firsthand why Graham's approach was not foolproof. He discovered that the price he received for selling the book value of poor economic companies that Berkshire owned was often less than desirable.

Using Graham's investment method of buying the common shares of companies, Warren accumulated several businesses for the newly reconstructed Berkshire Hathaway. Although buying cheap stocks of bad businesses during the partnership years worked out well, largely because Warren could quickly sell them and move on, he came to learn that buying and holding cheap assets of bad businesses for Berkshire was a failed strategy. "My punishment," he said, "was an education in the economics of short-line farm implement manufacturers, third-place department stores, and New England textile manufacturers."[12]

The farm implementation company was Dempster Mill Manufacturing, the department store was Hochschild Kohn, and the textile manufacturer was Berkshire Hathaway. Although Warren had the benefit of owning these companies outright, thereby in charge of capital allocation, the economic returns of these subpar businesses were, in a word, miserable. It was only when Warren, with Charlie's urging, bought See's Candies did he begin to appreciate the economics of a better business. "Charlie and I have found that making silk purses out of silk is the best we can do; with sow's ears, we fail. Our goal is to find an outstanding business at a sensible price, not a mediocre business at a bargain price."[13]

In the early 1970s, Berkshire Hathaway owned a company called Diversified Retailing, which in turn owned a company called Blue

Chip Stamps. Charlie via his investment partnership also owned Blue Chip Stamps. The company provided supermarkets and gasoline stations with trading stamps to give to their customers, who collected them in books that were later exchanged for merchandise. Like an insurance company, the unredeemed stamps were a form of float, which allowed Blue Chip Stamps to purchase other businesses, including a savings and loan, a newspaper, and a partial interest in a candy company—See's Candies, a West Coast manufacturer and retailer of fine boxed chocolates.

In 1972, Blue Chip Stamps was in a position to purchase the entire business of See's Candies from the founding family. The asking price was $40 million, which included $10 million on the balance sheet. See's had only $8 million in tangible assets, earning $4 million pretax annually. Charlie thought the deal was reasonable but Warren was not so sure. He noted the asking price was three times tangible assets, a price Ben Graham would have surely disapproved. Warren offered $25 million, still thinking he might have overpaid.

Looking back, we can now see that Warren did not overpay for See's Candies. Indeed, See's will go down in Berkshire history as one of the businesses with the highest economic returns. According to Will Thorndike, founding partner of Housatonic Partners and author of the popular book *The Outsiders: Eight Unconventional CEOs and Their Radically Rational Blueprint for Success*, between 1972 and 1999 (the last year Berkshire segmented See's Candies earnings) See's generated a 32 percent internal rate of return (IRR). "Remarkably, the IRR was both unlevered and without a terminal value," Will noted. "If you doubled the purchase price and held everything else constant including cash flow and time period, the IRR was 21 percent. Incredible."[14]

In the 2014 Berkshire Hathaway Annual Report, Warren updated shareholders on the See's investment. Over the 42 years, See's Candies returned to Berkshire $1.9 billion in pretax earnings, requiring only $40 million in additional capital investment. And the See's earnings were redeployed over the subsequent years, allowing Berkshire to buy other companies that, in turn, produced even more profits. It was like watching "rabbits breeding," said Warren.[15]

The lessons Warren learned from the See's acquisition were threefold. First, based on Graham's method of purchasing stocks, See's Candies was not overvalued but significantly undervalued. Second, from the experience of purchasing See's, Warren gained the insight that paying a high multiple for even a slow-growing company is a smart investment if the capital is rationally allocated. Lastly, he said, "I gained a business education about the value of powerful brands that opened my eyes to many other profitable investments."[16]

When Warren purchased See's Candies, he stepped away from Graham's stringent rule of buying only stocks with prices low in relation to earnings, dividends, and current assets. It is now understood as a significant turning point. The See's experience is in large part what motivated Warren to purchase other consumer products companies with strong brand value. Like The Coca-Cola Company.

When Berkshire purchased Coca-Cola in 1988, the stock was trading at 15 times earnings and 12 times cash flow, a 30 percent and 50 percent premium to the market averages. Warren paid 5 times book value for the stock. Those raised on the strict principles of value investing taught by Ben Graham howled. Warren, they cried, had turned his back on the master.

In 1989, Berkshire owned 7 percent of the outstanding shares of Coca-Cola. Warren invested one third of Berkshire's portfolio in the company, a $1 billion bet. Ten years later, Berkshire's investment in Coca-Cola was worth $11.6 billion. The same investment in the S&P 500 Index over the same time period was worth $3 billion. Was Warren's purchase of Coca-Cola a value investment? Or did he bow to the growth camp of investing, which during the 1990s had the support of the market's momentum?

Warren asks us to consider, how should we determine what is an attractive investment? Most investors, he said, choose between two customary approaches—"value" and "growth" investing—as if the two concepts are, by design, mutually exclusive. "Most analysts feel they must choose between the two approaches customarily thought to be in opposition: 'value' and 'growth.' Indeed, many investment professionals see any mixing of the two terms as a form of intellectual cross-dressing."[17]

"Value investing," Warren explains, "typically connotes the purchase of stocks having attributes such as a low ratio of price to book value, a low price–earnings ratio, or a high dividend yield. Unfortunately, such characteristics, even if they appear in combination, are far from determinative as to whether an investor is indeed buying something for what it is worth and therefore is truly operating on the principle of obtaining value in his investments. Correspondingly, opposite characteristics—a high ratio of price-to-book value, a high price-to-earnings ratio and a low dividend yield—are in no way inconsistent with a value purchase."[18]

The above paragraph, which appears on page nine in the 1992 Berkshire Hathaway Annual Report, in 102 words crystallizes Warren's sense of value investing. For him, value investing is not exclusively buying companies with low price-to-earnings ratios; neither is a value investor precluded from buying companies with high price-to-earnings ratios.

Warren did admit to suffering "fuzzy thinking" from the growth versus value debate when he was much younger. But he now understands "the two approaches are joined at the hip: Growth is always a component in the calculation of value, constituting a variable whose importance can range from negligible to enormous and whose impact can be negative as well as positive."[19]

In 1992, Warren publicly moved away from Ben Graham in one respect—not from Graham's fundamental investment philosophy, which emphasizes buying stocks with a margin of safety and nurturing the necessary temperament, but from the simple accounting-factor methods Graham used to identify value. Which then leads to an important question: what good are low price accounting factors in identifying value?

The essence of classical value investing (hereby defined as the methodology outlined by Graham and Dodd) is to locate low-valuation stocks that are down in price because investors have overreacted to recent bad news. Likewise, classic value investors believe this same overreaction can occur with popular growth stocks that are bid up in anticipation of better things to come. In their eyes, stocks that are priced high relative to current earnings are overvalued.

At the heart of value investing lies a contrarian spirit. Value inves-tors are driven to buy what the market is selling and sell what the market is buying. Indeed, the success of classic value investing rests on the concept of mean reversion, whereby low-priced stocks eventually go up while high-priced stocks eventually decline. On the cover page of *Security Analysis*, Graham inserted a quote from the Roman lyric poet Quintus Horatius Flaccus, known as Horace: "Many shall be restored that are now fallen and many shall fall that are now in honor."

However, Warren eventually learned a painful lesson: "What is required is thinking, rather than polling."[21] Over the years, classic value investing outlined by Graham and Dodd has been defended and promoted by leading academicians including Eugene Fama and Kenneth French. Their widely read and cited papers helped to launch and give credence to hundreds of value investment firms. Soon everyone who referred to themselves as a value investor was buying stocks with low prices-to-book value, earnings and dividends while avoiding high-multiple stocks. Warren did exactly the same, until his actual experience of owning wholly controlled business purchased at low prices based solely on these metrics sometimes generated poor economic results for Berkshire.

■ ■ ■

What slowly became evident to Warren Buffett 30 years ago is today troubling the classic value camp. Since the 2008 financial crisis, classic value stocks have dramatically underperformed the higher-multiple growth stocks. The persistence of this relative outperformance has now lasted for over 10 years. Classic value investors have bemoaned their plight, steadfastly arguing that once value investing returns they will again have their day in the sun. Many of them liken the underper-formance of classic value stocks to the period in the late 1990s when growth stocks, on the back of the technology and internet revolution, substantially outperformed their slower-growing classic value stocks. Value investors claim it is only a matter of time before the growth charge of outperformance will necessarily end badly as it did during the 2000–2002 bear market.

But there are fundamental differences between the technology companies of late 1990s and growth companies today. The price momentum of the growth stocks in the late 1990s was accompanied by little underlying economic fundamental support. At that time, investors were tabulating eyeballs, not earnings, to justify valuations. Unfortunately, the prices paid for eyeballs became grossly overvalued largely because those eyeballs did not translate into earnings. Today, however, we can measure the outperformance of growth stocks by clearly tabulated sales, earnings, and cash flows. A second important difference between today and 2000 is interest rates. The 10-year U.S. Treasury note yield was 6.00 percent in 2000. Today, it's less than 1.00 percent. Lower interest rates increase the value of stocks, particularly growth stocks.

There are now notable thinkers who are confronting this persistent tug-of-war between the performance of value stocks and growth stocks. In a widely circulated and thoughtful analytical paper, "Explaining the Demise of Value Investing", Baruch Lev at New York University's Stern School of Business and Anup Srivastava at the University of Calgary's Haskayne School of Business argue there is a perfectly reasonable and economically defensible reason why classic value stocks have struggled to outperform the market, a market that is increasingly becoming weighted to the faster-growing growth companies.[22]

Lev and Srivastava note that since the birth of value investing, marked by the publication of *Security Analysis*, the investments made by corporations were primarily in plant, property, and equipment. Tangible assets are defined by physical structures, largely brick and mortar. Accounting rules dictate the capitalization of these tangible assets must be fully reflected on a company's balance sheet net of depreciation charges. Accordingly, from the broad swath of American businesses, most were largely defined by their book value. By their calculation, Lev and Srivastava note the median market-to-book ratio of public companies hovered around 1.0 until the mid 1980s. In that world, the market value of a company reflected by its price being either higher or lower than its book value was a reflection of whether a stock was over- or undervalued.

However, in the 1980s, American business models began to change. The investment made in tangible assets—plant, property, and equipment—which had defined the growth of corporations since the Industrial Revolution was now giving way to the investment in intangible assets including patents, copyrights, trademarks and brand marketing. Whereas tangible assets are defined by physical properties, intangible assets are defined by intellectual property. Because accounting rules are still rooted in the industrial era, companies must immediately expense all intangible investments. In short, investments in intangible assets do not add to book value. Although it can be argued intangible investments do work to increase a company's intrinsic value, nowhere is this investment tabulated in the Graham and Dodd approach.

Lev and Srivastava note that since 1980, there has been a steady decline in the amount of money companies invest in tangible assets and a corresponding steady increase in the money invested in intangible assets. In the mid 1990s, the rate of growth of intangible investing surpassed the growth in tangible investing. "Currently in the U.S., the intangible investment rate of the corporate sector is roughly twice that of the tangible investment rate and it keeps growing."[23]

What does this mean for classic value investors? Simply put, a company that invests in intangible assets must subtract this cost from current earnings while not adding the investment to book value, which in turn makes a stock with a high price-to-earnings and a high price-to-book value appear expensive. But if one were to shift the valuation methodology from Generally Accepted Accounting Principles (GAAP) to the economic earnings of adjusted cash flow and return on capital, companies that look expensive from a GAAP perspective may actually appear attractive to an investor with a business-owner mindset.

What should not be lost is that Warren's revelation as a value investor coincided with his actual experience of owning companies decades before academicians finally reached the same conclusion. In this instance, we can say Warren's *a posteriori* knowledge based on his experience of owning businesses outwitted the *a priori* reasoning of financial mathematicians.

While classic value investors continue to pine for the good old days, Lev and Srivastava warn that better news may not be forthcoming. Examining the enterprise profitability of large value stocks compared to the returns of growth stocks, they discovered that the median return on equity (ROE) and the median return on net operating assets (RNOA) could not be more different. Whereas the growth stocks have achieved their highest profitability in the past 10 years, the classic value stocks have sustained their worse level of profitability in over 50 years. What makes matters worse, the profitability needed to help classic value stocks invest in innovation and growth in order to improve their economic performance is lacking. Without the internal funds from operations needed to invest in higher-returning projects, these classic value stocks are now trapped in their own low valuations. The margin of safety evidenced by the difference between price and current assets may at first look attractive but in reality many of these stocks are value traps.

On a side note, and recently cited, Eugene Fama and Kenneth French, who gained fame by introducing the Fama French Model in 1992, are now revisiting their previous assumptions. Fama and French claimed 28 years ago that value stocks, defined as low price-to-book-value companies, exhibited a "value premium" which drove their excess returns above the stock market. From 1963 to 1991, large-cap value stocks exhibited a 0.42 percent premium, leading to their outperformance over this time period. However, between 1991 and 2019, the value premium dropped to 0.11 percent, largely negating the relative outperformance of low price-to-book-value stocks.[24]

This data shows that the excess performance of value stocks, based on price-to-book ratios, has effectively declined over the last nearly 30 years, coinciding with Lev and Srivastava's observations as well. Professors Fama and French have reserved reaching a final conclusion. As French explained, "28 years of data on falling returns is not enough to determine whether the value factor has actually stopped working. It simply [could have] experienced a long run of bad luck."[25]

Ben Graham deserves all the high praise for his value formulas that worked exceptionally well for the better part of 50 years. He helped investors thoughtfully navigate the stock market when there were no navigational instruments. But today, the best we can say about Graham and Dodd accounting-factor multiples is that they are value markers. They represent the market's expectations for a stock. A high stock price relative to earnings or book value is a reflection of high investor expectation for a stock, while conversely a low price to earnings or book value reflects low expectations. However, we cannot determine whether or not a stock is mispriced merely by tabulating a simple ratio.

Michael Mauboussin, head of Consilient Research at Counterpoint Global, noted author of several books and adjunct professor of business at Columbia University, wrote an important research paper, "What Does a Price-Earnings Multiple Mean; An Analytical Bridge between P/Es and Solid Economics." It has helped to clarify the persistent confusion of using price-to-earnings multiples for valuation purposes.[26] Mauboussin points out that P/E ratios remain the primary tool analysts use to value stocks. A recent survey from a sample group of 2,000 investors found that 93 percent use multiples for valuation, with the overwhelming majority using P/E ratios. But Mauboussin is quick to point out the problem. "Multiples are not valuation. They are shorthand for the process of valuation."[27]

Investors simply don't spend enough time understanding what the price-to-earnings multiple means, explains Mauboussin. You have to reconcile how a multiple may actually miscalculate the current business model as well as the possibility the current multiple may change in the future. To make his point, Mauboussin loops in Aswath Damodaran, a professor of finance at the Stern School of Business at New York University and a leading expert on valuation. Damodaran says, "There's nothing wrong with pricing. But it's not valuation. Valuation is about digging through a business, understanding the business, understanding the cash flows and risk, and then trying to attach a number to a business based on the value of a business. Most people don't do that. They price companies. The biggest mistake in valuation is mistaking pricing for valuation."[28]

After Warren clarified his views on value investing as it relates to price-to-earnings ratios, he identified in clear language the critical variables investors must focus on to determine business valuation. "Leaving the question of price aside," he wrote, "the best business to own is one that over an extended period can employ large amounts of incremental capital at very high rates of return. The worst business to own is the one that must or will do the opposite—that is, consistently employ ever-greater amounts of capital at very low rates of return."[29] In Warren's Money Mind, it is always about the compounding. Most importantly, it is about value-creating, compounding companies.

■ ■ ■

To better appreciate the valuation differences between businesses with a high return on capital versus those with low return and their impact on price-earnings multiples, we need to return to Michael Mauboussin. In 1961, finance professors Merton Miller and Franco Modigliani published a paper titled "Dividend Policy, Growth, and the Valuation of Shares." Mauboussin believes this paper "ushered in the modern era of valuation."[30] Miller and Modigliani asked a rather simple question: "What does the market *really* capitalize?" They measured earnings, cash flows, the future opportunities to create value, and dividends. What did they learn? Surprisingly, all these measures collapsed into the same model. The value of a stock, they determined, is the present value of the future free cash flows. But it was what they did next that most warrants our attention.

To help investors grasp the valuation impact of future cash flows, Miller and Modigliani offer a formula that breaks down a company into two parts. The value of a firm (stock, business) is equal to "steady-state value + future value creation." They define the steady-state value of a company as being equal to the net operating profit after tax (normalized) divided by the cost of capital plus additional cash. Mauboussin explains, "The steady-state value of a firm, calculated using the perpetuity method, assumes the current net operating profit after tax (NOPAT) is sustainable and that incremental investments will neither add, nor subtract, value."[31]

Turning to future value creation, Miller and Modigliani calculate a company's future value as the investments the company makes multiplied by its return on capital minus the cost of capital times the competitive advantage period over the cost of capital. Said differently, the positive future value creation of a business becomes the cash it produces over time but only if the cash return as a percentage return on the company's invested capital is above the cost of that capital. Yes, this is a mouthful. But Miller and Modigliani are simply tabulating the same thing Warren has stated. The best business to own, the one that will create the most future value, is a company that generates high returns on incremental capital (above the cost of that capital) and then reinvests the cash profits back into the company to continually generate a high return on capital for an extended period of time.

Most important, Mauboussin thoughtfully helped his students appreciate Miller and Modigliani's future value creation returns as it relates to price-to-earnings multiples. The central thesis being that a company that earns on investment above the cost of capital creates value. A company that earns on investment below the cost of capital destroys shareholder value. And a company that generates returns equal to the cost of capital neither creates nor destroys shareholder value no matter how fast or slowly it grows.[32]

Rarely do investors ever think a faster-growing business can actually destroy their investment. But consider the following calculations: Assuming an 8 percent cost of capital, all equity financed for a period of 15 years, Mauboussin tells us a company that earns 8 percent return on capital is worth a 12.5 price-to-earnings multiple. And no matter whether the company grows at 4 percent per year or 8 percent or 10 percent, its multiple remains the same. But a company that earns only a 4 percent return on invested capital against a cost of capital of 8 percent is worth only 7.1 times earnings at a 4 percent growth rate or a 3.3 multiple for a 6 percent growth rate, and then summarily begins destroying shareholder value the faster it grows. Finally, a company that earns 16 percent on invested capital with an 8 percent cost of capital is worth 15.2 times at a 4 percent growth rate, 17.1 times for a 6 percent growth rate, 19.4 times for a 8 percent growth rate, and 22.4 times for 10 percent growth rate.

In a nutshell, when a company earns above the cost of capital, the faster it grows the more valuable it becomes. The lesson here is a rapidly growing company with a high price-earnings ratio can actually be a terrific value proposition if its cash returns on capital exceed its cost of capital.

When valuing stocks, if we first begin with a company's cash return, its return on capital and its growth rate, what can we say about price-to-earnings multiples? One thing is for sure, it is not a simple-minded claim that stocks with a high price-to-earnings ratio are overvalued while those with a low price-to-earnings ratio are undervalued. The next time an analyst or media commentator tells you a stock is selling for x times earnings per share, you should immediately be wondering how much actual cash does the company generate? What is the company's return on invested capital compared to its cost of capital? Finally, what is the future growth rate of these cash flows and how long will these returns last?

Classic value investors need to keep Michael Mauboussin, Aswath Damodaran, Merton Miller, and Frances Modigliani as well as Baruch Lev and Anup Srivastava in the forefront of their mind as they make a determination of the economic vitality of their companies, even those companies sporting low price-to-earnings-ratios.

Stage Two: Valuing a Business, Not a Stock

The tug of the war between calculating how much intrinsic value should be determined by present factors and how much by future factors is at the root of the evolutionary development of value investing. It's what moves us from Stage One to Stage Two.

Graham emphasized the present over the future. When Warren was captain of the Buffett Partnership, Graham's present factors were the navigation maps needed to reach his goal. But when he changed ships and began to steer his new vessel, Warren had to think about the future compounding factors needed to increase the value of Berkshire. He needed a new map. In doing so, Warren turned his attention to understanding the competitive position of companies, the future prospect of sales, earnings, and cash returns of these companies. And importantly, he focused on management's ability to allocate capital in order to maximize the compounding effect that comes with value creation.

To help us better appreciate the differences between booking the present and perhaps modest opportunity, over a future but greater investment return, Warren shared a surprising investment primer—the very first lesson written by Aesop the Greek storyteller 2,600 years ago.[33] In "The Hawk and the Nightingale," Aesop tells of a hawk who sets out to search for food one sunny afternoon when he spots a nightingale sitting on a branch. The hawk swoops down and quickly clutches the nightingale with its claws. The tiny nightingale turns to plead for his life; "I am such a tiny bird, I won't be able to satisfy your hunger." The hawk laughs. "Why should I let you go? It's always better to eat what you have than seek a larger catch that I have not yet caught." At that moment, the hawk made an investment calculation Aesop summarized as "a bird in hand is worth more than two in the bush."

But according to Warren a bird in hand is not always worth more than two in the bush until you have answered three important questions. First, "How certain are you that there are indeed birds in the bush?" Second, "When will they emerge and how many will there be?" Lastly, "What is the risk-free interest rate?"[34] Mathematically speaking, Warren tells us if there are two birds in the bush and it takes us five years to retrieve them with interest rates at 5 percent, then we should bet on the bush, for it provides a 14 percent compounded annual return.[35] Warren notes "Aesop's investment axiom, thus expanded and converted into dollars, is immutable. It applies to farms, manufacturing plants, bonds, and stocks."[36]

Setting aside for a moment the question of interest rates (which is not inconsequential, as higher interest rates can make an investment proposition unwise), let's focus instead on the first two questions: How certain are we there will be two birds in the bush and when exactly can we expect to get them? As this relates to stocks, Warren tells us "an investor needs some general understanding of business economics as well as the ability to think independently to reach well-founded conclusions."[37]

The time Warren spent attending Columbia University and studying with David Dodd and Ben Graham and even the two years he spent with Graham-Newman did little to advance his understanding of long-term business strategies and economic compounding. It wasn't part of the curriculum. Warren's eventual education in the inner workings of a company and management decision-making came from the school of hard knocks. The actual ownership of long-term businesses purchased by Berkshire left an indelible impression on Warren's thinking. It was real-life experiences, the kind of lessons that a college course and textbook could never fully explain.

In 1965, the Buffett Partnership took over the management of Berkshire Hathaway on the heels of a successful proxy battle for control. That year Warren added the responsibilities of an operating manager of a textile company to his position as general partner of his investment partnership. Even though Kenneth Chase had been appointed president of the company, replacing the outgoing Seabury Stanton, for all practical purposes Warren was overseeing Berkshire; he even wrote the company's annual report.

Ben Graham had long since moved on from Wall Street. He was living comfortably in California, no longer interested in investing. Charlie Munger, Warren's newfound friend, was in the early years of his own investment partnership. Although Warren and Charlie stayed in touch, the cement that bonded their partnership was still several years away. Warren was running solo and for the first time in his life he was in charge of a publicly traded company with stock-holders' equity of $22 million. But he was not alone.

In 1958, *Common Stocks and Uncommon Profits* by Philip Fisher was published. Warren read the book and a few years later went to visit Fisher. "I sought out Phil Fisher after reading his book. When I met him, I was as impressed by the man as by his ideas."[38] Phil Fisher also took an instant liking to Warren. When asked, he usually agreed to meet with up-and-coming investment professionals at least once, but rarely twice. Fisher divided people into two buckets; you got either an A or an F. Warren was one of the rare investors who got not only a second meeting but several thereafter. Phil Fisher was always proud he tagged Warren with an A long before his well-deserved fame.[39]

What did Fisher see in the young Warren Buffett? He was particularly impressed with how Warren evolved as an investor over the years without compromising his core principles—integrity, temperament, and an insistence on a margin of safety in his purchases. Most professional investors, Fisher noted, learn one craft, one approach to investing. For example they only buy stocks with low price-to-earnings ratios. They continue to build their craft but never change. In contrast, he watched Warren Buffett continue to evolve decade after decade.

For example, Fisher pointed out that no one would have predicted that Warren, with his original training in value investing, would invest in franchise media stocks in the 1970s. But what happened? Throughout the 1970s, Warren added The Washington Post Company, Knight-Ridder Newspapers, Capital Cities Communications, and American Broadcasting Company to Berkshire's portfolio. Nor, added Fisher, based on Warren's previous approach would they have predicted that in the 1980s he would be buying consumer-brand value stocks sporting above-average P/Es. Yet Warren began to populate Berkshire's portfolio with some of the best consumer-product companies in the world—General Foods, R.J. Reynolds, The Gillette Company, and The Coca-Cola Company. In Warren's mind, these stocks were cheap based on off-balance-sheet analysis. The brand value of these companies were worth billions but carried on the books at $1. It was clear to Warren there was more value in the intangible assets of these companies than cash, inventory, and real estate.

It was Warren's ability to change and to do it successfully that impressed Fisher. Most people who attempt to evolve, fail. Warren didn't fail, Fisher said, because he remained true to himself and never lost sight of who he was and where he was going.

For his part, what did Warren learn from Phil Fisher? It turns out, a lot.

While Ben Graham was teaching advanced security analysis at Columbia, Phil Fisher was beginning his career as an investment counselor. After graduating from Stanford's Graduate School of Business Administration, Fisher began work at the Anglo London & Paris National Bank in San Francisco. In less than two years, he was made head of the statistical department. Sound familiar? Fisher weathered the 1929 stock market crash, then undertook a brief career with a local brokerage firm before starting his own counseling firm. On March 31, 1931, six years after the launch of the Graham-Newman Corporation, Fisher & Company began soliciting clients.

At Stanford, one of Fisher's business classes required him to accompany his professor on periodic visits to companies in the San Francisco area. The professor would get the business managers to talk about their operations, and often helped them solve an immediate problem. Driving back to Stanford, the student and the professor would recap what they observed about the companies and managers they had visited. "That hour each week," Fisher later said, "was the most useful training I ever received."[40]

What Fisher learned from interviewing management and learning about their company's successes and challenges was applied to the investment process at Fisher & Company. At the core, Fisher believed superior long-term profits came from investing in companies with above-average economic potential and the most capable management. To isolate these companies, Fisher developed a point system that qualified a company according to the characteristics of its business and management. That point system became Chapter 3 of his landmark 1958 book *Common Stocks and Uncommon Profits and Other Writings*. No doubt Warren carefully studied Chapter 3, which is titled "What to Buy—The Fifteen Points to Look For in a Common Stock."

The one characteristic that most impressed Fisher was a company's ability to grow sales and profits over the years at rates higher than others in its industry. In order to do so, Fisher believed a company needed to "possess products or services with sufficient market potential to make possible a sizable increase in sales for at least several years."[41] Fisher's approach helped to further reinforce Warren's deep appreciation of compounding sales and earnings alongside the importance of a product's brand value in driving repeated consumer purchases year after year.

Fisher also believed superior investment returns were rarely obtained by investing in marginal companies. Those companies can produce adequate profits during expansion periods but see their profits decline rapidly during difficult economic times. Warren was already learning firsthand the dismal returns of marginal companies owned by Berkshire.

Fisher was also sensitive to a company's long-term profitability. He was attracted to companies that could grow into the future without requiring additional financing. Fisher knew if a company is only able to grow by issuing equity, the increase in the number of shares outstanding would cancel out any benefit that stockholders would receive from the company's growth. We will learn in the next chapter, "Business-Driven Investing," that the key for investors is to not focus solely on companies that are growing overall sales and earnings but to find those that are able to do so without issuing additional common shares.

Fisher was aware that superior companies possess not only above-average business economics but, equally important, are directed by people who possess above-average management capabilities. Fisher asked, Does the business have a management of unquestionable integrity and honesty? Do the managers behave as if they are in partnership with the stockholders, or does it appear they are only concerned with their own well-being? One way to determine management's intention, he said, is to observe how management communicates with its shareholders. All businesses, good and bad, will experience a period of unexpected difficulties. Commonly, when business is good, management talks freely; but we learn more when business declines. Fisher asks, Does management talk openly about the company's difficulties or does it clam up? How management responds to business difficulties, he said, tells you a lot about who is running the company.

Students of Warren Buffett can easily make the connection between Fisher's teachings and how Warren himself has learned to distinguish between good and bad managers. Additionally, we see Fisher's counsel of how managers ought to behave reflected in Warren's own behavior as the manager-partner of Berkshire.

Fisher also believed that to be successful, investors should invest only in companies that are well within an investor's ability to actually understand what the company does and how it generates profits for its shareholders. This is echoed in Warren's popular adage that investors should invest only within their "circle of competence." Fisher said that his early mistakes came from attempting "to project my skill beyond the limits of experience. I began by investing in outside industries which I believed I thoroughly understood but did not have comparable background knowledge."[42]

To show people how to strengthen and expand their circle of competence Fisher outlined in his book a random inquiry approach to gathering information he called "scuttlebutt." In *Common Stocks and Uncommon Profits* Chapter 2 is titled "What 'Scuttlebutt' Can Do." The chapter is only three short pages, but its message to investors was commanding. And I am sure when Warren read those three pages he broke out into a smile because it was the same advice he got when he was eleven years old reading Minaker's book *One Thousand Ways to Make $1000*—"read everything published about the business you intend to start, to get the combined experience of others, and begin your plans where they left off."

It is understood, said Fisher, that investors must read the financial reports of their companies, but that this research by itself is not enough to justify an investment. The essential step to prudent investing is to uncover as much as possible about the company from people who are familiar with the company. Think of it as a kind of business grapevine. Fisher's scuttlebutt investigation led him to interview customers and vendors. He sought out former employees as well as consultants who had worked for the company. He contacted research scientists in universities, government employees, and trade association executives. He also interviewed competitors. "It is amazing," Fisher said, "what an accurate picture of the relative points of strength and weakness of each company in an industry can be obtained from a representative cross section of the opinions of those who in one way or another are concerned with any particular company."[43]

Another investment principle Fisher imparted to Warren was to not overstress diversification. Although Fisher admitted diversification was widely acclaimed, he believed having too many eggs in too many baskets actually increased the risk of a portfolio. It never occurs to an advisor, he explained, that owning a stock without sufficient knowledge of the company, its products, and management team may be more dangerous than having what is thought to be inadequate diversification.

■ ■ ■

The differences between Graham and Fisher are apparent. Graham, the quantitative analyst, emphasized only those factors that could be measured with certainty: fixed assets, current earnings, and dividends. Graham did not interview customers, competitors, or managers. As we know, this playbook worked fine for Warren while managing the Buffett Partnership. But when he was running Berkshire, he required different thinking, a different education.

Fisher, the qualitative analyst, emphasized those factors that he believed increased the future value of a company: the competitive strategy of the company and management capabilities. To guide him toward compounding the future value creation of Berkshire, Fisher's book was like the postgraduate education Warren needed. It came at the right time from the right person.

The education of Warren Buffett is best understood as a synthesis of two distinct investment philosophies from two legendary investors. "I'm 15 percent Fisher and 85 percent Benjamin Graham," he once said.[44] But that was in 1969. Ahead for Berkshire was the purchase of See's Candies, The Washington Post Company, Capital Cities, and The Coca-Cola Company. "Although [their] investment approach differed," said Warren, they "parallel in the investment world." More important to him was the personal dimension.

"Much like Ben Graham, Fisher was unassuming, generous in spirit and an extraordinary teacher."[45]

There was, however, one important lesson Graham provided for Warren that was lacking from Phil Fisher's teachings—how to think about valuation and the criticality of always operating with a margin of safety. To this day, the margin-of-safety concept is of paramount importance for successful investing. It is, quite simply, nonnegotiable. But since buying stocks with low prices relative to earnings, book value, and dividend had been disqualified as valuation signals, Warren was left to take one more investment course to determine how to accurately value a stock.

■ ■ ■

John Burr Williams, an American economist, was born in Hartford, Connecticut, on November 27, 1900. He was educated at Harvard University where he studied mathematics and chemistry. Williams was drawn to investing and enrolled at Harvard Business School in 1923. He soon discovered that to be a good statistician, he also had to be a good economist, so he returned to Harvard in 1932 for a PhD in economics. His goal: to learn what had caused the 1929 Wall Street crash and the economic depression of the 1930s.

John Burr Williams had the great fortune to study with Joseph Schumpeter, an Austrian economist who had recently immigrated to the United States. Schumpeter would become famous for his book *Capitalism, Socialism, and Democracy* and for introducing the concept of "creative destruction." Williams signed up for Schumpeter's class "Economic Theory," and when it came time to choose a topic for his doctoral dissertation, he sought Schumpeter's advice. Schumpeter suggested "the intrinsic value of a common stock" would fit Williams' background and experience. Williams later commented that perhaps Schumpeter had a more cynical motive: The topic would keep Williams from "running afoul" of the rest of the faculty, "none of whom would want to challenge my own ideas on investments."[46]

Before winning faculty approval for his dissertation and to the great indignation of several professors, Williams submitted his work to Macmillan for publication. They declined. So did McGraw-Hill. Both felt the book was too long and had too many algebraic symbols. Finally, in 1938 Williams found a publisher in Harvard University Press, but only after he agreed to pay part of the printing cost. Two years later, Williams took his oral exam and, after some intense arguments over the causes of the Great Depression, passed.

Williams' book, *The Theory of Investment Value*, was published four years after Graham and Dodd published *Security Analysis*. In his book, Williams proposed an idea. The intrinsic value of an asset should be calculated using "the evaluation by the rule of present worth." Today, in finance, present worth is known as net present value (NPV) and is calculated as the value of an expected future income stream determined on the date of valuation. In *The Theory of Investment Value*, Williams suggested the intrinsic value of a common stock is the present value of its future net cash flows, in the form of dividends. Williams' model is called the dividend discount model (DDM).

For Warren, the appeal of John Burr Williams and his book resides in two important concepts. First, Williams referred to dividends as future coupons. This connects neatly to Warren's viewpoint that his company's profits each year were a form of coupon paid to Berkshire. Second, and very important, Williams linked his idea of the present value of future net cash flows to the margin-of-safety concept Warren learned from Graham.

Although Williams did not use the term "margin of safety," he did write this: "Investment value, defined as the present worth of future dividends, or future coupons and principal, is of practical importance to every investor because it is the *critical* [italics his] value above which he cannot go in buying and holding, without added risk. If a man buys a security *below* [italics his] its investment value he need never lose, even if its price should fall at once, because he can still hold for income and get a return above normal on his cost price; but if he buys it above investment value his only hope of avoiding a loss is to sell to someone else who must in turn take the loss in the form of insufficient income. Therefore all those who do not feel able to foresee the swings of the market and do not wish to speculate on the mere changes in price must have recourse to estimates of investment value to guide them in their buying and selling."[47]

In many ways, John Burr Williams was channeling Ben Graham back to Warren—two renditions of the same essential concept: how to think about purchasing common stock below intrinsic value while avoiding purchasing stocks above intrinsic value. But instead of using accounting-factor multiples (price-to-earnings, price-to-book value), Williams gave Warren a different method: calculating the net present value of the future profits of a business. It was perfect. It coincided with what Warren was doing at Berkshire and it was exactly what he needed to move forward.

In 1992, the same year Warren disavowed the low P/E method of picking stocks, he introduced John Burr Williams to the Berkshire shareholders. In that year's annual report, he wrote (including the italics), "In *The Theory of Investment Value*, written over 50 years ago, John Burr Williams set forth the equation for *value*, which we condense here: *The value of any stock, bond, or business today is determined by the cash inflows and outflows—discounted at the appropriate interest rate—that can be expected to occur during the remaining life of the asset.*" Warren, speaking for himself, continues: "The investment shown by the discounted-flows-of-cash calculation to be the cheapest is the one that the investor should purchase—irrespective of whether the business grows or doesn't, displays volatility or smoothness in its earnings, or carries a high price or low price to its current earnings and book value."[48]

Although John Burr Williams' theory is elegant and mathematically correct, it is far from simple to calculate. As Warren has said, "Every business is worth the present value of its future free cash flows and if you could tabulate all the money a company will disgorge between today and judgment day you would get a precise figure."[49] But therein lies the challenge. "A bond has a coupon and maturity date that define future cash flows; but in the case of equities," said Warren, "the investment analyst must himself estimate the future coupons."[50]

Williams recognized the same challenge. In Chapter 15 of *The Theory of Investment Value,* titled "A Chapter for Skeptics," Williams writes "Are long-range forecasts too uncertain?" He admits no one can possibly look into the future with certainty. Even so, Williams asks, "Does not experience show that careful forecasting—or foresight as it is often called when it turns out to be correct—is very often so nearly right as to be extremely helpful to the investor?"[51]

Warren agrees. Returning to Aesop's proposition, he empathizes. Sometimes making an estimate is a difficult task. How soon will the investor get the birds; how many birds are actually in the bush; and what will be the interest rates? "Usually, the range must be so wide that no useful conclusion can be reached," said Warren. "Occasionally, though, even very conservative estimates about the future emergence of birds reveal that the price quoted is startlingly low in relation to value. The investor does not need brilliance or blinding insights. Using precise numbers is, in fact, foolish; working with a range of possibilities is the better approach."[52] A rough approximation is enough for Warren. "Our inability to pinpoint a number doesn't bother us: we would rather be approximately right than precisely wrong."[53]

■ ■ ■

In *Value Investing: From Graham to Buffett and Beyond* the authors Bruce Greenwald, Judd Khan, Paul Sonkin, and Michael van Biema divide the value investing approach to selecting stocks into three distinct camps. The "classic" approach focuses on tangible assets. The "mixed" approach puts emphasis on private market value or replacement value. The "contemporary" approach is used by value investors like Warren Buffett, those described as business-owners. They favor franchise values and can spot value hiding in plain sight.[54]

The reference to "hiding in plain sight" is a nod to Edgar Allan Poe. "The Purloined Letter," written in 1844, is one of three detective stories written by Poe featuring the world's first literary detective, C. Auguste Dupin. Poe considered "The Purloined Letter" to be the best of his tales of ratiocination—the art of reasoning.[55]

The plot of the story is simple. A man steals a confidential, personally damaging letter in order to blackmail a woman. The police are engaged and search for the letter in the thief's home but they cannot find it. A senior police officer turns to Dupin for help.

In short order Dupin finds the letter lying in a card rack on the writing table in full view for all to see. The blackmailer, anticipating the police would assume the letter would be hidden in an elaborate place, did the exact opposite. He hid it in plain sight. Dupin explained why the police overlooked the obvious: "They consider their own ideas of ingenuity; and in searching for anything hidden, advert only to the modes in which they would have hidden it."

The beauty of a detective story is revealed by the reader's psychological limitations. In "The Purloined Letter" the preconceptions of the police were so powerful they were blind to see what was right in front of them. It is a form of confirmation bias. Investors also suffer from confirmation bias—forming preconceived ideas of what should be happening in the stock market without acknowledging what is obvious.

It reminds you of the story of two Wall Street bankers walking to lunch when one spots a $100 bill on the sidewalk and bends over to pick it up.

"What are you doing?" his friend asks.

"Picking up this $100 bill. What does it look like?"

"Don't bother," the friend replies. "If it was really a $100 bill someone would have already snatched it."

Investors have always been obsessed with what is hidden in the market, believing only that which is hidden has value. This is sometimes true, but not always. We can also say that which is transparent is often thought to be fairly priced but there are cases when it is not fully valued. Case in point, no pun intended, is the story of Warren's purchase of The Coca-Cola Company.

The first sale of a Coca-Cola bottle was in 1886. The company went public in 1919 at $40 per share. Seventeen years later, Warren was selling nickel bottles of Coke at his sidewalk table business. But he never bought a share of Coca-Cola for the Buffett Partnership, and it took 23 years before he pulled the trigger to buy a position for Berkshire.

"I carefully avoided buying a single share," said Warren. "Instead [I] allocated major portions of my net worth to street railway companies, windmill manufacturers, anthracite producers, textile businesses, and trading-stamp issuers. Only in the summer of 1988 did my brain finally establish contact with my eyes. What I then perceived was both clear and fascinating. After drifting somewhat in the 1970s, Coca-Cola became a new company with the move of Roberto Goizueta to CEO."[56]

During the 1970s, Coca-Cola was a fragmented and reactive company rather than an innovator setting pace with the beverage industry. Paul Austin, who had been president since 1962, was appointed chairman of the company in 1971. Although Coca-Cola continued to generate millions in earnings, those profits were not reinvested in the higher-returning soda business but allocated to water projects, shrimp farms, a wine business, and a modern art collection bought at the whim of Austin's wife. From 1974 to 1980, the company's market value rose an average rate of 5.6 percent, vastly underperforming the Standard & Poor's 500 Index.

In May 1980, Austin was ousted by Robert Woodruff, the company's 91-year-old patriarch, and replaced by Roberto Goizueta. Raised in Cuba, he became the first foreign-born chief executive officer of Coca-Cola. And he hit the ground running. Goizueta put forth the company's "Strategy of the 1980s," a 900-word pamphlet outlining the corporate goals for Coca-Cola. The plan was simple. Any division in the company that did not add substantially to earnings growth and effectively increase the return on equity of the company would be sold. The proceeds were to be reinvested back into the syrup business, the fastest growing and highest returning part of the company.

In 1980, when Goizueta took over, profit margins at Coca-Cola were 13 percent. By 1988, when Warren first bought shares in Coca-Cola, profit margins had climbed to a record 19 percent. In 1980, the return on equity for Coca-Cola was slightly above 20 percent. In 1988, return on equity had increased 50 percent to 32 percent. By 1992, it was near 50 percent.

Any money that could not be prudently reinvested back into the syrup business was earmarked for dividend increases and share repurchases. In 1984, Goizueta authorized the first-ever buyback, announcing it would repurchase six million shares of stock. Over the next 10 years, Goizueta repurchased 414 million shares of Coca-Cola, representing 25 percent of the company's shares outstanding at the beginning of 1984.

Warren observed what was happening at Coca-Cola and understood how Goizueta's actions would substantially increase the intrinsic value of the company. As long as Goizueta did not dilute the economic performance of Coca-Cola by adding subpar businesses and continued to use excess cash to buy back stock, the intrinsic value of Coca-Cola would be substantially higher than what the market was thinking.

Using John Burr Williams' dividend discount model to calculate the discounted present value of Coca-Cola's growth in owner-earnings, the company was worth $20.7 billion at a 5 percent growth rate for a 10-year forecast period followed by a 5 percent growth rate into perpetuity; $32.4 billion at a 10 percent growth rate; or $48.3 billion at a 15 percent growth rate. The market value of Coca-Cola when Warren was purchasing the stock averaged $15.1 billion. So depending on your estimate for growth, Warren was purchasing Coca-Cola "approximately" as low as a conservative 27 percent discount to intrinsic value and "approximately" as high as 70 percent. Stage One value investors observed the same Coca-Cola that Buffett purchased and because its price to earnings and price to book value were all so high, they considered Coca-Cola overvalued.[57]

To help investors appreciate the difference between the Stage One and Stage Two approaches to value investing, Tom Gayner, co-chief executive officer and chief investment officer of Markel Corporation, offers a thoughtful metaphor: it's the difference between a snapshot, which freezes one specific moment, and a full-length movie, which unfolds over time.[58]

Gayner was trained as an accountant and reminds us that accounting is important because it is the language of business. No surprise, then, that, when Gayner began investing he emphasized the quantitative approach he learned as an accountant—the same approach taught by Ben Graham.

Gayner calls quantitative investing "spotting value." It is like a camera that takes a snapshot. In that snapshot, time is standing still. This approach, said Gayner, worked spectacularly well after the Great Depression and World War II. Buying mathematically cheap stocks was a profitable investment approach for decades—until it didn't work any longer. Why? Because as the stock market evolves, the participants learn what is working. What began with just dozens of investors, then hundreds, then thousands, eventually became tens of thousands of investors all picking the same cheap stocks, and so the profit gap closed. Graham and Dodd's value approach to picking stocks no longer provided an excess return.

The evolution of value investing, Gayner said, can be seen as a segue from spotting value with a snapshot to understanding that value unfolds over time like a movie. Charlie Munger concurs. "The days of locating stocks selling at a 25%–50% discount to some liquidating value, a price that someone else would pay to buy the business, when it was easy as moving your Geiger counter over low multiple stocks is over. The world has wised up. The game has gotten harder. You have to get into Warren's thinking."[59] So let us say that how Warren thought about the intrinsic value of Coca-Cola was very much like watching a movie directed by Goizueta as it unfolds.

Moving from Stage One to Stage Two value investing is challenging. The fundamental movie-making in Stage Two is more difficult than taking a snapshot in Stage One. Financial missteps can be made if an investor's version of how they think their movie will turn out differs from reality. Even so, fundamental movie-making is the key component in understanding Stage Two value investing.

"It's extraordinary how resistant some people are to learning anything," said Charlie. What's really astounding," Warren added, "is how resistant they are even when it's in their self-interest to learn." Then in a more reflective tone, Warren continued, "There is just an incredible resistance to thinking or changing. I quoted Bertrand Russell one time saying, 'Most men would rather die than think. Many have.' And in a financial sense, that's very true."[60]

Stage Three: The Value of Network Economics

The transition from Stage Two to Stage Three value investing is less about adding new financial metrics and more about introducing new business models. In Stage One, business models were defined by their physical structure. To grow a business in Stage One required growing the physical aspects of the company—more plant and property. In Stage Two, growing a business was levered to the intangible components of a business—the attractiveness of the product, its brand value, and delivery of the product through various outlet channels. The service aspect in Stage Two, which drove the sales and earnings of the business, required significantly less capital than Stage One.

In Stage Three investors are learning, slowly at first but now more confidently, the value-creating aspects of knowledge, information, and entertainment, all of that made possible by new technologies including more powerful personal computers and smartphones all connected together to the global internet. In Stage Three, the cost of the physical input to business models has gone down while the value output has grown exponentially. In Stage Three, billions of dollars in market value is being created by companies generating hundreds of millions in earnings, all made possible by fractions of the capital employed compared to the Industrial Revolution.

Value investors have always been fascinated by growth but admittedly conflicted in how to confidently estimate a necessary margin of safety for that growth. For most, Aesop's two birds in a bush were always out of reach. Although most value investors were slow to learn how to value growth, nothing stopped academicians from studying the attributes of economic growth.

The first notable was Joseph Schumpeter. Schumpeter's view of the economy as being dynamic, innovative, and change-oriented came from involvement with the Historical School of Economics, a broad approach to economic theory that developed in Germany in the nineteenth century. According to Christopher Freeman, a British economist who is considered the preeminent researcher in innovation studies and who devoted much of his study to Schumpeter's work, "The central point of Schumpeter's whole life work is that capitalism can only be understood as an evolutionary process of continuous innovation and 'creative destruction.'"[61] Schumpeter came to believe economic growth occurred over a series of long cycles, what he called waves, with each picking up speed through time.

In 1962, Everett Rogers, an assistant professor of rural sociology at Ohio State University, published the first edition of *Diffusions of Innovation*. He was 31 years old. Today, Rogers is a renowned academic figure. His book, now in its fifth edition, was the second most cited book in all of social sciences in the early 2000s. Rogers sought to integrate Schumpeter's rolling waves into one distinct wave to explain how, why, and at what rate technological ideas spread. He categorized technology adopters as "innovators, early adopters, early majority, late majority, and laggards."

But it was Carlota Perez, a British-Venezuelan scholar, who connected the dots: Schumpeter's economic change begins first with innovation, which then attracts entrepreneurial activities, leading to a burst of financial investment. Perez's research focused on the concept of techno-economic paradigm shifts, showing how the financial markets paralleled, at times unevenly, the life cycle of technology revolutions.

In her book *Technological Revolutions and Financial Capital: The Dynamics of Bubbles and Golden Ages*, Perez identifies five technological revolutions from the 1770s to 2000s. The first, the Industrial Revolution, began in 1771 when Arkwright's water-powered cotton spinning mill opened in Cromford, England. The second, in 1829, the Age of Steam and Railways, opened with the test of the Rocket steam engine for the Liverpool-Manchester railway. The third is the Age of Steel, Electricity, and Heavy Engineering, which began when Carnegie's Bessemer plant opened in Pittsburgh in 1875. The fourth is identified as the Age of Oil, the Automobile, and Mass Production. It began in 1908 when the first Model-T rolled out of the Ford plant in Detroit. Today, says Perez, we are in the midst of the fifth technology revolution, which she calls the Age of Information and Telecommunications. It began in 1971 in Santa Clara, California, when Intel unveiled the microprocessor.[62]

The new technologies of the fifth revolution include microelectronics and computers, software, smartphones, and control systems. The new infrastructure includes global digital telecommunications with cable, fiberoptics, radio frequencies, and satellites providing internet, electronic mail, and other e-services.

The principles of the fifth technology revolution include information intensity, decentralized structures, and globalization. Information intensity means knowledge as capital is the value added. When the network structures are decentralized, markets can be segmented, creating a proliferation of powerful niches. Global communications enable instant globalized interactions between local operators, which lead to economies of scope and scale that in turn create a total addressable economic market that is unparalleled in history.[63]

Perez's life cycle of a technological revolution is not too dissimilar from Rogers' diffusion of innovations theory. Perez's life cycle comprises four different phases. In phase one, the paradigm begins to take shape. Products are invented, companies are formed, and industries are born. Growth is explosive; innovation continues at a high rate. In phase two, we see the full constellation of new industries, new-technology systems, and new infrastructure. In phase three, the innovations are fully reflected in the market's potential for these new products and services. Lastly, in phase four the last new products arrive in the marketplace while the earlier ones are fast approaching maturity and market saturation.[64]

Importantly, Perez goes further than Rogers and further than Schumpeter; she points out that the "trajectory of a technological revolution is not as smooth as the stylized curves" reflected in the textbooks.[65] The reason, she believes, is the participation of financial markets in the funding of a technological revolution.

Perez describes a standard flow of events that occur with all technological revolutions. Every revolution moves through two surges, each of which is in turn made of two phases. She defines the first surge as the *installation period*. "It is a time when the new technologies irrupt in a maturing economy and advance like a bulldozer disrupting the established fabric and articulating new industrial networks, setting up new infrastructure and spreading new ways of doing things." The second surge is called the *deployment period*. At this point, Perez says, "the whole economy is rewoven and reshaped by the modernizing power of the triumphant paradigm, which then becomes the normal best practice, enabling the full unfolding of this wealth generating potential."[66]

To some degree, that echoes what others have described. However, between the first surge (installation) and the second (deployment) is where Perez says the "stylized curve" gets interrupted. She calls it the *turning point*. She explains: in the first phase of the installation period, which she calls "irruption," there is a period of massive investment in the technological revolution. At this point "the revolution is a small fact and a big promise." Then, money is poured into new businesses and new infrastructure at a frantic pace; this is the second phase of the installation period, called "frenzy." The stock market booms, forms a bubble, then collapses—the turning point. With the collapse comes an economic recession. But the recession creates the conditions for institutional restructuring, a financial rebalancing of technology's future market potential. "The crucial recomposition happens at the turning point which leaves behind the turbulent times of installation and paradigm transition to enter the 'golden age' that can follow."[67]

In the second surge, the deployment period, there are two distinct phases—"synergy" and "maturity." Perez calls the synergy phase the "golden age," a time when companies achieve coherent growth with increasing externalities of production, employment, and customers. During this time, increasing real economic return in the form of sales, cash earnings and high returns on capital becomes evident. This is then followed by a "maturity" phase where the market becomes saturated, the technology matures and the last of the new entrants come to market.

Perez's roadmap allows investors to easily track the events of the 1970s and 1980s—first came the period of "irruption," followed by the "frenzy" investment period in the 1990s, leading to a stock market bubble, the 2000 market crash, and economic recession that followed. Now, says Perez, we are firmly on the other side of the turning point, and it appears we are in the midst of the golden age of investing in this fifth technological revolution. Synergies between capital, infrastructure, labor, service, and customers are now reaching a comprehensible level. It is quite possible the golden period of investing in the Age of Information and Telecommunications could last for many years to come. How long before the "maturity" phase begins is unknown, but for many industries and companies the total global addressable market remains quite large.

■ ■ ■

Schumpeter, Rogers, and Perez have all given investors a thoughtful way to think about growth from a macroeconomic perspective. What is still lacking is how to think about the competitive advantage of any one company in this technological revolution. For this insight, we must turn to another academician, a soft-spoken Irish economist named Brian Arthur.

Arthur was born in Belfast, Northern Ireland, in 1945. He received an electrical engineering degree from Queens University Belfast in 1966, then headed to the U.S. to continue his studies: a master's degree in mathematics from the University of Michigan, then a PhD in operations research and a master's in economics from the University of California at Berkeley in the same year. In 1996, he was named to the Morrison Chair of Economics and Population Studies at Stanford. He was 37 years old, the youngest person ever to hold that endowed chair. He was awarded the prestigious Schumpeter Prize in Economics in 1990 for his work in "Evolutionary Economics: Theory and Practice."

Soon after arriving at Stanford, Arthur began to record his observations about the economy in a personal journal. One page, entitled "Economics Old and New," was divided into two columns in which he began to list the characteristics of both concepts. Under "Old Economics" he wrote "rational" and "reversion to the mean." Everything was "in equilibrium." It was economics based on classical physics, on a belief the system was structurally simple. Under "New Economics" Arthur wrote people were "emotional not rational." The system was "complicated not simple" and it was "ever changing not static." In Arthur's mind, economics was more akin to biology than physics.

Brian Arthur made a personal connection to the Nobel-winning economist Ken Arrow, who introduced him to a close-knit group of scientists working at the Santa Fe Institute in New Mexico. Arrow invited Arthur to present his latest research at a conference of physicists, biologists, and economists at the Institute in the fall of 1987. The conference was organized in the hope that the ideas then percolating within the natural sciences, namely the science of complex adaptive systems, would stimulate new ways to think about economics. At the time, it was not widely known that John Reed, chairman and CEO of Citigroup, had funded the conference with the hope of finding new ideas about how capital markets actually work to offset the mistakes his own economists were continually making.

Common to the study of complex adaptive systems is the recognition the system is composed of multiple agents, each reacting and adapting to patterns the system itself creates. Complex adaptive systems are in a constant process of evolving over time. Although these types of systems were familiar to biologists and ecologists, the conference group at the Santa Fe Institute thought perhaps the concept should be expanded and maybe now was the time to include the study of economic systems and stock markets with an overarching idea of complexity.

Today, economics studied as a complex adaptive system is called "complexity economics," a term Arthur coined while writing an article for *Science* in 1999. In standard physics-based economic theory, markets exhibit diminishing returns. The law of diminishing returns is a fundamental principle of standard economics. It states that adding one more factor of production while holding constant other factors, namely demand, will at some point yield lower incremental returns per production unit. Said differently, the law of diminishing returns refers to a point at which the level of profits gained is less than the money invested.

However, complexity economics sees companies that are not destined to long market cycles of diminishing returns. According to Arthur, there are some companies that demonstrate increasing economic returns. "Increasing returns," he explains, "are the tendency for that which is ahead to get further ahead and for that which loses advantage to lose further advantage." Whereas diminishing returns is a feature of the older, brick-and-mortar economy, "increasing returns reign in the newer part—the knowledge-based industries."[68]

The principle of increasing returns, says Arthur, is especially significant in the technology-specific industries where *network effects* are common. A network effect is a phenomenon whereby a product or a service gains in value as more and more people use it. Networks have been around a long time, Arthur notes, but in the new knowledge-based economy the digital network is the value-creating symbol. And digital networks are far different from brick-and-mortar networks. There will certainly be competition between networks in the new-technology-based economy, Arthur predicts, but in the end, after the shakeout, "of the networks, there will be few."[69]

■ ■ ■

Each day after studying legal and political ethics in the doctorate program at Johns Hopkins University, Bill Miller stopped by the Baltimore office of Legg Mason Wood Walker brokerage firm. His wife, Leslie, was the assistant to Legg Mason's top stockbroker, Harry Ford. Waiting for Leslie to wrap up for the day, Miller could be found sitting in a corner, reading research reports.

A graduate student in philosophy spending afternoons reading stock reports might seem a bit odd. But for Bill Miller, who started out as a nine-year-old cutting grass with a push mower for a quarter in the hot Florida sun, finding new ways to make money was not out of bounds.

One day, a young Bill Miller noticed his father reading the newspaper—not the usual sports page but the finance section. When he asked his father to explain all those numbers, his father said, "If you'd owned a share of this company yesterday, you'd have 25 cents more today than yesterday." The stocks go up by themselves, his father continued.

"You mean if you know about stocks you can make money without doing any work?" Bill asked.

"Yes."

"Well, I want to make a lot of money but I don't want to do any work so I want to know about stocks."[70]

In high school Miller read his first investment book, *How I Made $2 Million in the Stock Market.* At age 16, he invested his $75 savings in RCA stock and made a handsome profit. He was hooked. From then on, investing was always a part of his life. Miller did not take the typical business school route. He attended Washington and Lee University in Lexington, Virginia, graduating with honors in 1972 with a degree in European history and economics. It was at Washington and Lee that he was introduced to Benjamin Graham and began to seriously study investing. "Once someone explains the value concept to you, either you get it or you don't." said Miller. "I found the concept to be congenial. It made sense."[71]

After graduating from college, Miller served overseas as an Army intelligence officer. From there, he pursued his doctorate in philosophy. Bill Miller was on a pathway to teach philosophy and one decision away from writing his doctoral dissertation at Johns Hopkins University when Professor Michael Hooker forewarned him there were no teaching jobs to be found. Hooker, who recalled seeing Miller in the faculty library every morning reading *The Wall Street Journal*, encouraged him to pursue a career in finance instead. That led Miller to take a position as a financial officer then treasurer at the manufacturing company J.E. Baker Company. One of the perks of the treasurer's position was the responsibility of overseeing the company's investment portfolio. Miller soon discovered this was the part of the job he enjoyed the most.[72]

Hanging around the Legg Mason office soon paid off for Miller. Raymond "Chip" Mason, the founder and chairman of Legg Mason, "recalls that Miller would show up and when his wife was ready to leave, he was so immersed in research reports that Leslie would prod him to go."[73] It wasn't long before Leslie introduced her husband to Ernie Kiehne, the head of research at Legg Mason. It so happened that Kiehne was planning to retire, and he and Chip Mason were looking for a successor. Thus, in 1981, Bill Miller joined Legg Mason and became Ernie Kiehne's understudy. The following year, Chip Mason launched the Legg Mason Value Trust mutual fund to showcase the firm's research prowess. Kiehne and Miller were named co-portfolio managers.

The Value Trust is the perfect case study to observe the evolution of the three different stages of value investing. In the beginning, Value Trust was managed based on the precepts outlined by Graham and Dodd, a classic Stage One. The mutual fund was widely diversified, owning over 100 stocks, and nearly all showed low price-to-earnings and low price-to-book-value ratings. The Graham and Dodd approach was favored by Ernie Kiehne and had been practiced by stockbrokers at Legg Mason since Chip Mason founded the firm in 1962. But soon after Value Trust was launched, Miller's influence slowly began to change the complexion of the portfolio. Miller focused on a company's future cash flows and return on equity, a hallmark of Warren Buffett's approach to value investing. Along the way, Miller steadily reduced the number of stocks in Value Trust and, like Warren, began to concentrate his positions around his best ideas. By the late 1980s, Value Trust had morphed into Stage Two value investing.

In October 1990, Ernie Kiehne turned the reins of Value Trust over to Bill Miller. He became the sole portfolio manager and starting in 1991 embarked on a record of outperformance that has never been equaled. From 1991 through 2005, the Legg Mason Value Trust beat its benchmark, the Standard & Poor's 500 Index, 15 years in a row.[74]

In hindsight, it is easy to see Value Trust evolving from Stage One to Stage Two value investing. After all, Warren Buffett had been illuminating the second approach for much of the 1980s. But when Miller took full control of Value Trust he was poised to move the portfolio to Stage Three, a value investing approach focused on companies that had never been thought as value propositions.

In 1993, Miller arranged to meet John Reed, CEO of Citigroup, in New York. At the time America's largest bank had been struggling but looked cheap in Miller's mind. His meeting with Reed confirmed the company was on the right approach, embracing cost controls and returning money to shareholders. Before leaving, Reed mentioned that Citigroup had funded a research project at the Santa Fe Institute that might interest the portfolio manager of the Value Trust. The lectures and presentations from the conference were now collected in a book titled *The Economy As an Evolving Complex Adaptive System*, edited by Phillip Anderson, Kenneth Arrow, and David Pines.

Miller got a copy, read the book, then headed to New Mexico.

■ ■ ■

High in the hills of the Sangre de Cristo Mountains, the southernmost tip of the Rocky Mountains, lies the Santa Fe Institute. It is a multidisciplinary research and education facility where physicists, biologists, mathematicians, computer scientists, psychologists, and economists have come together to study complex adaptive systems. These scientists are attempting to understand and predict immune systems, central nervous systems, ecologies, economies and the stock market, and they are all keenly interested in new ways of thinking.

When Miller arrived at the Institute he met Phil Anderson and Ken Arrow, both Nobel laureates. Anderson was studying the science of emergent properties. Arrow was laying the foundations for understanding the emergent growth theory and the economics of information. Miller was also introduced to Murray Gell-Mann, who had become a fixture at the Institute. Gell-Mann had collaborated with Richard Feynman and was awarded the Nobel Prize for his work on the theory of elementary particle physics, what he would call "quarks." Miller also met Geoffrey West, a British theoretical physicist, who was working on the universal laws of growth as it applied to organisms, cities, and companies. And it was here that Miller became friends with Brian Arthur.

Arthur explained to Miller his thoughts on increasing-returns economics. Then he went further, showing that companies that are experiencing increasing returns have certain attributes that further solidify their dominance within an industry. They talked about *network effects.* Arthur pointed out that people prefer being connected to a larger network rather than a small one. If there are two competing networks, one with 25 million members and one with five million members, a new member will tend to select the larger network because it is more likely to fulfill their need for connections to other members, offering more services and benefits.

Network effects are demand-side economies of scale. So for network effects to take hold, it is important to get big fast. This thwarts the competition from becoming established.

Miller and Arthur discussed the concept of *positive feedback,* a behavioral component of human nature described by B.F. Skinner, a behavioral psychologist. Positive experiences give us pleasure or satisfaction and we want to relive them. Someone who has a positive experience when using a technology product, or any product for that matter, will have a tendency to return to that product. The net effect of positive feedback in business is that the strong get stronger and the weak get weaker.

Another behavioral component of human psychology as it relates to technology investing is called *lock-in.* When we learn one way of doing something we have little interest in learning another. Technology products, specifically software, can be difficult to master in the beginning. Once we have become proficient using a certain product or software we fiercely resist changing to another. We become *path dependent*—more comfortable repeating the same technological functions. Changing requires learning a new set of instructions, often very difficult instructions. Consumers become satisfied, content with how they use technology. This is true even if a competitor's product is deemed superior.

All these factors—network effects, positive feedback, lock-in, and path dependency—result in high *switching costs.* Sometimes switching costs are literal, as when switching technologies and software costs so much money that customers can't be persuaded to change. But in many cases, attributes like positive feedbacks, lock-in, and path dependency also form a psychological dissuasion that is a form of high switching costs.

Warren Buffett taught us the best business with the best long-term prospects is called a *franchise*—a company that sells a product or service that is needed or desired and has no close substitute. Warren also said he believed the next great fortunes would be made by people who identify new franchises. After his first visit to the Santa Fe Institute, Miller came away with a strong belief the new-technology companies being added to the stock market were the modern-day equivalent of Warren's franchise factor.

When Miller returned to Baltimore he found the menu of value stocks in the market contained the usual suspects: banks, energy companies, industrials including depressed paper companies. Also on that menu—personal computer stocks. Investors had come to believe personal computer stocks were just another commodity product. The stocks historically traded between 6 and 12 times earnings. Value investors would buy PC stocks at 6 times earnings and then sell them at 12 times earnings. So, in 1996, during a slowdown in PC sales, value investors started buying again. So did Miller. He bought Dell Computer, which soon traded back to twelve times earnings along with the other personal computer stocks. At that point the value investors sold their stock. Value Trust held its position.

Many know the folklore of Michael Dell, the brilliant kid who sold personal computers from his college dormitory, turning a part-time job into a multibillion-dollar company. But few appreciate how Dell's model of direct selling to consumers generated historic levels of profitability. Most personal computer companies, like Gateway, Compaq and Hewlett-Packard, sold to retailers who in turned raised prices then sold to their customers. Because Dell sold its computers direct to the consumer, their prices were cheaper.

To buy a Dell Computer, a customer would call the 1-800 number (or later, connect via the internet), and order a monitor, keyboard, and desktop tower with specifications for memory and speed. The operator would take the order, ask for the customer's credit card for payment, and promise the computer would be delivered to their home or business in the coming weeks. That night, Dell received payment from the customer's credit card company for a computer it would assemble from components it had ordered from a supplier whose invoice it was not obligated to pay for 30 or maybe even 60 days. So the Dell business model was growing its direct PC business largely on the cash receivables from its customers. It is called "negative working" capital. Not only did Dell drive sales faster and higher than other competitors because its direct model allowed for cheaper prices, it also became the first corporation in history to generate a return on capital above 100 percent. It would eventually hit a high-water mark of 229 percent return on capital.

The fact that Miller didn't sell Dell Computer in lockstep with the other value investors was not big news. But when Dell became the largest position in Value Trust, selling at 35 times earnings, it caught the eye of many value investors and caused a fair amount of consternation. What was Miller thinking, they asked? If he wanted to own a personal computer stock why not Gateway, which was trading at 12 times earnings? Bill's answer was simple: Dell earns 200 percent return on capital while Gateway earned 40 percent. Dell was five times more profitable than Gateway but only three times the price-to-earnings ratio.[75]

Miller's investment methodology and approach were transparent. It was there for all to see. He was following the same investment approach as Warren—a discounted cash-flow model. But he was also channeling Warren's observation that "the best business to own is one that over an extended period can employ large amounts of capital at very high rates of return." Think back to Michael Mauboussin's illustration on justifiable price-to-earnings ratios. If a company was growing at a 10 percent rate earning 16 percent return on capital against a cost of capital of 8 percent, it was worth 22.4 times earnings. Dell Computer was growing much faster than 10 percent and it was earning 200 percent on invested capital with a capital cost of 10 percent. What should the stock have been selling for?

Miller was simply following the valuation of Dell Computer to its logical conclusion. "From a theoretical view," he said, "there are fundamental flaws using the backward-looking stuff" like price-to-earnings ratios. "At the end of the day, 100 percent of the value of any equity depends on the future, not the past."[76]

■ ■ ■

Miller's frequent trips to the Santa Fe Institute energized him. He knew the market was in the midst of a new-technology revolution and he also knew he had a roadmap in how to determine a technology company's competitive advantage. The literature on how to think about technology companies and investing was growing. Libraries were being formed. Geoffrey Moore, an organizational theorist, burst onto the scene in 1991 with the publication of his bestseller, *Crossing the Chasm*. Brian Arthur organized his research writing and published *Increasing Returns and Path Dependence in the Economy* in 1994. Ken Arrow wrote the foreword. In 1997, the highly respected Harvard management professor Clay Christensen wrote *The Innovators Dilemma: When New Technologies Cause Great Firms to Fail*. The following year Carl Shapiro, a professor of business strategies, and Hal Varian, an economist specializing in microeconomics and information economics, published the seminal book of the time—*Information Rules: A Strategic Guide to the Network Economy*. Hal Varian became the founding dean of the School of Information at Berkeley and later was appointed chief economist of Google.

That same year, Geoffrey Moore followed up his bestseller with another titled *The Gorilla Game: An Investor's Guide to Picking Winners in High Technology*, coauthored with Paul Johnson and Tom Kippola. In the book they outlined the investment case for Oracle and the relational database business; Cisco and the economics of network hardware; and a detailed analysis of the growing importance of customer service software. All turned out to be prophetic.

Paul Johnson earned his economics degree from the University of California, Berkeley, before obtaining his MBA from The Wharton School at the University of Pennsylvania. It was at Wharton that Johnson learned that value creation was a function of returns on capital. In class one day, he was asked how a company grows in value. Johnson was stumbling through the reasoning embedded in the Capital Asset Pricing Model when his professor cut him off and pointed him in the direction of William Fruhan, a Harvard Business School professor. Fruhan authored three books, but it was his second one, *Financial Strategy: Studies in the Creation, Transfer, and Destruction of Shareholder Value*, published in 1979, that planted the seed in corporate finance of a new way to think about what exactly was needed to increase a company's market value. In Chapter 2, "The Levers That Managers Can Utilize to Enhance Shareholder Values," Fruhan succinctly explained, "The economic value of any investment is a function of the future cash flows anticipated from that investment, and the cost of capital required to finance the investment." He went on to say, "Cash flow from an investment can also be increased if a firm can reduce the capital intensity of its business below that of its competitors."[77]

What Fruhan spotlighted was the notion that a firm's value was related not only to its cash-generating abilities but also to the cash return on its cost of capital. To the degree a firm earned high cash returns on capital, it increased the value of the firm. And one way to do this was to reduce the capital required to generate the cash return compared to competitors. Think Dell Computer. What Fruhan did for Johnson was to open his eyes to the value-creation levers—cash, return on capital, and cost of capital.

After Wharton, Johnson earned his analytical stripes at CS First Boston before moving to Robertson Stephens & Co., where he became managing director and senior technology analyst, following the telecommunications and computer networking equipment industries. In the 1990s, the Four Horsemen of the technology industry were Dell, Cisco Systems, Intel, and Microsoft. Johnson covered Cisco.

In December 1996, Johnson penned a research report titled "Networking Industry: A New Way to Listen to the Music: ROIC." It was Johnson's thesis that for long-term investors, value creation is a function of how much economic value is created by the funds a company invests and deploys. Johnson's viewpoint was that return on invested capital (ROIC) was the superior method to determine value creation, more informative than the traditional markers commonly used: earnings per share (EPS) or earnings before interest, taxes, depreciation and amortization (EBITDA).

Two months later, in February 1997, Johnson sent Warren Buffett an open letter pitching Cisco Systems. "Dear Warren, If you think Coke is a good investment," he wrote, "take a look at Cisco." Johnson's reasoning was that the strategy that helped drive Coca-Cola's intrinsic value higher—namely, reinvesting profits in a business with high return on capital—was also available with Cisco.

Coca-Cola, Johnson acknowledged, was indeed a great business. From 1991 to 1996, Coke had generated an annual ROIC between 25 and 35 percent against a weighted average cost of capital of 14 percent. But Cisco, he pointed out, had over the same period generated an annual ROIC in the range of 130 percent to 195 percent against a weighted average cost of capital Johnson estimated at 18 percent.

In his letter Johnson quoted Warren's own words from the Berkshire Hathaway 1992 Annual Report to Shareholders: "The best business to own is one that over an extended period of time can employ large amounts of incremental capital at very high rates of return. Growth benefits investors only when the business in point can invest at incremental returns that are enticing—in other words, only when each dollar used to finance the growth creates over a dollar of long-term market value."

Both Bill Miller and Paul Johnson were observing firsthand that for every one dollar that Dell Computer and Cisco Systems reinvested back into their companies, they were creating multiples of dollars in market value.

■ ■ ■

Bill Miller's definition of value comes from the finance textbooks outlined by John Burr Williams and emphasized by Warren. Value for any investment is the present value of the future free cash flows of that investment. Miller is quick to point out that nowhere in the textbooks does it say that value is defined in terms of low price-to-earnings ratios. But what Warren, Miller, and Johnson gleamed from their study of businesses is the value of the future cash flows is greatly enhanced by the high incremental returns on investment made possible by the cash flows.

What separates Miller from other value investors is not that he defined value differently but rather that he was willing to look for value anywhere it might be. Most important, he didn't rule out technology companies as businesses that might contain value. "We believe and continue to believe that technology can be analyzed on a business basis," he said, "that intrinsic value can be estimated, and that using a value approach in the tech sector is a competitive advantage in an area dominated by investors who focus exclusively, or mainly, on growth, and often ignored by those who focus on value."[78] Classic value investors, accustomed to relying on simple accounting metrics, were not able to get their hands around technology companies.

Having owned Dell Computer, Miller could have purchased another technology hardware company that earned high returns on capital like Cisco Systems, but he decided to move in a different direction. In late 1996, Miller began to purchase America Online (AOL) for the Legg Mason Value Trust. Steve Case, AOL's founder and chief executive officer, brought the internet to 29 million people in quick fashion. Once AOL's network reached 50 percent market share for online customers, Miller figured it had created an entity that was impregnable. Furthermore, he concluded, as strong as Microsoft was at the time, it couldn't overtake AOL.

Following Brian Arthur's roadmap, Miller could see the power of the network effect that was building inside AOL. It began as a simple communications system but then began to differentiate itself by the various channels it offered its members, including email, chat rooms, message boards, and instant messaging. AOL's positive feedback numbers were evident. As AOL offered more new features, more people had positive experiences and were eager to come back. Miller was able to measure individual usage, and he knew AOL subscribers were spending more and more time on the site.

From a technology perspective AOL was not daunting. Members quickly mastered sending and receiving email in a certain way and didn't care to change. Even when other providers offered more bells and whistles, AOL members were not interested in changing. The lock-in effect was working.

Even more interesting is what happened when the company switched to flat-rate prices. Hundreds of thousands of internet users recognized the good deal and the number of subscribers jumped astronomically, so much so that the system became hopelessly jammed. Anyone trying to access the service heard nothing but constantly busy signals. New customers were angry. Old customers were furious. Media coverage was intensely negative. But did people change to another provider? No. Despite the busy signals and the negative publicity, AOL membership continued to grow.

Miller employed a standard discounted cash flow model for determining the intrinsic value for AOL. To provide an ample margin of safety, he discounted the cash flows at 30 percent, three times as high as the discount rate he was using for IBM. Miller started purchasing AOL at average prices of $15 per share, but believed the business was worth approximately $30 per share. By 1998, he thought the value of AOL's business was near $110 on the low side and as high as $175, still using a conservative discounted cash flow. AOL split the stock four times between 1998 and 1999. Value Trust made 50 times its original investment in AOL. The position soon became a 19 percent weighting in the portfolio, and along with Dell Computer and other technology stocks, Value Trust's investment in the new-economy stocks reached 41 percent of its portfolio.

Miller had become an enigma in the value camp of investing. But what he did next stupefied Wall Street.

In 1994, Jeff Bezos left the venerable New York hedge fund D.E. Shaw. After reading a research report that forecast internet commerce growth would reach 2,300 percent, Bezos enacted what he called the "regret minimization framework"—a decision plan for avoiding any potential regrets he would have for not participating in the greatest business growth opportunity of our time. He made a list of the top 20 products that could be marketed online, then narrowed the list to the most promising five: computer hardware, software, computer discs, videos, and books. Bezos loaded his station wagon and drove to the state of Washington and was soon selling books out of the garage of his house on Northeast 28th Street in Bellevue.

Bezos incorporated his new company on July 25, 1994, under the name Cadabra. He soon changed the name to Amazon. com. A year later Amazon was selling books to all 50 states and 45 countries and within two months was ringing up sales of $20,000 per week. On May 15, 1997, Amazon offered a public offering of its stock at $18 per share. Miller bought Amazon on the IPO for Value Trust but then sold it after the stock quickly doubled. Two years later, in what *The Wall Street Journal* called the most audacious move of his career, Miller invested in Amazon again, this time at $88 per share.[79]

By the end of 1999, Amazon was trading at the lofty price of 22 times sales. It had been losing money since its launch, but Miller felt it was not losing as much money as the market was thinking. Cash was coming into Amazon by the bucketloads, but Bezos was reinvesting the money back into the business as fast as he could. Because Amazon had jumped out to an early lead in online sales of books, Miller believed the company had an unassailable lead on its competitors. The network effects were already in place. Furthermore, Miller understood the competitive advantage of Amazon's business model. It would be able to grow rapidly without the need for massive capital infusions either with debt or equity issuance.

Investment professionals at Legg Mason Capital Management would, of course, be expected to understand investment strategies and portfolio management as well as basics like accounting and finance. But to be on Bill Miller's team, more was expected; it also required an appreciation of the insights that can be gained from studying philosophy. William James, the father of American pragmatism, cast a bright light on Miller's investment team. So too did the teachings of Ludwig Wittgenstein.

Ludwig Josef Johann Wittgenstein, an Austrian-born philosopher who taught at the University of Cambridge from 1929 to 1947, is considered one of the preeminent philosophers of the twentieth century. The equally famous philosopher Bertrand Russell termed Wittgenstein "perhaps the most perfect example I have ever known of genius as traditionally conceived."[80] Wittgenstein's field of study included logic, mathematics, the philosophy of the mind and the philosophy of language. His theory of language has helped us appreciate that words have meaning—that the words we choose form a description, which ultimately provides an explanation.

In 1953, Ludwig Wittgenstein's second and last book, *Philosophical Investigations*, was published posthumously. After his death in 1951, his friends and colleagues gathered all his personal writings, notebooks, and papers, and organized them for publication. The resulting book is now recognized as one of the most important works of philosophy of the twentieth century.

On page 200 of *Philosophical Investigations* is a diagram, a simple triangle hand-drawn by Wittgenstein. Below this figure he wrote, "This triangle can be seen as a triangular hole, as a solid, a geometrical drawing, as standing on its base, as hanging from its apex; as a mountain, as a wedge, as an arrow or pointer, as an overturned object, which was meant to stand on the shorter side of the right angle, as a half parallelogram, and as various other things." In all, Wittgenstein tallied 12 different descriptions of a rather plain-looking three-sided pencil sketch. His point was clear. How we see the world is shaped by how we describe it. The world is compatible with many very different descriptions.

If there can be multiple descriptions of a simple one-dimensional triangle, imagine the number of descriptions for things with greater complexity. That is why, for example, there is not one description of what is occurring in the stock market, but several. Likewise, there is not only one description for a company. Analysts and portfolio managers who worked with Bill Miller were constantly challenged to come up with alternative descriptions, to redescribe the companies they were analyzing.

When Amazon became a public company Wall Street provided a simple description. The market believed Amazon was the online equivalent of the leading bookstore, Barnes & Noble. Analysts compared and contrasted the accounting factor multiples for both companies and concluded Barnes & Noble was much cheaper than Amazon. Hence, a smart investor should buy Barnes & Noble and sell Amazon. Later, as Amazon began to sell more than just books, analysts compared Amazon to Walmart. Using the same valuation markers, analysts recommended a pair trade of going long Walmart while shorting Amazon.

Miller also analyzed Amazon but what he saw didn't look much like Barnes & Noble. As an online retailer Amazon had minuscule capital expenditures per $100,000 sales compared to the brick-and-mortar competitors. Furthermore, Amazon collected revenues from its customers via online purchases but didn't need to pay the suppliers—book publishers—for three to six months. Often publishers would accept book returns with no penalty. Miller had seen this 'business model before. And after he met with Jeff Bezos to discuss Amazon's business model it confirmed what he thought. Amazon wasn't Barnes & Noble—it was Dell Computer.

Amazon and Dell had approximately the same gross and operating margins. They had the same direct-to-customer model and recognized revenues immediately while paying suppliers later. Amazon and Dell had the same capital velocity, the same negative working capital model and the same cash conversion cycle. Both companies were fueling their growth not through the income statement but via the working capital account on the balance sheet. Both had the same operating mantra—get the cash in the door as quickly as possible—meaning their customers helped pay for the company's expansion. Like Dell, Amazon became a company that generated returns on capital greater than 100 percent.

Miller also thought Wall Street was wrong in describing Amazon as a perpetual money-losing operation. At a Grant's Interest Rate Observer conference in 2000, Miller passed out a questionnaire asking the attending fund managers to guess the cumulative cash loss of Amazon since its initial public offering. Their estimates ranged from a low of $200 million to a high of $4 billion. The correct answer, said Miller, was $62 million. "We didn't believe the market was correctly analyzing Amazon," he insisted. "I mean, these guys were pros."[81]

Wittgenstein's lessons for investors are particularly acute—failure to explain is caused by failure to describe. Over the next 20 years (2000–2019), despite the 2000 technology bear market and the 2008 financial crisis, Amazon's stock price gained 2,327 percent compared to the S&P 500 Index, which posted a 224 percent total return.

Miller was once called a value investor who wrapped himself in the stripes of a momentum player. Today, he is universally considered to be one of the first investors to successfully tackle the value conundrum of technology companies. Miller never strayed from the basic principles of value investing. He calculated the value of businesses using the discounted cash flow model and only purchased stocks when there was a margin of safety. "With money managers turning their portfolios north of 100 percent per year in a frenetic chase to find something that works, our glacial 11 percent turnover is anomalous," said Miller. "Finding good businesses at cheap prices, taking a big position, and then holding for years used to be sensible investing. We are delighted when people use simple-minded, accounting-based metrics and then align them on a linear scale and then use that to make buy-and-sell decisions. It's much easier than actually doing the work to figure out what a business is worth, and it enables us to generate better results for our clients by doing more thorough analysis."[82]

Like Warren Buffett, Bill Miller is an educator. But unlike modern-day hedge fund managers who say little until good performance is revealed, Miller is an open book. He is happy to tell you what he is reading as well as what books are currently piled high on his desk in a Pisa-like to-be-read tower. Miller enjoys meeting colleagues at investment conferences and revels in the hours-long dinner conversations afterwards. And he is always delighted when portfolio managers and analysts ask to go to the Santa Fe Institute to study complex adaptive systems.

Looking back, we can see that Miller's success is a result of three distinct influences. First, he was an accomplished student of accounting and finance and studied the approaches of other successful investors including Warren Buffett. Second, in his tireless pursuit of seeking to always understand what works best, he was willing to jump full force into the teachings of the Santa Fe Institute long before any Wall Street regulars showed up. Last and most important, Bill Miller is a philosopher-investor. Better yet, he is a pragmatist.

Most investors who have been successful, but only for a limited period of time, hold a correspondence theory of truth. They believe their viewpoint corresponds to some deep, well-founded structure of how markets operate. The correspondence theory of truth relies on absolutes. Stubbornness is a medal of honor. Now contrast this to a pragmatic approach. If you are a pragmatist, you typically have a shorter time period in which you will hold an ineffectual model. Pragmatists realize a model, any model, is there only to help you with a certain task. They apply the test of usefulness and utility while discounting the infatuation others have for absolutes.

Brian Arthur once asked Miller how a doctoral student in philosophy found his way to the business of investing. Miller replied that he wasn't an investor despite studying philosophy but rather he was intrigued with money management precisely because of his exposure to the study of philosophy. "Thanks to that training," he said, "I can smell a bad argument miles away."[83]

■ ■ ■

In the second quarter of 2019, Warren announced Berkshire had purchased 537,300 common shares of Amazon.com worth then about $947 million. It was not a big purchase in terms of the size position. Indeed, Warren let it be known it was not he who bought the stock but one of his investment managers, Todd Combs or Ted Weschler. Combs joined Berkshire in 2010 to help manage a slug of Berkshire's investment portfolio. Two years later, Weschler was added to the team. Together, they manage collectively approximately 10 percent of Berkshire's common stock portfolio.

Warren met Jeff Bezos soon after Amazon went public. In 2003, Berkshire owned $459 million in Amazon bonds. At the time, there were only three things Warren purchased over the internet: *The Wall Street Journal*, online bridge, and books from Amazon. "I don't know if Amazon is going to weigh 150 pounds or 300 pounds," said Warren, "but one thing I do know is that they are not anorexic. Here is a guy [Bezos] who took something that is right in front of us—selling books—and put it together with new technology to create, in a couple of years, one of the biggest brand names in the world."[84]

Fifteen years later, at the Berkshire 2019 Annual Meeting, Warren was still singing Bezos' praise. It is Olympic for someone to build from scratch a business that became the biggest in the world. Bezos, Warren noted, had done it twice, first with online retailing then later with Amazon Web Services (AWS), the world's largest on-demand cloud computing platforms for individuals, companies, and governments on a metered pay-as-you-go basis. "I have always admired Jeff," Warren said. "I've been an idiot for not buying. I always thought he was special, but I didn't realize you could go from books to what happened here. He had a vision and executed it in an incredible way."[85]

At the annual meeting, Charlie Munger was more reserved. "We are a bit older than most," said Charlie, "and we are not as flexible as others." Warren added that he and Charlie grew up studying John Rockefeller and Andrew Carnegie, two of the twentieth century's greatest industrialists and richest men in history. They could have never imagined someone could build a trillion-dollar business generating billions in earnings with so little capital employed. It was unimaginable.

At that same meeting, Charlie gave himself a pass for not buying Amazon but said he "felt like the horse's ass for not buying Google." Now called Alphabet, Google went public in August 2004 at $85 per share and today is one of the world's largest companies, worth over $1 trillion. For years, Warren and Charlie watched GEICO send checks to Google to pay for the clicks consumers hit on the Google search engine to learn about GEICO Insurance. "We just sat on our hands," said Charlie. Then, in an unapologetic tone, he added, "Maybe Apple is our atonement."[86]

Berkshire began buying Apple in 2016. It was announced the company purchased 9.8 million shares on May 16, 2016. By the end of the year, Berkshire owned 67 million shares at a cost of $6.7 billion for an average price of about $100 per share. The following year Warren purchased an additional 100 million shares, making Apple the second largest holding at Berkshire. At a market value of $28 billion, Apple was only slightly less than the market value of Wells Fargo at $29 billion. Then in 2018, Warren added another 90 million shares, making Apple Berkshire's largest holding by far. Twice as big as Wells Fargo. Twice as big as Bank of America. Twice as big as Coca-Cola. In a CBS interview with Jane Pauley, Warren admitted he had been keeping an eye on Apple for several years. "I don't need to know things instantaneously. I'm not making buy-and-sell decisions based on instant news. When we bought Apple, it'd been something I'd looked at a long time."[87]

Warren was coming around to the idea that Apple was a very valuable product and that people were building their lives around the iPhone. "That's true of 8-year-olds and 80-year-olds. People want the product," he said. "And they don't want the cheapest product."[88] Today, Apple sells annually about 13 percent of the world's cell phones but captures 85 percent of the world's profits because it charges a premium price customers are willing to pay. When Warren first bought Apple, many were scratching their heads wondering why Berkshire wanted to buy a company like Motorola or Nokia, two cell phone manufacturers that had seen better days. But in another case of "failure to explain is caused by failure to describe," Apple wasn't Motorola or Nokia, it was Louis Vuitton. There is a reason why the Apple Store on Fifth Avenue in New York and on the Avenue des Champs-Elysees in Paris is next to the Louis Vuitton store. Apple is the luxury goods manufacturer of cell phones, and consumers have a strong affinity for its products.[89]

The second value-added component of Apple is its growing network. Over the years, Apple has built a wide array of products including the Mac computer, iPod, the iPhone, and the iPad. Next came the wearables, Apple Watch and AirPods. All these products were connected to a service component that includes the App Store, Apple Music, Apple TV, and the iCloud. Next came Apple Pay, a financial services component, and Apple Health. Today, Apple's services unit is the fastest-growing part of the company. And that growth is the principal reason for the rapid growth in Apple's stock price over the last several years. In 2016, when Berkshire first purchased Apple, the market was assigning no value to the implied growth of the company. Today, over a third of Apple's enterprise value is attributed to future growth.[90]

Apple's iPhones are profitable, but the economic returns of its service businesses are triple digit. At year-end 2019, Apple's return on invested capital (ROIC) was 143 percent against a weighted-average cost of capital (WACC) of 7 percent.[91] The company is gushing cash. At the end of the second quarter 2020, Apple had $192 billion in cash, about 15 percent of the $1.3 trillion market value of the company. What is Apple doing with its cash? A good deal goes to maintenance capital expenditures as well as future investment opportunities. But the lion's share of Apple's cash earning is going directly to shareholders in dividends and share repurchases. Apple pays a $13 billion current annual dividend to owners of the company. However, much more is going to share repurchases. When Berkshire first purchased Apple in 2016, the company had 5.3 billion shares outstanding. At year-end 2019, Apple's total shares outstanding tallied 4.4 billion. In the last four years, Apple repurchased 17 percent of its shares outstanding. Warren's investment in Apple is increasing each year without Berkshire having to spend a dollar.

If we step back and examine Apple, we find it is the perfect investment that straddles Stage Two and Stage Three value investing. It is a global consumer products company with strong brand value that continues to attract customers year after year. It generates high returns on capital and uses its excess cash to repurchase stock. In many ways, Apple is the Coca-Cola Company Warren purchased 30 years ago. Furthermore, it is noteworthy that Apple, like Coca-Cola, was "hiding in plain sight."

Apple is also a new-economy stock. All of Apple's products and services are powered by Apple's iOS operating system. Once a product becomes a part of Apple's ecosystem the network effects take over, and positive feedback, path dependence and lock-in create a powerful global franchise. The switching cost for Apple's customer base is simply too high.

Interestingly, Warren does not think of Apple as being part of Berkshire's stock portfolio, but rather as one of Berkshire's own separate businesses. He refers to Apple as Berkshire's third business, alongside GEICO and Burlington Northern Santa Fe railroad. "Apple is probably the best business I know of in the world," said Warren. "It has a valuable product which is central to people's lives." At the 2019 Berkshire Annual Meeting, Charlie pointed out that Buffett's willingness to invest in Apple was a good sign for Berkshire. "Either you've gone crazy or you're learning," he quipped. "I prefer the learning explanation."[92]

One of the greatest rewards that come from studying Warren Buffett has been to observe how he evolved, both rationally and pragmatically, over the last 65 years as an investor—from Stage One to Stage Two and now to Stage Three value investing. We heard Warren explain to his limited partners at the Buffett Partnership the investment rationale of owning Commonwealth Trust Company of Union City, New Jersey (1958), the outsized bet on Sanborn Map Company (1960), and his controlling interest in Dempster Mill Manufacturing Company (1962). Later, at Berkshire Hathaway, he explained the reasoning behind the See's Candies' acquisition and the billion-dollar bet on Coca-Cola. He discussed the strategic importance of owning franchise media companies and the benefit that comes from investing the float of an insurance company. Now Warren is illustrating the value of owning Apple, the largest company in the world, in the midst of the fifth technological revolution.

Philip Fisher was right. It is rare that a successful investor can evolve from one approach to a second, much less a third. To be successful past one market cycle requires mental flexibility, the proper temperament, and a burning desire to continually learn how to make money. This is an essential part of the mental construct of how a Money Mind works.

■ ■ ■

When Ben Graham retired from investing and left New York in 1956, Roger Murray took over the Value Investing Program at Columbia. Murray not only taught Graham's spring semester value investing seminar, he added David Dodd's fall class in 1961 when Dodd retired.[93]

Murray was well known on Wall Street and enjoyed a respectable career at Bankers Trust as the chief economist, becoming the youngest vice president in the bank's history. He advised members of Congress and was the originator of the concept of the Individual Retirement Account (IRA). He was the founding director of the Investor Responsibility Research Center (IRRC) and became the 23rd president of the American Finance Association. But despite the long list of professional accolades, Murray found that being a teaching professor was the most rewarding. He was immensely liked by his students and always took great pride in the professional successes they achieved after graduation. Among Roger Murray's notable students are some of the best-known names in our industry: Mario Gabelli, Chuck Royce, Leon Cooperman, Art Samberg, and Robert Bruce.

By the late 1960s, investment thinking across the country was beginning to change. On the heels of World War II and with the birth of the baby boom generation, the United States entered into a period of prolonged prosperity. The Dow Jones Industrial Average broke through 1,000 for the first time. Growth, not value, became the new investment mantra. A new breed of investment managers surfaced to lead the charge.

Gerald Tsai, Jr., was born in Shanghai. He moved to the United States with his parents in 1947 and graduated from Boston University with a bachelor's and master's degree in economics. Tsai began his career at Bache and Company but soon moved to Fidelity Management and Research, where he was named the fund manager of the newly formed Fidelity Capital mutual fund. Tsai's portfolio management style was momentum investing, which at the time helped to build Fidelity Investments into a mutual fund juggernaut. In 1965, Tsai left Fidelity and founded his own aggressive growth strategy, the Manhattan Fund.

Tsai's approach to investing was to concentrate his bets on growth stocks, in contrast to the value investing approach, which preached broad diversification. Tsai bought the glamour stocks like Xerox, Polaroid, and Avon Products; while value portfolios were full of slower-growing industrials, utilities, and energy companies. Soon the published performance of Tsai's Manhattan Fund was trouncing the returns of value stocks. In short order, investors gravitated to what became known as the Nifty Fifty stocks, the fastest-growing companies in the United States; the tried and true value stocks were left behind. It all worked out very well for investors, until it didn't. The brutal bear market of 1973–1974, the worst since the Great Depression, wiped out the Nifty Fifty growth investors, causing massive losses for individuals and their portfolios.

One might have thought value investing would have flourished again to fill the void, but the rally call for value approaches went unanswered and into the breach came a new group of investment thinkers—not investors but academicians. Born out of the University of Chicago in 1956, Modern Portfolio Theory (MPT) provided the salve for investors' wounds. MPT preached conservative returns and low price volatility. Investors rushed toward the emotionally soothing strategy. When Roger Murray retired from Columbia University in 1977, the Value Investing Program started by Ben Graham and David Dodd 50 years earlier was gone.

In 1984, Columbia Business School hosted a conference to celebrate the 50th anniversary of the first publication of *Security Analysis*. Warren was asked to present Ben Graham's value investing approach. Michael Jensen, a finance professor from the University of Rochester, argued on behalf of the efficient market hypothesis. Jensen, along with other academicians including Eugene Fama, believed the market quickly and accurately priced stocks, hence active management was a waste of time. No one could beat the stock market. Warren believed otherwise and offered evidence in a speech he titled "The Superinvestors of Graham-and-Doddsville."[94]

Warren began by recapping the central argument of Modern Portfolio Theory: The stock market is efficient, all stocks are priced correctly, and therefore anyone who beats the market year after year is simply lucky. Maybe so, he said, but I know some folks who have done it, and their success can't be explained away simply by random chance.

Still, to give the must-be-luck argument its fair hearing Warren asked the audience to imagine a national coin-flipping contest in which 225 million Americans bet $1 on their guess. After each flip, the losers dropped out and the winners kept the pot and advanced to the next round. After 10 events, there would be 220,000 winners left who, by letting their winnings ride, would have gained $1,064. After another 10 tosses, there would be 215 winners, each with $1 million.

Now, Warren continued, the business school professors, analyzing this national contest, would point out that the coin-tossers demonstrated no exceptional skill. The event could just as easily be replicated, they would protest, with a group of 225 million coin-flipping orangutans.

Slowly building his case, Warren granted the statistical possibility that, by sheer chance, the orangutans might get the same results. But imagine, he asked the audience, if 40 of the 215 winning animals came from the same zoo. Wouldn't we want to ask the zookeeper what he feeds his now very rich orangutans?

The point, Warren said, is that whenever a high concentration of anything occurs in one specific area, something unusual may be going on at that spot, and bears investigation. And what if—here comes the clincher—the members of this one unique group are defined not by where they live but by whom they learned from.

And thus we come to what Warren called the "intellectual village" of Graham and Doddsville. All the examples he presented that day were centered on individuals who had managed to beat the market consistently over time—not because of luck but because they all followed the principles learned from the same source: Benjamin Graham and David Dodd.

Each of these investors called the flips differently, explained Warren, but they were all linked by a common approach that seeks to take advantage of discrepancies between the market price and intrinsic value. "Needless to say, our Graham and Dodd investors do not discuss beta, the Capital Asset Pricing Model, or covariance returns," Warren said. "These are not subjects of any interest to them. In fact, most of them would have trouble defining those terms."

Warren's 1984 speech was the intellectual defibrillator Columbia Business School needed to revive its Value Investing Program. That same year, David Dodd's family made a substantial financial contribution to the school, establishing the Graham and Dodd Asset Management Program. Robert Heilbrunn's family established a professorship in his name at the school. Heilbrunn had met Ben Graham in the 1930s, took his class and eventually became an early investor with Warren in the Buffett Partnership. Later, Helaine Heilbrunn along with Sid Lerner endowed The Heilbrunn Center for Graham and Dodd Investing, creating a permanent home for value investing at the Columbia Business School.

Mario Gabelli also took significant interest in reviving the Value Investing Program. Gabelli Asset Management Company (GAMCO) sponsored a series of four lectures in 1993 on value investing at the Museum of Television and Radio. The speaker was Roger Murray, the retired professor. He was 81 years old at the time but was said to have delivered each 90-minute lecture without notes.

But it was Bruce Greenwald who has received the most credit for taking the helm of the newly rejuvenated Value Investing Program at Columbia and ably steering the study of value investing for the next quarter century. Greenwald joined the Columbia Business School in 1991 and was named the Robert Heilbrunn Professor of Finance and Asset Management in 1993. Later he became the Heilbrunn Center's first academic director. Greenwald attended Roger Murray's GAMCO's lectures and soon after convinced Murray to resurrect his professorial talents in a coteaching role. Together, Greenwald and Murray relaunched the value investing course Ben Graham started in 1927 and that Murray had himself taught for 21 years.

The newly resurrected value investing course at Columbia included 12 three-hour lectures. Murray and Greenwald cotaught five, and invited seven guest speakers, including Mario Gabelli, Chuck Royce, Michael Price, Walter Schloss, and Seth Klarman, to present the final lectures. Roger Murray retired from Columbia for the second time in 1995, leaving Greenwald to manage the value course for the next 20 years.

Bruce Greenwald's intellectual firepower and determination remade the Value Investing Program at Columbia in two distinct ways. First, instead of teaching value investing as a single course in the fall and spring, Greenwald greatly enlarged the program into a wide branch system. In the 2020 academic year, there were 32 different but interrelated courses on value investing taught by 42 different professors, not including guest speakers. In addition, in 2002 Greenwald convinced Paul Johnson to initiate a value investing seminar for the Executive MBA program at Columbia. It was not only the students Greenwald was interested in teaching about value investing but the hundreds of professionals who were returning to Columbia to continue their education. Paul Johnson had taught Greenwald's value investing course twice when Greenwald was on sabbatical. You might recall Johnson as the 36-year-old technology analyst at Robertson Stephens who sent the open letter to Warren Buffett recommending Cisco Systems in 1996. Johnson proved to be a popular professor at Columbia so Greenwald knew he had the right teacher for the Executive program. Today, Johnson holds the record for teaching at Columbia Business School, 47 semester-long courses.

The second initiative Greenwald undertook in remaking the Value Investing Program was to address, head on, the question of growth, especially the important question of how to value growth. For decades, growth investing was treated as the misaligned outsider never invited into the value club. But when Warren Buffett, in 1992, legitimized growth as a component to the calculation of value, Greenwald knew he had to accommodate the teaching of growth as it related to value. It seemed everywhere Greenwald looked, more and more prominent value investors were including growth companies in their portfolio.

When Greenwald joined Columbia in 1991, he was singularly focused on reenergizing the study of value investing. But behind the scenes he was already thinking about how to incorporate growth in the Value Investing Program. Greenwald publicly stepped up with the release of his soon-to-be popular book, *Value Investing: From Graham to Buffett and Beyond*, first published in 2003. He began writing the book in the late 1990s and had already decided to include a section on Intel Corporation with a chapter titled "The Value of Growth within the Franchise." Four years later Greenwald, along with Judd Kahn, published *Competition Demsytified: A Radically Simplified Approach to Business Strategy*. In Chapter 16, "Valuation from a Strategic Perspective," Greenwald summarized his view of valuation as something that should include "assets value, earnings power value, assessment of competitive advantages, and the value of growth."

At the same time, Greenwald also began to expand the coursework at the Value Investing Program to include how to think about valuing growth companies. Michael Mauboussin joined the faculty. He had worked with Paul Johnson at Credit-Suisse, then joined Bill Miller at Legg Mason Capital Management as chief investment strategist and later became chairman of the board of trustees at the Santa Fe Institute. Mauboussin brought the teaching of complex adaptive systems to Columbia along with how to think about the value of the new-economy network companies. Paul Johnson needed no convincing. He was already teaching his students how to think about growth. Today, his seminar in value investing includes case studies on Apple, Amazon, and Uber Technologies. Paul's recent book, coauthored with Paul Sonkin, *Pitch the Perfect Investment: The Essential Guide to Winning on Wall Street*, has become popular with students at Columbia. Chapter 3 is titled "How to Evaluate Competitive Advantage and Value Growth." Paul Sonkin was a former student of Paul Johnson at Columbia, had taught in the Business School for 16 years, and launched the school's Applied Value Investing course in 1998. Sonkin was also a coauthor with Bruce Greenwald on his book *Value Investing and Beyond*.

Today, a student at Columbia Business School can take a course on distressed value investing alongside a course on compounders, a study of companies that are rapidly compounding the growth of intrinsic value. Tano Santos, David L. and Elsie Dodd Professor of Finance, faculty codirector and head of research at the Heilbrunn Center, teaches a course on modern value that includes the study of disruptors, newly formed businesses that are taking market share from older, established companies. Students at Columbia can take a course on value investing in credit markets, on special situations investing, or on economics of strategic behavior, all based largely on Greenwald's book *Competition Demystified*. In all, the purview of value investing taught at Columbia Business School has widened dramatically.

For far too long, investors have erred by narrowly defining value investing. Warren Buffett, Charlie Munger, Bill Miller, Bruce Greenwald, Paul Johnson, and Michael Mauboussin, along with many others, have worked to widen the lens in the search for value. And in doing so, they enlarged the opportunity set for individuals to invest thoughtfully. Value does not hibernate, remaining hidden from the market's forces for years at a time. Value migrates. Sometimes value can be discovered in rapidly growing, high-return-on-capital businesses. At other times it resides in the slower growing, more capital-intensive companies. More often than not, value can be found in both camps. When a value investor claims their performance will improve once the market again recognizes value, this is an open admission that their view of value is confined, restricted to a small subset of all possible value opportunities.

As Warren and Charlie so powerfully remind us, "all intelligent investing is value investing." They point out "the very term 'value investing' is redundant. What is 'investing' if it is not the act of seeking value at least sufficient to justify the amount paid?"[95]

In the next chapter, "Business-Driven Investing," we examine in detail Warren's Money Mind construct as it relates to buying not a value stock, but a valued business.

Business-Driven Investing

"Investment is most intelligent when it is most *businesslike*."[1]

That's Ben Graham in his landmark book, *The Intelligent Investor*.

"These are the nine most important words ever written about investing."[2]

That's Warren Buffett, Graham's most famous pupil.

Although we have moved past Graham's methods for valuing stocks, his counsel for how to think about stocks as businesses is both enduring and invaluable.

As far back as 1917, when Graham wrote his first article for *The Magazine of Wall Street*, he held a steadfast belief that there was a better way to think about investing, and it was *not* speculating about what the next fellow was going to do with his shares. At the heart of Ben Graham's approach was an appreciation that, in the world of investing, the temperament of a businessperson was far superior to that of a speculator. Having said this, he was dismayed to "see how many capable businessmen try to operate in Wall Street with complete disregard of all sound principles through which they have gained success in their own undertakings."[3]

Graham believed that someone who purchased common shares in a company had earned "double status" and that it was their choice to decide which action to take. They could view themselves as a "minority stockholder in a business" whose fortune was "dependent on the profits of the enterprise or on a change in the underlying value of its assets." Or they could see themselves holding "a piece of paper, an engraved stock certificate, which could be sold in a matter of minutes at a price which varies from moment to moment—when the market is open, that is—and often far removed from the balance-sheet value."[4] That is, they have to choose between being a business-owner or a stock speculator.

The tug-of-war between those points of view was a matter of deep concern for Graham. Throughout his life, he made note of the losing battle. "The development of the stock market in the recent decades," he wrote in 1973, "has made the typical investor more dependent on the course of the price quotations and less free than formerly to consider himself merely a business-owner."[5] It seemed to him that the news of the moment—any moment—obscured the more important financial data that would determine one's long-term prospects. "The investor who permits himself to be stampeded or unduly worried by unjustified market declines in his holdings," he wrote, "is perversely transforming his basic advantage into a basic disadvantage. That man would be better off if his *stocks had no market quotation at all* [italics mine], for he would then be spared the mental anguish caused him by other persons' mistakes of judgment."[6]

It should come as no surprise that Warren Buffett, Graham's most famous student, adopted the same thinking. "Stocks as businesses" has been the cornerstone of Warren's investment approach for 65 years. A stock market, he once said, "is by no means essential; a prolonged suspension of trading in the securities we hold would not bother us any more than does the lack of daily quotations on World Book or Fechheimer," two of Berkshire's wholly owned businesses. "Eventually, our economic fate will be determined by the economic fate of the businesses we own, whether our ownership is partial or total."[7] "As far as I am concerned," he adds, "the stock market doesn't exist. It is there only to see if anybody is offering to do something foolish."[8]

So, we are left with a conundrum. The father of financial analysis and the world's greatest investor are telling us the same thing:

The daily quotations of the stock market are unnecessary for an investor to be successful. Indeed, for most investors they can cause more harm than good. At the same time, investors around the world are consumed with what is happening in the stock market. Every day they watch financial news programs and carry their mobile phones loaded with real-time quotes, especially the upticks and downticks of their personal holdings.

Ben Graham and Warren Buffett barely think about the stock market. The vast majority of investors can think of nothing else.

As a mental exercise, imagine this for a moment. How would you change your behavior if there was no daily stock market pricing? What if the stock market was open only once a year? On that one day, and only then, investors could buy and sell common stocks. For the other 364 days of the year, the only stock-specific information available would be quarterly financial reports and any other news deemed material for the owners of the company.

In this hypothetical world, we would inhabit a new financial dimension. In appreciation of Rod Serling, for purposes of this chapter we will call it the *Investment Zone.*[9] Everything you would need to know about buying and selling stocks can be found in the Investment Zone. Lessons can be learned; an education can be obtained. All the necessary ingredients for becoming a successful investor are available for those who are willing to cross over to the Investment Zone. But if you do so, you will not be alone. It is a world where Warren Buffett has lived since 1956.

Investment Zone

When Warren buys common stocks for Berkshire he doesn't think in terms of share price. For him, stocks are an abstraction.[10] "We approach a transaction," he says, "as if we are buying into a private business"—the entire business. Furthermore, once he has purchased shares in a company Warren does not have in mind some future date or a higher price at which he would sell the stock. "We are willing to hold a stock indefinitely so long as we expect the business to increase in intrinsic value at a satisfactory rate."[11] Although

Wall Street is full of market analysts and security analysts, this is not Warren's role at Berkshire. Rather, he says, "we view ourselves as business analysts."[12]

When Warren invests, he sees a business. Most investors see only a stock price. They spend far too much time and effort watching, predicting, and anticipating price changes and far too little time understanding the business they now own a part of. Warren believes the investor and the businessperson should look at the company in the same way, because they both want essentially the same thing. The businessperson wants to buy the entire company; the investor wants to buy portions of the company. Both will profit from the growth of the intrinsic value of the business they own.

Owning and operating businesses has given Warren a distinct advantage. "Can you explain to a fish what it's like to walk on land?" he asks. "One day on land is worth a thousand years of talking about it and one day running a business has exactly the same kind of value."[13] Over the years Warren has experienced both success and failure in his business ventures and has applied to the stock market the lessons he learned. Most other investors have not been given the same beneficial education. While they were busy studying capital asset pricing models, beta, and Modern Portfolio Theory, Warren studied income statements, capital reinvestment require-ments, and the cash-generating capabilities of his companies.

The objective of this chapter is to give you the mental construct of investing in a business without the daily inputs of the stock mar-ket. Like Warren, let's think about investing in a company as if the stock market doesn't exist.

It's impossible to overstate this: the bedrock to forming a Money Mind is a purposeful detachment from the stock mar-ket. Mentally you must put on blinders so that the stock market does not absorb your attention during every waking moment. It is no longer your primary focus. It is secondary at best, only to be acknowledged periodically when market prices gyrate wildly up and down. That is the only sensible time when a business-owner with a Money Mind should turn their attention to the stock market, to gauge whether there is a profitable opportunity to buy or sell shares of their businesses. But at all other times, the daily, weekly, monthly news about the stock market is of little interest.

In *The Warren Buffett Way*, we outlined the investment tenets Warren applies in analyzing companies. Whether he is considering buying a company outright or buying its stocks, the process is the same. The tenets are divided into four categories: Business, Financial, Market, and Management.

Business Tenets

In Warren's view, an investor's success is in direct proportion to the degree to which they understand the investment. Remember Minaker's advice: the first step in starting or buying a business is to know something about it. Those with a Money Mind read the annual and quarterly reports of the companies they own, as well as other articles written about their businesses, their competitors, and industry observations. Remember, in the Investment Zone the only information you have about your investments is company specific. There are no daily stock prices. This understanding is a distinguishing trait that separates investors with a business orientation from hit-and-run speculators who merely buy shares of stock.

Warren is able to maintain a high level of knowledge about the businesses he purchases, both public and private, because he purposely limits his selections to companies that are within his area of intellectual understanding. "Invest in your circle of competence," he counsels. "It's not how big the circle is that counts, it's how well you define the parameters."[14] Warren tells us investment success is not a matter of how much you know but how realistically you define what you don't know. "An investor needs to do very few things right so long as he or she avoids big mistakes."[15] Above-average results, he explains, are often produced by doing ordinary things. The key is to do those ordinary things exceptionally well.

Warren not only avoids the complex, he avoids purchasing companies that are either attempting to solve difficult business problems or fundamentally changing the company's direction. Regarding the latter, it has been Warren's experience that the best returns are achieved by companies that have been producing the same product or service for several years—think Coca-Cola and Apple. He believes that "severe change and exceptional returns usually don't mix."[16] As regards major problems, his experience in business operations and investment has taught him that "turnarounds" seldom turn. "Charlie and I have not learned how to solve difficult business problems. What we have learned is to avoid them. To the extent that we have been successful, it is because we concentrated on identifying one-foot hurdles that we could step over rather than because we acquired any ability to clear seven-footers."[17]

To be a successful business-owner does not require you to become an expert on every type of business available for investment, but it does require you to understand *a* company. Do you understand the objective of the company? Do you know what products and services it sells and who its customers are? Better yet, do you know the competitors and are they doing a better or worse job than the business you own? Finally, as a business-owner investor you should avoid turnaround stories no matter how exciting it might seem to resurrect a failed business.

Warren tells us the best business to own is one that has favorable long-term prospects. "The definition of a great company is a company that will be great for 25 to 30 years."[18] He calls them franchises. They sell a product or service that is needed or desired and has no close substitute. These traits, explains Warren, allow the franchise to regularly increase prices of products or services without fear of losing market share or unit volume.

Businesses with favorable long-term prospects typically operate in large and growing markets. The total addressable market, defined as the sales a company could achieve if it had 100 percent market share, is a critical component that determines a company's potential value. How large the company can become and still create shareholder value is linked to the size of its market. Since 1960, about a third of the increase in value of the S&P 500 Index has been a result of the payoff from future investment.[19] So, to understand value creation we need to understand a company's reinvestment potential and the size of the market landscape.

Another benefit that comes from owning a franchise is the ability to endure an economic mishap and still survive. It is comforting, says Warren, to be in a business where mistakes can be made and above-average returns can still be achieved. "Franchises," he tells us, "can tolerate mismanagement. Inept managers may diminish a franchise's profitability but they cannot inflict mortal damage."[20]

Here's a succinct recap, in Warren's own words: "What I like is economic strength in an area where I understand it and I think it will last."[21]

Financial Tenets

If there were a financial Moses, he would have come down the mountain carrying one tablet with three commandments—cash earnings, return on invested capital, and a margin of safety. We will discuss the third financial commandment in the market tenets section; for now, let's focus on the two most important financial yardsticks for a business-owner.

If you were to ask a business-owner what is their primary objective, they would tell you it's to generate a profit, specifically cash. Business-owners understand and appreciate the importance of cash. Each month, or at year end, the owner of the business takes the cash profits and pays personal obligations, spends some on leisure activities, and invests the rest for retirement. At Berkshire, Warren takes the cash from his businesses and either reinvests back into the businesses or reallocates funds to better investment opportunities. But he can do so only with cash.

We need to remember that the earnings per share that a company reports is not always equal to the cash earnings a business-owner would expect to receive. Warren cautions investors that accounting earnings per share are the starting point for determining the economic value of business, not the ending point. "The first point to understand," he explains, "is that not all earnings are created equal."[22] Companies with high assets to profits tend to report ersatz earnings. The earnings of these businesses take on a mirage-like quality. In sum, accounting earnings—the earnings per share reported by the company—are only useful to the investor if they approximate the expected cash flow.

Even the concept of "cash flow" as that term is popularly used is not a perfect tool for getting the cash dollar bills the business-owner is expecting. Cash flow is an appropriate way to measure businesses that have large investments in the beginning and smaller outlays afterwards, says Warren. To this list we can add new-technology companies that have been able to generate high cash profits with little capital expenditures. However, industrial and manufacturing companies require ongoing capital expenditures and are not accurately valued using only cash-flow numbers.

A company's reported cash flow is customarily defined as net income after taxes plus depreciation, depletion, and amortiza-tion—all noncash charges. The problem with this definition, Warren explains, is that it leaves out a critical economic element—capital expenditures. How much of the company's yearly earn-ings must be used for new equipment, plant upgrades, and other improvements needed to maintain its economic position and unit volume? Warren estimates that about 95 percent of America's industrial-manufacturing businesses require capital expenditures that are roughly equal to their depreciation rates. You can defer capital expenditures for a year or so, he says, but if over a long period you don't make the necessary expenditures, your busi-ness will decline. Necessary capital expenditures are as much an expense to a company as are labor and utility costs.

Warren also warns us not to be seduced by the EBITDA (earnings before interest, taxes, depreciation, and amortization) numbers that are widely passed off as cash-flow equivalents. Warren believes these numbers "are frequently used by marketers of business and securities in attempts to justify the unjustifiable and thereby sell what should be unsalable. When earnings look inadequate to service debt of junk bonds or justify a foolish stock price, how convenient it becomes to focus on cash flow."[23] But you cannot focus on cash flow, he warns, unless you are willing to subtract the necessary capital expenditures.

Instead of cash flow, Warren prefers to use what he calls "owner-earnings"—a company's net income plus depreciation and amortization, less the amount of capital expenditures and additional working capital that might be needed to operate the business as a going concern. Warren's owner-earnings are equivalent to the cash that business-owners demand from their businesses.

Just how important are cash earnings? Empirical Research Partners, an independent research boutique founded by Michael Goldstein in 2002, studied a universe of 750 large-capitalization stocks from 1952 through 2019, comparing the "free cash-flow yields" (similar to owner-earnings) from the highest quintile to the lowest quintile. What did they discover? Calculating monthly returns and annualizing the results, the highest quintile free cash-flow stocks outperformed the lowest quintile by 850 basis points per year. Even for the higher second quintile, the top free cash-flow stocks outperformed this group by 200 basis points a year.[24]

What should not be lost on us is this: owner-earnings is the fuel that allows a company to expand its business in the total addressable market. So a Money Mind operating in the Investment Zone is laser-focused on a company's owner-earnings.

Wall Street analysts measure a company's annual performance by tabulating earnings per share (EPS). Did the company increase EPS over the past year? Are they high enough to brag about? Did they beat the market's expectations for earnings growth? Despite the market's obsession, Buffett considers EPS growth a smoke-screen. Since most companies retain a portion of their previous year's earnings as a way to increase their equity base, he sees no reason to get excited about record EPS. There is nothing spectacular about a company that increases EPS by 10 percent if at the same time it is growing its equity base by 10 percent. That's no different, he explains, from putting money in a savings account and letting the interest accumulate and compound.

"The primary test of managerial economic performance," Warren argues, "is the achievement of a high earnings rate on equity capital employed (without undue leverage, accounting gimmickry, etc.) and not the achievement of consistent earnings gains in earnings per share."[25] To measure a company's annual performance, Warren prefers return on equity—the ratio of operating earnings to shareholder's equity. His objective is to isolate, specifically, the annual performance of the business. He wants to know how well management accomplished its task of generating a return on operations of the business given the capital it employed. That, he says, is the single best judge of management's economic performance.

Warren believes that a business should achieve good returns on equity while employing little or no debt. He knows a company can increase returns on equity by increasing its debt-to-equity ratio. But he reminds us, "Good business or investment decisions will produce quite satisfactory results with no aid of leverage."[26] Warren is not phobic about borrowing money. He is just leery of companies that pile on debt to increase returns. Highly leveraged companies are vulnerable to economic slowdowns.

Business-owners operating in the Investment Zone will come across companies that have borrowed money from banks or bondholders. Indeed, there are companies in the consumer staples space that can operate safely with debt on their balance sheet. As such, we need to tally our economic returns not just on shareholder's equity but the company's total invested capital: equity sold to investors, retained earnings, and debt.

Return on invested capital (ROIC) is a measure of value creation. If the return of our business is above the weighted average cost of capital, both equity and debt, then management is increasing the intrinsic value of the business. But if the returns on invested capital are below the cost of capital, a company is destroying shareholder value.

Whether you are measuring results on shareholder's equity or return on total invested capital, it is important to tally these returns alongside growth in earnings per share to get a complete picture of a company's economic performance. Investors in the Investment Zone demand not only growth in owner-earnings cash, they also insist the return of owner-earnings divided by the capital invested in the company must be above the cost of capital. Never forget, a return above the cost of capital is the *minimum* rate of return that a business must earn in order to generate long-term value for its owners.

Once we have isolated a business that generates owner earnings above the cost of capital, we can next turn our attention to sales growth. We know a key indicator for companies with favorable long-term prospects is the potential for future growth. Hence, for a company with an optimal economic business model, sales growth becomes an important driver for growth in intrinsic value.

We studied the relationship between sales growth and returns on capital, defined as economic value added, for companies that were members of the S&P 500 Index over a ten-year period, 2009–2018. We divided the stocks into four groups: companies with above-average sales growth, with below-average sales growth, with positive economic value added (returns above the cost of capital employed), and with negative economic value added (returns below the cost of capital employed). What did we discover?

Stocks with above-average sales growth, measured over a trailing three-year period, generated a 14.0 percent average annual return; those with below-average sales growth produced a 12.3 percent return. Stocks with positive economic value added posted a 16.0 percent annual return; those with negative economic value added delivered an 11.3 percent return. During this period, the compounded annual growth return of the S&P 500 Index was 13.0 percent.

But what were the results when we combined both sales growth and economic value added? Stocks with below-average sales growth and negative economic value added produced a return of 11.0 percent, well below the average return of the S&P 500 Index. Stocks with above-average sales growth but negative economic value added generated a 12 percent annual return, still below the Index return. However, when we combined sales growth with positive economic value added, the performance returns were substantially better. Even companies with below-average sales growth but with positive economic value added posted a 15 percent average annual return, above the market return. The best-performing group was the stocks with above-average sales growth *and* positive economic value; they produced a 17.1 percent average annual return—4 percentage points above the S&P 500 Index over the decade.[27] When a company earns above the cost of capital, the turbocharger for increasing intrinsic value is sales growth.

Lesson learned—business-owners should focus on companies with favorable long-term prospects operating in large total addressable markets. This allows a company to grow sales at solid rates, producing owner-earnings that generate a return on capital above the cost of capital.

All combined, this drives the growth in the intrinsic value of our investment.

Market Tenets

A business-owner's third commandment is to purchase a company only if the price of the stock is below the intrinsic value of the company. Price is established by the stock market. Value is determined by the business analyst. When the difference between the two numbers is in the investor's favor, that is your margin of safety. Ben Graham's recommendation to buy only stocks with a margin of safety is timeless.

But how should we calculate the intrinsic value of a business? Warren gives us a simple formula: owner-earnings expected to occur over the life of a business discounted at the appropriate rate. "So valued," Warren says, "all businesses, from manufacturers of buggy whips to operators of cellular telephones, become economic equals."[28]

This mathematical exercise, Warren says, is very similar to valuing a bond. A bond has both a coupon and a maturity date that determine its future cash flow. If you add all the bond's coupons and divide by the appropriate discount rate, the price of the bond will be revealed. To determine the value of a business, the business analyst must estimate the coupons—owner-earnings—that the business will generate for a period into the future, and then discount all the coupons back to the present.

The next question then becomes, what is the appropriate discount rate? Abbreviated answer: cost of capital. In the standard cash-flow model, a company's cost of capital is used as the discount rate for determining the value of future cash flows. And so how do we determine a company's cost of capital? The cost of debt is straightforward: the weighted-average interest rate of its debt outstanding. But determining a company's equity cost of capital requires some additional thinking.

Today, the basic model for determining cost of capital is deeply rooted in mainstream academic finance. It is called the capital asset pricing model (CAPM) and was first proposed by William Sharpe in the 1960s. We will reintroduce Sharpe along with the other High Priests of Modern Finance in the next chapter. According to CAPM, a firm's cost of equity capital is a product of individual stock price volatility multiplied by the risk premium of the overall equity market. The risk premium is the expected return of the market over the risk-free rate, which is defined as the 10-year U.S. Treasury yield.

However, those who have studied Warren Buffett know his view that risk defined by price volatility is, to put it mildly, nonsensical. Thus, it is no surprise that both Warren and Charlie have jettisoned the concepts embedded in CAPM.

"I don't know our cost of capital," said Warren. "It's taught in business schools, but we're skeptical. I have never seen a cost of capital calculation that makes sense to me." Charlie weighed in: "The rest of the world has gone off on some kick—perfectly amazing mental malfunction."[29]

When *The Warren Buffett Way* was first published in 1994, Warren explained that he used the risk-free rate, the 10-year U.S. Treasury, to discount stocks. During the decade of the 1990s, the average yield of the 10-year Treasury was 8.55 percent. We wrote that Warren used the risk-free rate and adjusted his purchase price, the margin of safety, relative to the riskiness of the business. Warren said, "I put a heavy weight on certainty. If you do that, the whole idea of a risk factor doesn't make any sense to me. Risk comes from not knowing what you're doing."[30] In Warren's mind, the predictability of a company's future free cash flow should take on a coupon-like certainty like that found in bonds. However, with interest rates now near 0 percent, Warren has had to think of a different discount rate.

It appears both Warren and Charlie have a solution. "We just look to do the most intelligent thing we can with the capital we have," said Warren. "We measure everything against our alternatives," Charlie adds. "It's your alternatives that matter."[31]

Charlie, by speaking of alternatives, frames the question as opportunity cost. Paul Sonkin and Paul Johnson see it the same way, In their book *Pitch the Perfect Investment* they write, "The 'correct rate' to use in the discounting process is the company's cost of capital, which also represents investor's opportunity cost, making the returns opposite sides of the same coin. The cost of capital is the rate of return an investor demands to make an investment, while the opportunity cost is the forgone return the investor gives up when he chooses one investment opportunity over another one."[32]

People who invest in the stock market have an expectation of earning at least a 10 percent return, which is the average historical rate of return of stocks since 1900.[33] Thus, we can say an investor's cost of capital for "lending" their money to the stock market is 10 percent. Conversely, someone who decides not to invest in the stock market has made a decision to forgo a 10 percent annual return. "All capital has an opportunity cost," say Sonkin and Johnson.[34]

A quick word on discounting stocks using an average weighted cost of capital for both equity and bonds. For many companies, debt is part of the capital structure. And with interest rates for high-grade, 10-year corporate debt near 3 percent, the mathematics of discounting a business that is 75 percent equity and 25 percent debt suggests an 8.25 percent discount rate. With companies that have greater than 25 percent debt, the discount rate would be even lower. Investors should recognize that with very low interest rates, such as we have now, discounting stocks using a weighted-average capital cost of equity and debt may make for a perilous calculation. My solution is this: I continue to discount stocks at 10 percent regardless of capital structure, then adjust the margin of safety for the predictability for future free cash flows.

Intrinsic business value, Warren explains, is an economic calculation based on the future cash flows of a business discounted back to present value. "We define intrinsic value as the discounted value of cash that can be taken out of a business during its remaining life," he says. "Anyone calculating intrinsic value necessarily comes up with a highly subjective figure that will change both as estimates of future cash flows are revised and interest rates move. Despite its fuzziness, however, intrinsic value is all-important and is the only logical way to evaluate the relative attractiveness of investments and businesses."[35]

Warren is not the only one to recognize intrinsic value as an elusive concept. Although Ben Graham did not apply the discounted-present-value model, he also cautioned that intrinsic value was not a precise estimate. "The essential point," he said, "is that security analysis does not seek to determine exactly what is the intrinsic value of a given security. It only needs to establish either that the value is adequate to protect a bond or justify a stock purchase. For such purposes an indefinite and approximate measure of the intrinsic value may be sufficient."[36] Seth Klarman thinks along the same lines. In his book *Margin of Safety*, he writes, "Many investors insist on affixing exact values to their investment, seeking precision in an imprecise world, but business value cannot be precisely determined."[37] Warren echoes both Graham and Klarman: "Intrinsic value is an estimate rather than a precise figure."[38]

With Wall Street's obsession over target prices and single-point estimates, Warren's admission that the calculation of intrinsic value lacks precision sounds anomalous, but it is perfectly logical. Although Warren likes to buy certainties at discounts, in reality business returns can and do fluctuate. So business analysts must think in a range of possibilities, knowing full well there are various scenarios that can occur. How does Warren think about the different outcomes? "We take the probability of loss times the amount of possible loss from the probability of gain times the amount of possible gains. It is imperfect, but that's what it is all about."[39] Thus, expected intrinsic value is the weighted average value for a distribution of possible outcomes. Warren has often said, "I would rather be approximately right than precisely wrong."[40]

Management Tenets

The highest compliment Warren can pay a manager is that they unfailingly behave and think like an owner of the company. Managers who behave like owners do not overlook the company's primary objective—increasing the intrinsic value of the business. Warren admires managers who openly and fully report to shareholders and have the fortitude to resist what he has termed the "institutional imperative"—blindly following the behavior of industry peers.

In reporting the financial performance of the business, Warren holds in high regard those managers who admit the mistakes they have made as readily as they share successes. Over time, every company makes mistakes, both large and inconsequential. Too many managers report with excess optimism what has gone right with the business and not enough time examining what went wrong. Warren has set an example by openly discussing Berkshire's economic performance, both good and bad. In 1989, he started a formal practice of listing his mistakes, initially called "Mistakes of the First Twenty-Five Years" and now referred to as "Mistakes Du Jour." It is Warren's belief that candor benefits the manager at least as much as the shareholder. "The CEO who misleads others in public," he says, "may eventually mislead himself in private."[41] Warren credits Charlie with helping him understand the value of studying one's mistakes, rather than concentrating only on success.

The most important management act is the allocation of the company's capital. It is the most important because allocation of capital, over time, determines shareholder value. Deciding what to do with the company's earnings—reinvest in the business or return money to shareholders—is, in Warren's mind, an exercise in logic and rationality.

If allocation of capital is simple and logical, why is it so poorly done? The answer, says Warren, is an unseen force he calls the institutional imperative—the lemminglike tendency of corporate management to imitate the behavior of other managers, no matter how silly or irrational it may be. According to Warren, the institutional imperative exists when "(1) an institution resists any change in its current direction; (2) just as work expands to fill available time, corporate projects or acquisitions will materialize to soak up available funds; (3) any business craving of the leader, however foolish, will quickly be supported by detailed rate-of-return and strategic studies prepared by his troops; and (4) the behavior of peer companies, whether they are expanding, acquiring, setting executive compensation or whatever, will be mindlessly imitated."[42]

The question of how to allocate earnings is linked to where the company is in its life cycle. During the growth stage, companies that are profitable rightly decide to reinvest profits back into the business to compound growth in intrinsic value. When a business reaches its maturity stage, growth is slowing and the company begins to generate more cash than it can optimally reinvest. At this point management is then left with three choices: continue to reinvest in a business that is not generating returns above the cost of capital in hopes their managerial prowess will return the company to profitability; buy growth; or return the money to shareholders. It is at this crossroad that Warren keenly focuses on management's behavior. It is here that management will behave rationally or irrationally.

Warren is suspect of most managers' ability to resurrect a declining business. Even though shareholders are mesmerized by the idea the company is going to be resurrected, managers too often overestimate their turnaround skills. Result: failure. Warren is also skeptical of managers who feel the need to buy growth with acquisitions. They typically overpay and then struggle to integrate the new company into the legacy business. In both cases, lots of shareholder money is spent and lots of shareholder value is destroyed.

In Warren's mind, the only reasonable and responsible course for companies with a growing pile of cash that cannot be reinvested at above-average returns on capital is to return the money to shareholders. There are two methods available: pay dividends or buy back shares. With cash in hand from dividends, shareholders have the opportunity to look elsewhere for higher investment returns.

But management can also decide to return money to shareholder via share repurchases. Although the benefit of repurchasing stock is in many respects less direct, less tangible, and less immediate, the impact on shareholder value can be dramatic, if executed smartly over time.

When management repurchases stock, Warren feels the reward is twofold. If the stock is selling below its intrinsic value, repurchasing shares makes good business sense. If a company's stock price is $50 and its intrinsic value is $100, then each time management buys its stock, they are acquiring $2 of intrinsic value for every $1 spent. Transactions of this nature can be very profitable for remaining shareholders.

Furthermore, says Warren, when management actively buys the company's stock, they are demonstrating that they have the best interest of their owners at heart, rather than a careless need to expand the corporate structure. That kind of behavior sends positive signals to the market, attracting other investors looking for a well-managed company that is intent on increasing shareholder wealth.

A word of caution at this point. Be alert for repurchases made when the stock price is *above* the intrinsic value of the company; ultimately this destroys shareholder value. Thinking the very act of buying back stock is judicious, management's senseless behavior actually causes the stock price to decline over time.

Share repurchases have the added benefit of returning money to shareholders in a tax-efficient manner. When a company pays a dividend to shareholders, those with taxable accounts must share the economic benefit with the government. However, share repurchases accrue 100 percent to the shareholder with the added benefit that the shareholder now owns a greater percentage of the company than they did before the repurchase. When the company's profits are next recorded, the shareholder thus will share more in the company's profits without having spent a dollar more to buy the company.

Like long-term compounding, repurchasing shares at first appears to have little impact on one's investment. But over the long term, thoughtful share repurchases by management can substantially increase the investor's beneficial ownership in a company. After Warren purchased Coca-Cola in 1988 and 1989, investing one billion dollars, Berkshire owned 7 percent of the company. But over time, the management of Coca-Cola strategically repurchased shares when its stock price was below the company's intrinsic value. Today (year end 2019), Berkshire's $1.3 billion investment in Coca-Cola (Warren added additional shares in 1994) is worth $22.1 billion. Currently, Berkshire's 400 million shares represent 9.3 percent ownership of Coca-Cola. Warren increased his ownership and also increased his share of the company's profits by 32 percent without having spent one dollar, based solely on management's thoughtful share repurchases.

We can see the benefit of share repurchases even more strongly with Berkshire's investment in American Express. Warren built his position in American Express over 1994 and 1995. By 1996, Berkshire owned 10.5 percent of the company. At year end 2019, Berkshire's ownership in American Express, without adding one more dollar of investment, equaled 18.7 percent of the company. American Express has dutifully repurchased shares over the past 20 years with its excess cash, which means that Berkshire's investment in the company has almost doubled without Warren having to lift a finger.

On a side note, you might also be interested to know that the dividends paid by Cola-Cola to Berkshire over the past 30 years have paid for Warren's initial $1.3 billion investment several times over. In 2019, based on Warren's initial investment, Berkshire received $656 million in paid dividends. The dividends paid by American Express in 2019 equaled $248 million. Since 2000, American Express has returned to Berkshire $2.1 billion in dividends, almost twice the dollar amount Warren invested in the company. Granted, dividends paid are a taxable event for Berkshire, but even so we can clearly see that the combination of dividends paid and share repurchases has substantially increased Berkshire's investment in both Coca-Cola and American Express based on management's rational allocation of capital.

Will Thorndike, author of *The Outsiders*, rightly points out that it is "the denominator that matters." The best-performing CEOs, he tells us, "shared an intense focus on maximizing *value per share*. To do this, they didn't simply focus on the numerator, total company value. They also focused intently on managing the denominator through the careful financing of investment projects and opportunistic share repurchases. These repurchases were not made to prop up stock prices but rather they offered attractive returns as investments in their own right."[43]

Warren Buffett was highlighted in Thorndike's book in a chapter titled "The Investor as CEO." Thorndike explains that Warren's exceptional results are derived from business operations that upstream cash to Berkshire, bequeathing to Warren the opportunity to allocate capital. Warren linked intrinsic value to capital allocation in the 1994 Berkshire Hathaway Annual Report. "Understanding intrinsic value is as important for managers as it is for investors. When managers are making capital allocation decisions—including decisions to repurchase shares—it's vital that they act in ways that increase per-share intrinsic value and avoid moves that decrease it."[44] Warren codified the importance of per-share value in Berkshire Hathaway's *Owner-Related Business Principles*. "Our long-term economic goal is to maximize the average annual rate of gain in intrinsic value on a per share basis," he wrote. "We do not measure the economic significance or performance of Berkshire by its size; we measure by share progress."[45]

■ ■ ■

The components that form a Money Mind are many. We have looked at some of them in detail, and there are still others yet to learn. But make no mistake—a critical element is the skill of capital allocation, which in itself is an investment act.

Remember that when Warren first mentioned the concept of a Money Mind, he was answering a shareholder's question about capital allocation, asked in the broader context of Berkshire's succession plans. In his answer, Warren was clearly reflecting the mandate from Berkshire's board when he said that the next CEO must have "proven capital allocation abilities."

It is well understood that the cash profits of Berkshire's operating businesses are the fuel that ultimately powers the growth in the company's intrinsic value. And the process of determining how those profits are handled—whether reinvesting them or using them to repurchase shares or pay dividends—is a textbook definition of capital allocation.

How, precisely, does someone who is responsible for allocating capital decide which way to go? It's not really complicated. Think about it as an exercise whose outcome is preordained by mathematical logic. If a business earns above the cost of capital and there seems little doubt that it can continue to do so, the smart decision is to reinvest the profits back into the company. However, if the business is struggling to earn rates of return above the cost of capital, the logical thing is to return the money to shareholders. If the stock price is below the intrinsic value of the business, buy back shares. If not, return the money to shareholders via dividend payouts. As I said, not that complicated.

So, if the allocation of capital is so logical and straightforward, what causes CEOs to make such grievous mistakes? The failure of capital allocation, Warren explains, is a failure of business judgment. And the most common cause is the inability to resist the urge to imitate one's peers. Warren, you may remember, calls this the "institutional imperative."

Think back to Charlie's "Psychology of Human Misjudgment," described in Chapter 2, specifically the Social-Proof Tendency— the tendency to behave exactly like others without taking the time to consider whether their way is worthwhile. Charlie's antidote for avoiding this mistake is to simply ignore the bad behavior in others when it is so obviously wrong.

From our readings in philosophy and psychology, we now know that the ability to ignore bad behavior is all about having the self-confidence to do what is right despite the pressure to conform. Ralph Waldo Emerson taught us that self-confidence is directly linked to self-reliance, the core principle Warren learned from his father. And self-reliance, in turn, is the foundation of a Money Mind.

So yes, the next CEO of Berkshire, the next Money Mind, must have proven abilities at capital allocation. But in the end, what we are really saying is that Berkshire's next CEO must demonstrate the uprightness of self-reliance.

Thus far we have discussed how business-owners should analyze an individual business, purchase shares of that business, and monitor the business—without needing a stock market to tell them how well their investment is performing. Next, let's turn our attention to the best way to measure the performance of a *portfolio* of businesses, namely publicly traded companies, without relying on the stock market. Once again, Warren Buffett is our tutor.

In 1980 Warren said, "The value to Berkshire Hathaway of retained earnings is not determined by whether we own 100 percent, 50 percent, 20 percent, or 1 percent of business in which they reside. Rather, the value of those retained earnings is determined by the use to which they are put and the subsequent level of earnings by that usage."[46] In addition to the companies it owns outright, Berkshire also owns a portfolio of common stocks of which it owns partial positions, 20 percent or less of the outstanding shares. Although Berkshire receives, and accounts for, the dividends paid by these companies, Berkshire's financial statement does not account for the retained earnings these public companies keep and reinvest back into their business.

The value of the public companies Berkshire owns "is no way affected by the inclusion or non-inclusion of those retained earnings in our own reported operating earnings," Warren explains. "If a tree grows in the forest partially owned by us, but we don't record the growth in our financial statements, we still own part of the tree."[47] He later added, "In our view, the value to all owners of the retained earnings of a business enterprise (common stock) is determined by the effectiveness with which those earnings are used—and not by the size of one's ownership percentage."[48]

Warren believes the best way to think about the retained earnings is to measure them as what he calls *look-through earnings*. In 1991, he tallied Berkshire's top seven common stock holdings and then calculated Berkshire's ownership in these companies to determine how much Berkshire would have received if the undistributed earnings were passed through the company. That year, Berkshire's share of undistributed earnings of its major investees totaled $230 million. In 2019, Berkshire's share of the undistributed earnings of its top 10 holdings amounted to $8.3 billion. This money was left with the companies and reinvested, thereby compounding the intrinsic value on behalf of Berkshire.

But it was what Warren said next that helped crystallize investors' thinking on how they should measure the progress of their investments. "Investors can benefit by focusing on their look-through earnings. To calculate these, they should determine the underlying earnings attributable to the shares they hold in their portfolio and total these. The goal of each investor should be to create a portfolio (in effect, a "company") that will deliver him or her the highest possible look-through earnings a decade or so from now."[49] Warren makes it clear: if an investor wants to increase the intrinsic value of their portfolio at 10 percent annual rate, the look-through earnings need to grow at a 10 percent rate.

One additional idea on how to think about portfolio management independent of the stock market comes from Charlie Munger. For Charlie, it's a question of opportunity cost. We might think of it as the return we forgo, he explains, but it can also be thought of as the return we already own. When evaluating an investment to add to Berkshire, Charlie asks, Is this better than what we already own? And there are multiple answers. In addition to look-through earnings, Charlie considers the weighted-average return of sales growth, return on capital, and even the margin of safety. All these returns, weighted-average for the portfolio, become the economic benchmark for Berkshire. So then for Charlie the question becomes: Does adding a new stock to the portfolio increase our economic benchmark, pushing forward the growth of intrinsic value? A policy like this, he argues, works to concentrate Berkshire's portfolio into fewer names, its best ideas.

You might have noticed something here. Warren and Charlie are both counseling investors to think about their portfolio as a mini-Berkshire Hathaway. Analyze and purchase common stocks, as does Berkshire. Measure the economic returns of your common stocks as does Berkshire. And finally, calculate the performance return of your companies based on economic returns, including look-through earnings, as does Berkshire. Warren points out, "An approach of this kind will force the investor to think about the long-term business prospects rather than short-term market prospects, a perspective likely to improve results."[50] The look-through earnings approach to measuring investment performance is the perfect method for an investor who is operating in the Investment Zone.

■ ■ ■

In managing a portfolio of businesses—that is to say, a portfolio of common stocks—the number of stocks you own and how long you own them will have a significant impact on your returns. At Berkshire, Warren's policy is to concentrate his positions in common stocks and hold onto these companies for many years, maybe even indefinitely.

"The strategy we've adopted," explains Warren, "precludes our following standard diversification dogma. Many pundits would therefore say the strategy must be riskier than that employed by more conventional investors. We disagree. We believe that a policy of concentration may well *decrease* risk if it raises, as it should, both the intensity with which an investor thinks about a business and the comfort level he must feel with its economic characteristics before buying into it."[51] This mirrors Warren and Charlie's central premise of investing—know what you own and why you own it.

Warren quotes John Maynard Keynes, the famous British economist who was also a legendary investor. In a letter to a business associate, F.C. Scott, Keynes wrote, "As time goes by, I get more and more convinced that the right method in investment is to put fairly large sums into enterprises which one thinks one knows something about and in management of which one thoroughly believes. It is a mistake to think one limits one's risk by spreading too much between enterprises of which one knows little and has no reason for special confidence.

One's knowledge and experience are definitely limited and there are seldom more than two or three enterprises at any given time in which I personally feel myself entitled to put *full* confidence."[52]

We can see a direct correlation between the number of stocks an investor owns and the level of understanding the investor has about their business. Both Warren and Keynes would argue that risk, defined as permanent loss of capital, is reduced by limiting the number of stocks in one's portfolio. Put differently, someone who owns too many stocks and is overdiversified has actually *increased* the risk of capital loss. Owning 50-plus companies makes it difficult to thoughtfully monitor which companies are increasing and which are destroying shareholder value.

In addition to owning few stocks in Berkshire's portfolio, Warren's strategy is to own these companies for the long term. "We need to emphasize, however, that we do not sell just because they have appreciated or because we have held them for a long time. Of all Wall Street maxims the most foolish may be 'you can't go broke taking a profit.' We are quite content to hold any security indefinitely, so long as the prospective return on equity capital of the underlying business is satisfactory, management is competent and honest, and the market does not overvalue the business."[53]

It is Warren's intention not to interfere with the compounding of intrinsic value that is occurring in the companies Berkshire owns, whether they are privately held or publicly traded. In Berkshire's 2019 Annual Report, Warren introduced shareholders to Edgar Lawrence Smith and his book *Common Stocks as Long Term Investments*. Before writing the book, Smith was a little-known economist and financial advisor. But after the book was reviewed by John Maynard Keynes, all this changed.

"I have kept until last what is perhaps Mr. Smith's most important and certainly most novel point," Keynes wrote. "Well-managed industrial companies do not, as a rule, distribute to the shareholders the whole of their earned profits. In good years, if not in all years, they retain a part of their profits and put them back into business. Thus *there is an element of compound interest* [Keynes' italics] operating in favor of a sound industrial investment. Over a period of years, the real value of the property of a sound industrial is increasing at a compound interest, quite apart from the dividends paid out to the shareholders."[54]

"And with that sprinkling of holy water," Warren wrote, "Smith was no longer obscure."[55]

Warren admitted that he is baffled why the idea of compounding retained earnings, which can lead to increasing shareholder value, is so totally lost on investors. "After all," he wrote, "it was no secret that mind-boggling wealth had earlier been amassed by such titans as Carnegie, Rockefeller, and Ford, all of whom had retained a huge portion of their business earnings to fund growth and produce ever-greater profits. Throughout America, also, there had long been small-time capitalists who became rich following the same playbook."[56]

Looking back on the mistakes of investors, and there are many, perhaps the one most often violated is the tendency to sell stocks too soon, thus losing the ultimate payoff that comes from compounding retained earnings. At first, compounding may appear unimpressive to the investor, but as time goes by it picks up momentum when true wealth creation is finally achieved. Investors have never seemed to have the patience to stick with good businesses over time. Warren quotes Pascal, "It has struck me that all the misfortunes of men spring from the single cause that they are unable to stay quietly in one room."[57]

We will give Edgar Lawrence Smith the last words. There is a "distinction which is to be drawn between the meaning of the terms 'Investment' and 'Investment Management.' Investment implies a simple act, and implies sound judgment only at the time the investment is made. Investment Management is a continuing act and implies the continuous application of judgment. It includes the act of investment, but also a great deal more."[58] As we are coming to learn, "the continuous application of judgment" is strengthened by the Money Mind.

■ ■ ■

You may not know the name Jack Treynor, but he was an intellectual giant in the field of financial management. First trained as a mathematician at Haverford College, he graduated with distinction from Harvard Business School in 1955 and began a career in the research department at Arthur D. Little, a consulting firm. Treynor was a prolific writer whose articles won many awards, including the *Financial Analysts Journal's* Graham and Dodd award and the Roger F. Murray Prize. In 2007, he won the prestigious CFA Institute Award for Professional Excellence. Treynor's writings were once loosely noted, but now can be found collected in a 574-page volume titled *Treynor on Institutional Investing*. Tucked near the back, on page 424, is an article called "Long-Term Investing." It first appeared in the May-June 1976 issue of *Financial Analysts Journal*.

Treynor begins by talking about the ever-present puzzle of market efficiency. Is it true, he wondered, that no matter how hard we try we'll never be able to find an idea that the market hasn't already discounted? To address the question, Treynor asks us to distinguish between "two kinds of ideas: (a) those whose implications are straightforward and obvious, take relatively little expertise to evaluate and consequently travel quickly, and (b) those that require reflection, judgment, and special expertise for the evaluation and travel slowly."[59]

"If the market is inefficient," he concluded, "it will not be inefficient with respect to the first kind of idea, since by definition, the first kind is unlikely to be misevaluated by the great mass of investors."[60] Think back to Ben Graham's low accounting factors and Charlie's confession that these types of ideas no longer generate excess investment returns. "If there is any market inefficiency, hence any investment opportunity," said Treynor, "it will arise with the second kind of investment idea—the kind that travels slowly. The second idea—rather than the obvious, hence quickly discounted insight relating to 'long-term' business developments—is the only meaningful basis for long-term investing."[61] Recall Tom Gayner's analogy of the difference between taking a quick financial snapshot and analyzing a movie that is unfolding slowly over time.

All market activity lies on a time continuum. Moving from left to right, we observe buy–sell decisions that occur in microseconds, minutes, hours, days, weeks, months, years, and decades. Although it is unclear where the demarcation line is located, it is generally agreed that activity on the left side (shorter timer frame) is more likely to be speculation, while activity on the right side (longer time periods) is considered investing. What we have come to recognize is that more and more people are scrambling on the far left side of the line, trying to make as much money as possible in the shortest period of time, while the number of people on the right side has declined year after year.

The seminal work on comparing short-term and long-term strategies was written over 20 years ago by Andrei Shleifer, a Harvard economics professor and winner of the John Bates Clark Medal, and Robert Vishny, professor of finance at the University of Chicago's Booth School of Business. In 1990, Shleifer and Vishny wrote a research paper for the *American Economic Review* titled "The New Theory of Firm: Equilibrium Short Horizons of Investors and Firms."[62] In it, they compared the cost, risk, and return of short-horizon and long-horizon arbitrage.

The cost of arbitrage is the amount of time your capital is invested; risk is the amount of uncertainty over the outcome; and return is the amount of money made on the investment. In short-horizon arbitrage, the time you are invested is short, the outcome is known quickly, and the return on your investment is less. With long-horizon arbitrage, your capital is invested longer, the knowledge about when the payoff occurs is more uncertain, but the returns should be higher.

According to Shleifer and Vishny, "In equilibrium, the net expected return from arbitrage in each asset must be the same. Since arbitrage in long-term assets is more expensive than it is for short-term assets, the former must be more mispriced in equilibrium for net returns to be equal."[63] Put differently, because long-horizon arbitrage is more expensive, the investment return must be greater.

It should be noted that in order to generate substantial returns from short-term arbitrage, the strategy must be employed frequently and successfully, over and over again. Shleifer and Vishny also explain that, to increase your investment return beyond what a speculator would likely receive, you must be willing to increase the cost of the investment (the amount of time your money is invested) as well as take on more risk (uncertainty as to when the outcome will be resolved).

The controlling variable for both speculators and investors is time horizon. Speculators work in short-horizon periods and accept smaller returns. Investors operate over long-horizon periods and expect larger returns.

This leads us to the next question. In long-horizon arbitrage, do large returns from buying and holding common stocks actually exist? In a simple mathematical exercise, we took a look at the evidence.

We calculated the one-year return, trailing three-year return, and trailing five-year return (price only) between 1970 and 2012. During this 43-year period, the average number of stocks in the S&P 500 Index that doubled in any one year averaged 1.8 percent, or about nine stocks out of 500. Over three-year rolling periods, 15.3 percent of stocks doubled, about 77 stocks out of 500. In rolling five-year periods, 29.9 percent doubled, or about 150 out of 500.[64]

So, back to the original question: Over the long term, do large returns from buying and holding stocks actually exist? The answer is yes. And unless you think a double over five years is trivial, this equates to a 14.9 percent average annual compounded price return.

Who is best to close the price-value gap over the rolling five-year periods? Answer: long-term investors. However, the legion of long-term investors is declining while the market's constituency is increasingly being dominated by short-term traders.

Between 1950 and 1970, the average holding period for stocks was between four and eight years. Beginning in the 1970s, the holding period has persistently declined. Today, the average holding period for common stocks held by mutual funds is measured in months. Our research indicates that the greatest number of opportunities to achieve high investment returns occurs after three years.

No doubt, with portfolio turnover ratios near 100 percent, this all but guarantees that most investors will be excluded from these outsized returns.

By all appearances, the stock market does not often efficiently price long-term sustainable growth. Because there are so few companies that are able to achieve sustainable growth over a multiyear period, perhaps the market's skepticism is understandable. But this much is certain: for those companies with favorable long-term prospects that generate positive economics and drive above-average future value creation, many of their stocks are likely mispriced.

Of course, the value of this research is relevant only to the degree investors have the ability to select beforehand which stocks have the potential to outperform. The answer obviously lies in the robustness of their selection process and portfolio management strategy. But there can be no doubt that those who follow the investment tenets outlined by Warren Buffett stand a good chance of isolating a fair number of outperforming companies.

■ ■ ■

When investors think about diversification they customarily think about the number of stocks in their portfolio and the different industrial sectors they own. Some investors also diversify by style—choosing both value and growth—or by market capitalization, selecting large-cap and small-cap stocks. But rarely do investors think about diversifying by time horizons.

Short-horizon arbitrage strategies differ from long-horizon strategies. The two sets of anglers are fishing in different profit ponds. What is observable is that most investors, regardless of investment style or market cap, are hanging around the short-horizon pond. Over at the long-horizon pond there is plenty of room. At the short-horizon pond, traders are jammed together reeling in minnows, while at the long-horizon pond business-driven investors patiently keep an eye on their bobbers until it is time to pull in a trophy fish.

Business-driven investing is best suited for long-horizon arbitrage. Business-driven investors don't need the stock market to tell them they are winning or losing. The economic progress of what they own is the only gauge they need. Investors who operate in the Investment Zone are rarely disheveled because the economic returns of what they own instill a sense of confidence, a calm reminder they are on the right path.

Without a stock market and the ever-ringing change of stock prices, there is little to distract a business-driven investor. Alas, for most people the Investment Zone is only a temporary stop, a "fifth dimension" where they can take a short break to reset their bearings. Soon they feel the urge to cross back over to the Market Zone. But even there, the rules of business-driven investing still apply. Everything Warren taught us in the Investment Zone is applicable in the Market Zone.

It is important to realize the Market Zone is a carnival full of different actors playing different games with different time horizons. Some are investors, some are traders, but most are speculators. And almost all are easily distracted by the endless streaming of financial news telling all who will listen how best to proceed. But the business-driven investors mentally distance themselves from this noise. Our game does not change. All that is required is that we not forget the lessons we learned in the Investment Zone. All of these still apply.

Back in the Market Zone, it is imperative that business-driven investors not allow themselves to be pulled into the vortex of short-term nonsense. They must never lose sight of this truth: they are managing a portfolio of value-creating companies, all of them compounding their intrinsic value over time.

In a sense, we are managing our own conglomerate in the same way that Warren is managing Berkshire. In the weeks, months, and years ahead our progress and performance will be measured not by flickering stock prices but by the economic returns of our businesses. This is of paramount importance, whereas the roller-coaster ride of ever-changing stock prices is of little to no importance.

Whenever business-driven investors operating in the Market Zone are most seriously challenged, they will find value in the teachings of Ralph Waldo Emerson passed from Howard Buffett to his son Warren, and on to us. His words can help strengthen our own Money Mind.

> Why should we assume the faults of our friends because they have the same blood? All men have my blood and I have all men's. Not for that will I adopt their petulance or folly, even at the extent of being ashamed. Our isolation must not be mechanical, but spiritual, that is, must be elevation. At times the whole world seems in conspiracy to importune you with emphatic trifles, all knock at once at thy closet door and say "come unto us." Do not spill thy soul, do not descend, keep thy state; stay at home in thine own heaven; come not for a moment into their facts; into their hubbub of conflicting appearances.

CHAPTER 5

It's Not That Active Management Doesn't Work

At the 1997 Berkshire Hathaway Annual Meeting, Charlie Munger asked an important question. The Berkshire style of investing "is so simple," he remarked. "But it is not widely copied. I do not know why. It is not the standard in investment management even at great universities and other intellectual institutions. It's a very interesting question. If we are so right, why are so many imminent places so wrong?"

Why indeed? In a world where people are so keenly focused on smart investing, why are there so few Berkshire copycats? Yes, there are a recognized few but as a percentage of the global industry the number of firms that follow Berkshire's approach to investing is minuscule. The others cling to a different approach, one that is generally characterized as "active management." Their success is less than stellar.

Unhappy investors increasingly complain that active management costs too much, trades too much, and underperforms too much. Their solution is to switch over to passive index funds instead, and as a result hundreds of billions of dollars are being liquidated each year from active management strategies and many of those managers are losing their jobs.

But, as we will soon learn, it's not that active management doesn't work. It is the strategies used by most active managers that don't work.

■ ■ ■

If you asked people what they know about the history of investing, I suspect most would begin by recounting the infamous Crash of 1929. The Roaring Twenties, the decade following World War I, was a period of double-barreled economic activity: great wealth building and great speculation. The latter of these culminated in the biggest stock market crash in American history.

Others might answer that American investing actually began on May 17, 1792, when 24 stockbrokers gathered under a buttonwood tree outside 68 Wall Street to sign an agreement, later known as the Buttonwood Agreement, that founded what is now the New York Stock Exchange. But history buffs would tell you that in actuality, the clock of the investing world began with the Amsterdam Stock Exchange in 1602. An invention of the Dutch East India Company, the exchange not only allowed joint-stock companies to attract capital from investors, but also allowed investors to buy and sell their shares in these companies. So in all, the history of modern investing is about 420 years old.

Today, that which passes for the standard of investment management, called Modern Portfolio Theory, is barely 40 years old. We can trace its root back to 1952, some 70 years ago, although for the first 30 years no one outside academia gave it much thought.

Modern Portfolio Theory (MPT) assumes investors are risk averse and that given the choice of two portfolios with the same expected return, investors will always prefer the less risky one. Understanding this, investors can build an optimal portfolio of stocks and bonds that reflects their risk tolerance, defined as the emotional wherewithal to withstand price volatility. As we will see, MPT is all about the bounciness of a stock price and the individual investor's ability to handle bad news. To say this in other, blunter terms: the driving force for the standard investment management is the paramount objective of solving a psychological discomfort—an objective deemed more important than achieving higher investment returns.

Central to Modern Portfolio Theory is the belief that a portfolio's overall risk and return is more important that the risk and return of an individual investment. In MPT, the whole becomes more important than the individual parts, and over the years numerous strategies have been developed to guide investors toward their goals with a minimum of angst. But as we will soon learn, all those strategies fail to find the answer to reaching that goal because they emphasize the wrong question.

Modern Portfolio Theory puts investors' emotional well-being—there is no other way to describe risk tolerance—ahead of investment returns, which are given second place on the priority list. Thus grounded in risk, standard active management cannot, as a general rule, outperform passive index funds. No value is added. No wonder investors are turning sour on active management.

By misprioritizing what is critical for outperformance, Modern Portfolio Theory has sowed the seeds of its own demise. It is a theory built on straw legs that today is wobbling as investors rush to take money away.

How did we get here, and how do we get out of this dangerous mindset? First, by taking an honest look back and then by listening to, and emulating, those who operate from the secure foundation of a Money Mind.

■ ■ ■

The question of how we got into this self-defeating mindset starts with Harry Max Markowitz, born in Chicago on August 24, 1927. By all accounts he was a good boy. Played the violin and studied hard. His interests included physics, mathematics, and philosophy. It was said that his hero was David Hume, the English philosopher, and that his favorite essay was "Skeptical Doubts Concerning the Operations of Understanding" in which Hume drew a distinction between the "relations of ideas" and "matters of fact."[1]

Markowitz attended the University of Chicago—the only college he applied to—where he earned a bachelor's degree in liberal arts and continued graduate studies in economics. As a graduate student, Markowitz gravitated to the Cowles Commission for Research in Economics, which was then embedded at the University of Chicago. Alfred Cowles had established the commission in 1932. Having subscribed to several investment services, none of which had predicted the 1929 stock market crash, Cowles set about to determine whether market forecasters could actually predict the future direction of the market. In one of the most detailed studies ever conducted, the commission analyzed 6,904 forecasts between 1929 and 1944; the results, Cowles noted in a model of understatement, "failed to disclose evidence of ability to predict the future course of the stock market."[2]

In the early 1950s, the University of Chicago was a hotbed of economic talent. The faculty included Milton Friedman, Tjalling Koopsman, Jacob Marschak, and Leonard Savage. When it came time to decide on a topic for his doctoral dissertation, Markowitz chose as his advisor Professor Marschak, a recent director of the Cowles Commission. One afternoon, Markowitz was sitting outside Marschak's office when he introduced himself to an older, distinguishing-looking gentleman sitting nearby. In the casual conversation that ensued, the gentleman mentioned that he was a stockbroker and suggested that Markowitz might consider writing his dissertation on the stock market. When Markowitz mentioned the idea to his advisor, Marschak enthusiastically agreed—and then reminded his student that Alfred Cowles was himself interested in markets.[3]

Jacob Marschak's field of expertise was economics, not the stock market, so he directed Markowitz to Marshall Ketchum, dean of the Graduate School of Business and coeditor of the *Journal of Finance*. Ketchum, in turn, sent Markowitz to the university library to read *The Theory of Investment Value* by John Burr Williams, which you may recognize as the same book that Warren studied to better help him determine a company's intrinsic value.[4]

Markowitz was instantly intrigued. He was fascinated by Williams' net present value (NPV) model for valuing stocks but was left perplexed. Markowitz believed Williams' suggestion to use the NPV model would logically drive an investor to own a portfolio of just a few stocks, possibly only one. That led Markowitz to wonder what Williams thought about risk. Surely, no sensible investor would own only one or two stocks, he thought. The uncertainty of what could happen in the world would argue against taking such risk.

Going deeper, Markowitz could not see how Williams was controlling for risk. In Chapter 3 we noted that Williams had aligned with Ben Graham's idea of a margin of safety. In the preface of his book he advised the reader to select stocks that were selling below net present value and avoid stocks selling at prices above it. Other than this, Williams did not expound on risk management in his book. Even so, it is puzzling why Markowitz made no note of Williams' view on risk management. Nonetheless, Markowitz strongly believed investors should be interested in risk as well as return. The theory that he ultimately developed, with refinements from others, is that risk to investors is wholly a function of the volatility of stock prices. That understanding of "investment risk" becomes the first leg of Modern Portfolio Theory.

In March 1952, "Portfolio Selection" by Harry Markowitz, a graduate student in search of his PhD, appeared in the *Journal of Finance*. Markowitz would receive his doctorate in economics two years later. The article was not long—only 14 pages—and, by the standards of academic journals, it is unremarkable: only four pages of text (graphs and mathematical equations consume the rest) and only three citations: J.B. Williams, *The Theory of Investment Value* (1938); J.R. Hicks, *Value and Capital* (1939); and J.V. Uspensky, *Introduction to Mathematical Probability* (1937). From Markowitz's standpoint, it didn't take volumes to explain what he believed was a rather simple notion: risk and return are inextricably linked. As an economist, he believed it was possible to quantify the relationship between the two and thus determine the degree of risk that would be required for various levels of returns.

To illustrate his point, Markowitz simply drew a trade-off graph with the expected return on the vertical axis and the risk on the horizontal axis. A simple line drawn from the bottom left to the top right is referred to as the efficient frontier, a staple in Modern Portfolio Theory. Each point on the line represents an intersection between the potential reward and the corresponding level of risk. The most efficient portfolio is one that gives the highest return for a given level of risk. An inefficient portfolio exposes the investor to a level of risk without a corresponding level of expected return. The goal for an investor, said Markowitz, was to match portfolios to an investor's risk tolerance while limiting or avoiding inefficient portfolios.

However, the slippery slope that Markowitz introduced was the idea that the best measure of risk is variance, which is price volatility. In the first paragraph of his paper, Markowitz writes, "We consider the rule that the investor does (or should) consider expected return a desirable thing and the variance of return an *undesirable thing* [my italics added]."[5] Markowitz goes on to say, "This rule has many sound points, both as a maxim for, and hypothesis about, investment behavior. We illustrate geometrically relations between beliefs and choice of portfolio according to the 'expected returns—variance of returns' rule."[6] Markowitz notes that the "terms 'yield' and 'risk' frequently appear in financial writings but are not always used with precision." He suggests that "if the term 'yield' were replaced with 'expected yield' or 'expected return,' and 'risk' by 'variance of return,' little change of apparent meaning would result."[7]

If you stop and think about Markowitz's reasoning, it's obvious it was a gigantic leap—and arguably a pretentious position for a 25-year-old graduate student—to assume that which is undesirable (the unpleasantness of price volatility) is in fact *risk*, without any corresponding economic explanation or evidence that an asset which has high variance actually leads to permanent loss. It is also noteworthy that Markowitz ignores the issue of a company's value as it relates to a stock price, which, as we know, is the centrality of Ben Graham's approach to investing. Nowhere does Markowitz equate risk to capital loss—only to price variance.

It is not clear why Markowitz in writing his paper did not cite, nor did his advisor or the dissertation committee suggest he make reference to, the leading textbook at the time, *Security Analysis*. In 1951, just one year earlier, the third edition of Benjamin Graham and David Dodd's masterwork had been published. Neither did Markowitz reference Graham's *The Intelligent Investor*, at the time a popular investment book that had been widely reviewed two years earlier. Graham had made the important point that there is a difference between short-term quotational loss and permanent capital loss. Markowitz did not. In two separate cases, Markowitz ignored the advice and viewpoint of both John Burr Williams and Benjamin Graham as it related to risk management.

The bedrock of Markowitz's theory of risk is the way assets behave, pricewise. According to Markowitz, the risk of the portfolio depends on the price variance of its holdings with no mention of the financial risk to the value of the underlying company. With each step in Markowitz's thinking he moved further away from understanding the value of stocks owned and further toward constructing a portfolio solely on the price volatility of its stocks. Hence, the primary objective of his approach became an exercise in managing a portfolio of prices rather than a portfolio of businesses.

Initially, Markowitz's reasoning suggested the riskiness of a portfolio is simply the weighted average variance of all its individual stocks. Although variance may provide a gauge to the riskiness of an individual stock, the average of two variances (or one hundred variances) will tell you very little about the riskiness of a two-stock (or a hundred-stock) portfolio. To measure the riskiness of the entire portfolio, Markowitz introduced the formula for "covariance" to portfolio management.

Covariance measures the direction of a group of stocks. Two stocks exhibit high covariance when their prices, for whatever reason, tend to move together. Two stocks that move in opposite direction are said to have low covariance. In Markowitz's thinking, the risk of a portfolio is not the variance of the individual stocks but the covariance of the holdings. The more they move in price in the same direction, he reasoned, the riskier the portfolio becomes. Conversely, a portfolio of low covariance stocks would be more conservative.

In 1959, Markowitz published his first book, *Portfolio Selection: Efficient Diversification of Investment*, based on his PhD dissertation. Two years later, a young PhD student named William Sharpe approached Markowitz, who was then working on linear programming at the Rand Institute. Sharpe was in need of a dissertation topic and one of his professors at UCLA had suggested tracking down Markowitz. We introduced Sharpe and his Capital Asset Pricing Model (CAPM) in Chapter 4. You may recall that Sharpe argued that a company's cost of capital is related to the volatility of its stock price. Markowitz told Sharpe about his work in portfolio theory and the burden it was to estimate countless covariances for stocks. Sharpe listened intently, then returned to UCLA.

The next year, 1963, Sharpe's dissertation was published: "A Simplified Model of Portfolio Analysis." While fully acknowledging his reliance on Markowitz's ideas, Sharpe suggested a simpler method that would avoid the countless covariant calculations.

It was Sharpe's contention that all securities bear a common relationship to some underlying base factor. For any specific security this factor could be a stock market, the gross domestic product, or some other price index, as long as it was the single most important influence on the behavior of the security. Using Sharpe's theory, an analyst would need only to measure the relationship of the security to the dominant base factor. It greatly simplified Markowitz's approach.

According to Sharpe, the base factor for stock prices, the single greatest influence on their behavior, was the stock market itself. Also important, but less influential, were industry groups and unique characteristics about the stock. Sharpe's argument was if the price of a particular stock is more volatile than the market as a whole, then the stock will make the portfolio more variable and therefore more risky. Conversely, if a stock price is less volatile than the market, then adding this stock will make the portfolio less variable, less volatile, and less risky. The volatility of the portfolio, based on Sharpe's methodology, could be determined easily by the simple weighted average volatility of the individual securities.

Sharpe's volatility measure was given a name—beta factor. Beta is described as the degree of correlation between two separate price movements: the market as a whole and an individual stock. Stock prices that rise and fall exactly with the market are assigned a beta of 1.0. If a stock rises and falls twice as fast as the market, its beta is 2.0; if a stock's move is only 80 percent of the market's move, the beta is 0.8. Based solely on this information, Sharpe was able to ascertain the weighted average beta of the portfolio. His conclusion, perfectly in line with Markowitz's view of price variance, was that any portfolio with a beta greater than 1.0 will be more risky than the market, and any portfolio with a beta less than 1.0 will be less risky.

What would someone with a Money Mind make of all this? Let's think back for a minute. When Harry Markowitz was researching and writing his paper "Portfolio Selection" in 1951, Warren was enrolled at Columbia University, sitting for Ben Graham's spring investment seminar. When William Sharpe published his dissertation in 1963, Warren was in his seventh year managing the Buffett Partnership, posting outstanding investment results. At the time, Markowitz and Sharpe were both warning of the dangers of stock price volatility as something an investor should guard against. For his part Warren had learned how to take advantage of price volatility from his mentor, Ben Graham, and was applying the lessons learned to his partnership. While Markowitz and Sharpe sought to promote their theories of risk as volatility, Warren was already firmly planted in a different direction.

In 1974, Berkshire Hathaway purchased 467,150 shares of The Washington Post Class B stock for $10,628,000. At the time, it was Berkshire's largest equity investment. By the end of the year, the stock market was down nearly 50 percent in the midst of a brutal bear market, its worst showing since the Great Depression. The share price of Washington Post declined along with everything else, but Warren remained steadfast and calm. Writing in the 1975 Berkshire Hathaway Annual Report, he said, "Stock market fluctuations are of little importance to us—except as they may provide buying opportunities—but business performance is of major importance. On this score we have been delighted with the progress made by practically all of the companies in which we now have significant investments,"[8] the Washington Post shares included.

In a 1990 lecture to a class at Stanford Law School, Warren laid out his thinking. "We bought The Washington Post Company at a valuation of $80 million in 1974. If you'd asked any one of the 100 analysts how much the company was worth when we were buying it, no one would have argued about the fact it was worth $400 million. Now, under the whole theory of beta and modern portfolio theory, we would have been doing something riskier buying stock for $40 million than we were buying it for $80 million, even though it's worth $400 million—because it had more volatility. With that, they've lost me."[9] That's just about as perfect a rendition of his feeling about Modern Portfolio Theory as I can imagine.

Warren has always perceived a drop in share price as an opportunity to make additional money, not something to avoid. The way he looks at it, after you determine a company's intrinsic value, a drop in price *reduces* your risk. "For owners of a business—and that's the way we think of shareholders—the academic's definition of risk is far off the mark, so much so that it produces absurdities."[10]

Warren has a different definition of risk. For him, risk is the possibility of harm or injury. And that, he says, is a factor related to the intrinsic value of the business, not the ongoing short-term price behavior of the stock. In Warren's view, harm or injury comes from misjudging the primary factors that determine the future profits of your investment.

This is a perfect spot to lay out those factors, in Warren's own words. First, "The certainty with which the long-term economic characteristics of the business can be evaluated." Second, "The certainty with which management can be evaluated, both as to its ability to realize the full potential of the business and to wisely employ its cash flows." Third, "The certainty with which management can be counted on to channel the rewards from the business to the shareholder rather than to itself." And fourth, "The purchase price of the business."[11]

Importantly, Warren tells us risk is inextricably linked to an investor's time horizon. If you buy a stock today, he explains, with the intention of selling it tomorrow, then you have entered into a risky transaction. The odds of predicting whether share prices will be up or down in a short period are the same as the odds of predicting the toss of a coin—you will lose half the time. However, he says, if you extend your time horizon out several years, the possibility that a stock is a risky transaction declines meaningfully, assuming of course that you have made a sensible purchase in the first place.

The best we can say about the Modern Portfolio Theory of risk, the use of beta, is that it is applicable for short-horizon investors but meaningless for long-horizon investors. The Modern Portfolio Theory's definition of risk—how much a stock price bounces around the market's price—is relevant for someone who treats their investment portfolio like a money market account, flinching every time their portfolio's net asset value drops below $1.

But this begs a question, why would an investor be short-term reactive if their investment goals and objectives are long term? We can make a good argument that managing a portfolio to minimize short-term price volatility has the unhappy effect of suboptimizing long-term investment returns. Secondly, and more problematic, an investor who obsesses over the short-term price dips is more likely to embrace speculative habits, frenetically buying and selling stocks in a vain attempt to keep their portfolio from declining. Warren as usual puts it succinctly: "If the investor fears price volatility, erroneously viewing it as a measure of risk, he may, ironically, end up doing some very risky things."[12]

For the business-driven investor a better way to gauge risk taking is the size of the margin of safety, which is the discount to intrinsic value they pay for an investment. The deeper the discount between the stock price and the value of the business, the less risk that investor is taking on.

"If you asked me to assess the risk of buying Coca-Cola this morning and selling it tomorrow morning," said Warren, "I'd say that's a very risky transaction."[13] But in his mind there was little risk when he bought Coca-Cola in 1988 with the thought of holding it for 10 years. In much the same way, when he bought The Washington Post Company in the midst of the 1974 bear market he also believed he was taking little risk because he intended to hold the stock for 10 years or longer. Modern Portfolio Theory academicians would have said Warren had increased the risk to Berkshire's portfolio by buying the Washington Post in 1974. Ten years later, in 1985, Berkshire's $10 million investment in the Washington Post was worth $200 million—a 20-bagger.

"To invest successfully," said Warren, "you need not understand beta [or] modern portfolio theory. You may, in fact, be better off knowing nothing of these. That, of course, is not the prevailing view at most business schools, whose finance curriculum tends to be dominated by such subjects. In our view, investment students need only two well-taught courses: How to Value a Business, and How to Think About Market Prices."[14] This is a cornerstone of the Money Mind.

Business-driven investors look upon the price volatility occurring in the Market Zone as a periodic opportunity. Otherwise, they rarely give stock price variance much thought, if at all. In a nutshell, business-driven investors do not obsess over ever-changing stock prices. Instead they choose to focus on the economic progress of the companies they own. Just because a business-driven investor operates in the Market Zone does not mean they have to worship at the altar of Modern Portfolio Theory.

■ ■ ■

The second leg to Modern Portfolio Theory is portfolio diversification. In his paper, "Portfolio Selection," Markowitz says the reason he rejected John Burr Williams' net present value rule, which he called the expected returns rule, was "that it never implied the superiority of diversification." Markowitz then adds, in no uncertain terms, that an investor must reject the idea of a concentrated portfolio. In his view, because error rates do occur, a diversified portfolio is always preferable to a nondiversified one. But not just any diversified portfolio. "It is necessary to avoid investing in securities with high covariances among themselves. We should diversify across industries because firms in different industries, especially industries with different economic characteristics, have lower covariances than firms within an industry."[15]

In summary, then, Markowitz fiercely believed that a widely diversified portfolio, so long as its stocks had negative covariance, was always preferable to a concentrated portfolio. "Diversification is both observable and sensible," he wrote. "A rule of behavior which does not imply the superiority of diversification must be rejected both as a hypothesis and as a maxim."[16] Another bold statement coming from a graduate student who had never managed money.

How does this square with the perspective of a Money Mind? Not surprisingly, Warren has a different view on portfolio diversification and it is the polar opposite of Modern Portfolio Theory. According to MPT, the primary benefit of a broadly diversified portfolio is that it mitigates the price volatility of individual stocks. But if you are not concerned with price volatility, as Warren is not, then you see diversification in a totally different light.

In his typical clear fashion, Warren deftly illustrates the folly of owning a widely diversified portfolio compared to the sensibility of owning only a few outstanding businesses. "If my universe of business possibilities was limited, say, to private companies in Omaha, I would, first, try to assess the long-term economic characteristics of each business; second, assess the quality of the people in charge of running it; and, third, try to buy into a few of the best operations at a sensible price. I certainly would not wish to own an equal part of every business in town. Why, then, should Berkshire take a different tack when dealing with the larger universe of public companies?"[17]

Building a portfolio of common stocks that is equally weighted by every company independent of their economic return, as MPT would have us do, prioritizes price volatility over maximizing returns. Warren tells us, "If you are a know-*something* investor, able to understand business economics and to find five to ten sensibly-priced companies that possess important long-term competitive advantages, conventional diversification makes no sense for you. It is apt simply to hurt your results and increase your risk."[18]

So, to recap: Warren first rejects the idea that risk equals price volatility and now soundly disavows the idea that broad diversification is the optimal portfolio strategy. "I cannot understand why an investor elects to put money into a business that is his 20th favorite rather than simply adding that money to his top choices—the businesses he understands the best and that present the least risk, along with the greatest profit potential."[19]

How, then, can we characterize Warren's strategy for managing his portfolio? What should we call it? He once said to me, "Robert, we just focus on a few outstanding companies. We're focus investors."[20] So when I decided to write a book about Warren's strategy of portfolio management, published as *The Warren Buffett Portfolio*, I subtitled it *Mastering the Power of the Focus Investment Strategy.*

I knew it would be insufficient simply to say, in effect, focus portfolios work for Warren and therefore you should just follow his approach; most people would want more solid information, and I wanted to deliver it. So I began an intensive, multilevel research study to see if actual market data would support the premise. If you're interested, the full scope of that research is spelled out in great detail in *The Warren Buffett Portfolio*, but for our purposes in *this* book, a couple of points warrant our attention.

For one thing, it is important to realize that focus, low-turnover portfolios customarily suffer periods of underperformance as the stock market continually gyrates around different stocks and industries. In fact, it is not unusual for a focus investor to underperform the stock market, on a short-term basis, a third of the time or more. The point to remember is this: it is not how many times you are right minus how many times you are wrong that counts; it is how much money you make when you are right minus how much money you give back when you are wrong. It is a frequency versus magnitude argument.

In our study, the focus portfolios demonstrated much higher highs and lower lows than the larger diversified portfolios. As such, a focus portfolio has a much better chance of performing worse than a broadly diversified portfolio, but you also have a much higher probability of outperforming a broadly diversified portfolio.

All told, our research demonstrated that the probabilities of beating the market go up as the number of stocks in a portfolio is reduced. And the reverse is true: the chances of underperforming the market increase to the degree you increase the number of stocks you own. Once you own a portfolio of 100 to 250 stocks, you have become the market—and this is *before* subtracting management fees and trading expenses.

Of course, the controlling factor for successfully managing a focus portfolio is stock selection. If you cannot competently purchase stocks that will outperform the market over time, it is in your best interests to own a broadly diversified portfolio, like a passive index fund. But if you are able to isolate stocks that are compounding intrinsic value and are also mispriced by the market it is definitely in your best interest to manage and optimize a focused portfolio.

"Diversification serves as protection against ignorance," explains Warren. "If you want to make sure that nothing bad happens to you relative to the market, you should own everything. There is nothing wrong with that. It's a perfectly sound approach for somebody who doesn't know how to analyze businesses." In many ways, Modern Portfolio Theory protects investors who have limited knowledge and understanding of how to value a business. But that protection comes with a price. According to Warren, "It [Modern Portfolio Theory] will tell you how to do average. But I think almost anybody can figure out how to do average by fifth grade."[21]

■ ■ ■

It is completely understandable that so many investors are abandoning active-management strategies. Eventually, people tire of paying for bad outcomes when they can pay less money for better results. The data are uncontestable. Cheaper passive index funds continue to outperform most active managers. But passive index funds do not outperform *all* active managers.

Twenty-five years ago, we wrote about focus portfolios. Today, academicians are engaged. The most notable thinkers on nondiversified portfolios are K.J. Martijn Cremers and Antti Petajisto. But they no longer call it focus investing. It is now referred to as "high active-share investing."

In 2009, Cremers and Petajisto, at the time both at the International Center of Finance at the Yale School of Management, coauthored a landmark paper on portfolio management; "How Active Is Your Fund Manager? A New Measure That Predicts Performance." First a definition. Active share is the percentage amount of a portfolio that is different from the performance benchmark, calculated by tabulating the differences in names and weights in a portfolio compared to the benchmark. A portfolio that has no names in common with a benchmark has an active share of 100 percent; a portfolio that has exactly the same holdings and weights as the benchmark will have an active share of 0 percent. If a portfolio has an active share of 75 percent, then 25 percent of its holdings are identical to the holdings of the benchmark and 75 percent of the holdings are different.

Cremers and Petajisto examined 2,650 mutual funds from 1980 to 2003. What did they discover? Those portfolios with high active share, defined as 80 percent or higher, beat their benchmark indices by a range of 2.0 percent to 2.7 percent before fees and 1.5 percent to 1.6 percent after fees.[22] In addition, those funds with low active share, commonly referred to as closet indexers because they are actively managed portfolios that closely resemble the benchmark, were unable to outperform the index after expenses.

It is now understood that portfolios with the highest active share outperform their benchmarks while funds with the lowest active share underperform. Today, active share is considered a predictor of fund performance.

On a side note, Cremers and Petajisto pointed out that tracking error volatility, which measures the standard deviation of the difference between a manager's return and the index returns—the standard MPT approach to measuring active management—does not predict future returns. Whether a manager has a portfolio with low tracking error or high tracking error only implies what actions are occurring in the portfolio, not how different the portfolio looks compared to the benchmark.

In a follow-up to his paper, Cremers, along with Ankur Pareek at the Rutgers Business School, wrote an article in 2016 for *Journal of Financial Economics* titled "Patient Capital Outperformance: The Investment Skill of High Active Share Managers Who Trade

Infrequently." Here the authors examined the performance results of portfolios that were both high active share and low turnover—in other words, portfolios managed by and for buy-and-hold investors. They found that "among high active share portfolios—whose holdings differ substantially from their benchmark—only those with patient investment strategies (with holding durations over two years) on average outperformed." Importantly, they discovered high active-share portfolios with high turnover ratios actually underperformed the market.[23]

Collectively, Cremers, Petajisto, and Pareek have made it clear that the worst portfolio management approach is a widely diversified portfolio that trades a lot, and the best approach for beating the market is to own high active-share portfolios run by managers who buy and hold stocks. Exactly the same type of portfolio Warren manages at Berkshire.

You would think that with such a growing body of evidence, we would find high active share, low-turnover portfolios on the upswing. Indeed, Cremers and Pareek wrote, "Our results suggest that US equity markets provide opportunities for longer-term active managers because of the limited arbitrage capital devoted to patient and active investment strategies."[24] But the facts say otherwise.

In fact, the percentage of assets managed by high active-share portfolios has been in a steady decline. In 1980, high active-share portfolios accounted for 58 percent of total equity assets. In 2003, the number dropped to 28 percent and continues to decline today. According to Cremers and Petajisto, this is true even of high active-share portfolios that outperformed their benchmarks.

What could possibly explain investors' indifference to an investment approach that we *know* helps them outperform the market? Cremers sought to untangle this paradox in a 2017 article written for the *Financial Analysts Journal* titled "Active Share and the Three Pillars of Active Management: Skill, Conviction, and Opportunity." Cremers links those three traits—skill, conviction, and opportunity—to a line of reasoning he traces back to Plato and Aristotle, who argued that "practical wisdom involves the triad of right knowledge (skill), good judgment (conviction) and effective application (opportunity)."[25]

We can say, therefore, that the first pillar of successful high active-share investing is having the right knowledge, the skill to identify stocks with those properties (business, financial, and management) that lead to long-term compounding of intrinsic value. The second pillar is conviction, the good judgment to apply the skill of picking stocks linked to a strategy that best provides the opportunity to outperform. Cremers specifically pointed to strategies subject to long-horizon arbitrage outlined by Schleifer and Vishny, who had argued that long-horizon investing provides higher returns than short-horizon investing (see Chapter 4).

But it is not enough for a portfolio manager to have skill and conviction. Without the third pillar, effective application, high active-share low-turnover portfolios cannot succeed if not given "the practical ability to do so effectively." Cremers argues that for high active-share portfolios to grow assets under management they must be given "sufficient opportunity or (at a minimum) the lack of practical obstacles to do so persistently."[26]

In thinking about the challenges for high active-share portfolios, Cremers acknowledges an increased risk for the portfolio manager who is on the right track: "the possibility that a profitable long-term strategy may underperform in the short term." I would go further and say it is not a possibility but a near certainty. And the impact of doing so can have dire consequences for the well-being of a firm and the employment of its portfolio manager. Cremers writes, "Short-term underperformance may jeopardize the manager's ability to retain assets and continue the long-term investment strategy especially in the case of impatient investors."[27] Shleifer and Vishny get to the heart of the matter. "Strategies subject to limited (long-horizon) arbitrage include those that trade on long-term pricing," which they consider "riskier for the manager because they require stronger convictions and investor trust."[28]

Today, the challenge for managers of high active-share portfolios does not reside in the viability of the strategy itself but in connecting investors to the approach in a way that builds trust and patience. When that happens, a kind of upward spiral takes effect. The trusting support of the investors strengthens the portfolio manager's fortitude to continue the strategy, which in turn brings further profit from long-horizon arbitrage and thereby provides the excess returns investors expect from active management.

This "trust gap" is not going to be narrowed by providing additional investment studies on the benefits of high active-share portfolio management. There is not much more to say. If trust between an investor and the portfolio manager is going to be made stronger it will come about when investors realize there are many different reasons why stock prices rise and fall. Along with this we may see them begin to recognize the need for a better way to think about investment performance.

■ ■ ■

Each year, investors step back to evaluate the performance of their portfolio managers. The annual reports tally the percentage return of different strategies, all compared to their relative benchmarks. Managers that outperformed are ranked at the top; those that underperformed sit at the bottom. You would think the decision to replace a manager would be a thoughtful exercise—evaluating outcomes and the performance returns, along with understanding the investment process, the strategies that drove the returns. Unfortunately, this is not often the case.

Amit Goyal, a finance professor at Emory University, and Sunhil Wahal, a finance professor at Arizona State University, analyzed 6,260 institutional portfolios managed by 1,475 investment management firms between 1991 and 2004. They discovered the consultants in charge of hiring and firing portfolio managers followed a rather simple approach. They fired managers who had, in the most recent past, underperformed their benchmark and consistently hired managers who had outperformed their benchmarks. There was only one problem with this simple metric: it wasn't a smart decision. In subsequent years, many of the managers who were fired ended up outperforming the new managers hired to replace them.[29]

It is not that outcomes don't matter; of course they do. But the obsession of wanting only winners each and every year inevitably puts investors' portfolios in harm's way. It forces investors to become performance chasers, which leads to buying a strategy only after it works and avoiding strategies that have lagged. But without understanding the process that drove the results, an investor could easily buy a strategy which employs a bad process but stumbled into good performance. The technical term for that is "dumb luck." Conversely, good investment processes sometimes experience bad outcomes, what are called "bad breaks."[30] Robert Rubin, former U.S. Treasury Secretary, said it best. "Any individual decision can be badly thought through, and yet be successful, or exceedingly well thought through, but be unsuccessful. But over time, more thoughtful decision-making will lead to better results, and more thoughtful decision-making can be encouraged by evaluating how well they were made rather than an outcome."[31]

It is clear that if investors are going to benefit from high active-share investing they will have to come to understand and appreciate the process that is involved in managing that kind of portfolio and its corresponding outcomes. In the short term, the performance returns of high active-share portfolios are variable; the long-term performance results are predictive.

But if short-term results are largely uninformative, what should an investor rely on? If not stock prices, what else? The answer goes back to Chapter 4 and the use of Warren's look-through earnings to gauge the economic return of one's portfolio of businesses, independent of prices. It is here that the business-driven investor must apply the lessons learned in the Investment Zone while operating in the Market Zone. It is here the Money Mind must rise to the occasion.

The question becomes, what would inspire investors to shift their view of how portfolio performance is measured? Can they be persuaded to gauge their investment managers from the perspective of economic returns rather than market price returns? The challenge is not so much the acceptance of look-through earnings as a meaningful measuring stick; who would not want to know the economic progress of their investments? Rather it requires a deeper mental shift, and one that in my opinion is long overdue: to recognize that short-term stock prices, in and of themselves, often represent more noise than signal.

Thinking of this important issue as a problem of communication could be useful.

In July 1948, the mathematician Claude E. Shannon published a groundbreaking paper for *The Bell Systems Technical Journal* titled "A Mathematical Theory of Communication." Shannon wrote, "The fundamental problem of communication is that of reproducing at one point either exactly or approximately the message selected at another point."[32] In other words, communication theory is very much about getting information, accurately and completely, from point A to point B.

A communication system consists of five parts. An *information source*, which produces a message or a sequence of messages. A *transmitter*, which deciphers the message to produce a signal that is transmitted to a channel. A *channel*, the medium that receives the signal from the transmitter and passes it along to the receiver. The *receiver*, which reconstructs the message from the transmitter before it reaches the final *destination*.

What is the communication system of investing? The stock market. For the most part it is stock prices that continually produce messages or sequences of messages. The transmitters of information include analysts, writers, reporters, advisors, portfolio managers, television reporters, and anyone else who is moved to relay the information of what is happening in the stock market. The channel might be television, radio, the internet, websites, newspapers, magazines, journals, analyst's reports, and even casual conversations; all these have taken the information from the transmitter and passed it along to the receiver. A receiver is the investor's mind, which works to reconstruct and process the meaning of all the signals produced by the transmitter and shipped by the channel. The final destination is an investor's portfolio, which takes the reconstructed information and acts on it.

Let's go back to the beginning, the information source. How can we best think about the stock market as the first link in the communication system? We could begin by adding up all the stocks in all the exchanges around the world but this sounds a bit overwhelming. We could limit our study to the 3,671 stocks listed in the United States, or better yet the largest stocks included in the Russell 1000 Index, which represents about 92 percent of US stock market capitalization. That's still a lot of data to absorb and make sense of. What else might we do?

■ ■ ■

Lately I've been thinking a great deal about ways to illuminate the mysteries of the stock market, and I keep coming back to one analogy. The game of chess.

A chess board has 64 (eight by eight) two-inch squares. To construct a communication system for the stock market, we could build a chess board that is 1,000 squares wide and 3,000 squares long. The 1,000 represent all the stocks in the Russell 1000 Index. Each of the 3,000 squares is equal to one dollar in market per-share value; for the sake of simplicity, each share price is rounded to the nearest one dollar. Why 3,000? So that we can include the higher-priced stocks such as Alphabet, Amazon, and others; Berkshire Hathaway is represented by its "B" shares. Our stock market chess board is 55 yards wide, slightly wider than a football field, and approximately 165 yards long.

We will play this game of chess with only pawns; no need for kings, queens, bishops, knights or rooks. Each pawn represents one thousand stocks, and each pawn lines up on the chess board organized left to right by the market's major sectors, largest to smallest capitalizations. To begin the game, each pawn moves out onto the board to the square that represents its share price. Then, with a snap of a finger, the stock market turns on. The pawns advance up and down the board based on the buy and sell tickets that are entered. Your job as an investor is to figure out why the pawns are moving and what the moves mean. As always in the game of chess, you must try to grasp what whoever is on the other side of the board is thinking, and plan your moves accordingly.

Investors have the tendency to think about the movement of stock prices as it relates to their personal viewpoint of the stocks they own. If a stock price goes up, investors believe others are in agreement. If a price goes down, then most investors think someone must disagree. When the market goes off on a tangent, with manic buying or selling, investors will attribute the exaggerated moves to the market's momentary lapse in judgment and not take it personally. But most other times, investors interpret changes in their stock prices as a judgment call on themselves being either right or wrong.

However, it is important we understand that the "who" on the other side of the trade, sitting on the opposite side of the chess board, is not just one mindset betting contrarily. No, the stock market is surrounded by multiple mindsets all executing different strategies, the consequence of which is moving stock pawns on the board for reasons that have nothing to do with an investor's original investment bet. Make no mistake, the stock you own is also owned by others executing different strategies, most of which have nothing whatsoever to do with a calculation for the value of a stock.

How many of those different strategies do you think are occurring in the stock market at the same time? This list is in no way exhaustive but would include:

1. Momentum: Exploits a tendency for a stock's prior price return to predict future returns.
2. Technical: A technician uses historical patterns of trading data to predict what might happen to stocks in the future.
3. Asset allocation: An investment strategy that divides and continually reallocates between asset classes, not bets on individual stocks.
4. Indexing: Attempts to mimic the return of the broad market by buying a basket of stocks, or a group of stocks that reflect a market sector.
5. Hedging: Risk-management strategy employed to offset short-term price losses by taking opposite positions in a related asset typically involving derivatives such as options and futures.

This strategy, in turn, impacts individual stock prices as others arbitrage the differences. Today, option volume is greater than stock volume.

6. Tax-loss selling and gifting: A strategy to minimize the penalty of paying taxes on the potential sale of stocks and the transfer of wealth in a tax-efficient manner. Recipients in turn indiscriminately sell stocks to fund needs.

7. ESG: Selling stocks that do not meet the criteria designated by environmental, social, governance standards while buying stocks that comply.

8. Macroinvesting: Buying or selling stocks based on the overall economic and political views of countries or their macroeconomic policies.

9. High-frequency trading: Quantitative, algorithmic high-speed trading that is able to transact large number of orders in fractions of seconds.

10. Speculation: Buying or selling stocks based on a belief of what other individuals or institutions will be buying or selling.

All of the strategies listed above are moving stocks up and down the chessboard for reasons that have little to do with a value proposition. This being the case, we have to ask just how important are short-term stock prices in determining whether or not someone has made a smart value investment? To this day, investors continue to believe the change in a stock price is a signal that they are either right or wrong. But in reality, the change in short-term stock prices is not a signal as much as it is just noise. And in a communication system, noise can have a profound impact on our perception and our interaction with others as well as our own analysis of the proficiency of the communication system itself.

Claude Shannon tells us a communication system is charged with getting information accurately and completely from point A to point B. Based on what we have learned, I do not believe a long-term value investor can look upon short-term price changes with any confidence that it is a reflection of value interpreters. As Richard

Cripps, senior investment strategist at EquityCompass Investment Management, rightly points out, nonvalue-based short-term strategies, high-frequency trading included, are exerting tremendous pressure on stock prices, obscuring the fundamentals of what investors own and leaving them to react emotionally to the consequences of intense price volatility. With this being said, the rationale for using price changes as a signal of an investor's well-being, including the use of short-term performance returns, becomes nonsensical.

To overcome noise in a communication system, Shannon recommended placing a "correction device" between the receiver (the investor's mind) and the destination (the investor's portfolio). This correcting device would take information from the channel (financial news media), separate out the noise, and then reconstruct the message so the information most needed arrives correctly to the destination, one's investment portfolio.

Shannon's correction system is a perfect metaphor for how investors should process information, and the correction system they need is Warren's look-through earnings. That concept, remember, emphasizes the need to focus on the *economics* of the business you own rather than obsessing over its *stock price*. This Buffett-designed correction device filters out the garbled signal that comes from the channel and reconfigures it into the information that is most needed. The process for doing this is within in our control. It is simply the lessons we learned in the Investment Zone, taught by Warren, that we must apply while operating in the Market Zone.

■ ■ ■

Fischer Black, an American economist trained at Harvard, is today best known as one of the authors, along with Robert Merton and Myron Scholes, of the famous Black-Scholes formula now used for option pricing. But I remember him most for his presidential address to the American Finance Association in 1986. In his talk, titled simply "Noise," this well-respected academician fearlessly took exception with his colleagues and challenged the widely accepted thesis that prices are efficient.

Rather than pure information leading to rational prices, Black believed that most of what is heard in the market is noise, leading to nothing but confusion, which in turn further escalates the noise level. "Noise," he said, "is what makes our observations imperfect."[33] The net effect of noise in the system, he explained, makes prices less informative for the producers and consumers who use them to guide their economic decisions. Likewise, noise also means stock prices are less informative as a guide to understanding intrinsic value. The total effect is to render suspect the notion, much in favor with his colleagues, that market prices are inherently and consistently efficient.

The efficient market hypothesis, alternatively referred to as the efficient market theory, is the third leg of the stool that holds up Modern Portfolio Theory. Although several academicians have written about efficient markets, including the economist Paul Samuelson, the person most credited with developing a comprehensive theory of stock market behavior is Eugene Fama.

Born in Boston in 1939, Fama attended Malden Catholic High School where he became an honoree of the school's Athletic Hall of Fame, lettering in football, basketball, and baseball. In 1960 he graduated magna cum laude from Tufts University with a degree in romance languages, then moved to the University of Chicago for graduate study, earning both an MBA and PhD in economics and finance.

Fama began studying the change in stock prices the minute he arrived in Chicago. An intense reader, he absorbed all the written work on stock market behavior then available, but it appears he was especially influenced by the French mathematician Benoit Mandelbrot. Mandelbrot was a maverick. He spent 35 years at IBM's Thomas J. Watson Research Center before moving to Yale, where, at the age of 75, he became the oldest professor in the university's history to receive tenure. Along the way he received more than 15 honorary degrees.

Mandelbrot developed the field of fractal geometry (he coined the term) and applied it to physics, biology, and finance. A fractal is defined as a rough or fragmented shape that can split into parts, each of which is at least a close approximation of its original self. Examples of fractals include snowflakes, mountains, rivers and streams, blood vessels, trees, ferns, and even broccoli. In studying finance, Mandelbrot argued that because stock prices fluctuated so irregularly, they would never oblige any fundamental or statistical research; furthermore, the pattern of irregular price movements was bound to intensify, causing unexpectedly large and intense shifts.

Like Harry Markowitz and William Sharpe, Eugene Fama was a newcomer, a graduate student looking for a dissertation topic who was neither an investor in the market nor the owner of a business. Like Markowitz and Sharpe, Fama was an academician through and through. Even so, his PhD dissertation, "The Behavior of Stock Prices," caught the attention of the finance community. The paper was published in *The Journal of Business* in 1963 and later excerpted in *The Financial Analysts Journal* and *The Institutional Investor.*

Fama's message was very clear: stock prices are not predictable, because the market is too efficient. Essentially, an efficient market is one in which at any given time stock prices reflect all available information and trade at exactly their fair value. In an efficient market, as soon as market information becomes available, a great many smart people (Fama called them "rational profit maximizers") aggressively apply that information in a way that causes prices to adjust instantaneously, before anyone can profit. Predictions about the future therefore have no place in an efficient market, because the share prices adjust too quickly.

In May 1970, Fama wrote an article for *The Journal of Finance* titled "Efficient Capital Markets: A Review of Theory and Empirical Work." In it, he proposed there were three different types of market efficiency: strong-form; semi-strong; and weak-form. The strong-form of market efficiency states that all information, public and private, is completely accounted for in current stock prices. The semi-strong form believes that information in public use is immediately reflected in the price of the stock but information that is nonpublic might help investors boost their returns above the market return. The weak-form of market efficiency suggests that today's stock prices reflect all past prices, hence no form of technical analysis can be used to help investors.

However, some advocates for the weak-form of market efficiency believe Fama left a crack in the door. They suggest that if thoughtful fundamental analysis and research are employed, an investor might be able to gain insight as to which stocks are over- or undervalued. Those that subscribe to this view believe it is the information that is not easily and readily available to the public that can enable an investor to outperform the market. This is equivalent to Jack Treynor's "slow-moving ideas"—ideas that require reflection, judgment, and special expertise for evaluation that might lead to above-average returns.

What would a Money Mind make of these three forms of market efficiency, indeed of the whole efficient market theory? It's not hard to answer that question.

In Berkshire's 1988 Annual Report, Warren wrote, "This doctrine [the efficient market hypothesis] became highly fashionable—indeed, almost holy scripture in the academic circles during the 1970s. Essentially, it said that analyzing stocks was useless because all public information about them was appropriately reflected in their prices. In other words, the market always knew everything, As a corollary, the professors who taught EMT said that someone throwing darts at the stock table could select a stock portfolio having prospects just as good as one selected by the brightest, most hard-working security analyst."[34]

Warren went on to remind shareholders of the investment returns achieved by the Graham-Newman Corp. between 1926 and 1956, as well as performance of the Buffett Partnership and Berkshire itself. To this, we can add the revelatory evidence of outperformance of the "Superinvestors of Graham and Doddsville" and the track record of the "Superinvestors of Buffettville" outlined in *The Warren Buffett Portfolio*. Lastly, we can add the academic work of Cremers, Petajisto, and Pareek to the list. In all, we can cite decades of outperformance from investors who selected stocks based on value principles and who, in varying degrees, managed focus, low-turnover portfolios.

Proponents of the efficient market hypothesis point out if the market was indeed inefficient, then many more investors would outperform the market. But they never took into consideration a reason *why* most investors don't outperform—not because the market is efficient but because the strategies used by most investors are inept.

If the efficient market hypothesis is valid, there is no possibility, except random chance, that any person or group could outperform the market, and certainly no chance the same person or group could consistently do so. Yet Warren Buffett's track record, along with the others listed above, is prima facie evidence that it is possible to do so. What does that say about the efficient market hypothesis?

Warren's problem with the efficient market hypothesis rests on one central point: it makes no provision for investors who analyze all the available information and gain a competitive advantage by doing so. "Observing correctly that the market was frequently efficient," said Warren, "they went on to conclude incorrectly that it was *always* efficient. The difference between these two propositions is night and day."[35]

One side note. Paul Samuelson, an American economist and early proponent of the efficient market hypothesis, was an early investor in Berkshire Hathaway. In an article written for *The Wall Street Journal* titled "From a Skeptic, a Lesson on Beating the Market," Jason Zweig pointed out that Samuelson invested in Berkshire Hathaway, at an average price of $44 per share in 1970, the same year he won the Nobel Prize. Samuelson learned about Warren Buffett and Berkshire Hathaway from Conrad Taff, a private investor who attended Columbia Business School and studied with Ben Graham. Although Taff trumpeted Warren's track record, it appears that Samuelson was most attracted to the idea of compounding money tax-free since Berkshire didn't pay a dividend.

Even so, "Professor Samuelson—who for years had been blasting the mediocrity of most fund managers—knew lightning had struck. He soon began buying shares, adding more over the years."[36] According to his son, Samuelson bequeathed his shares

of Berkshire to his children and grandchildren and various chari-
ties. If he had kept the Berkshire shares they would have been
worth over $100 million. "Professor Samuelson believed the same
[as I do]," said Warren, "Markets are efficient but not perfectly
efficient."[37]

■ ■ ■

The intertwined threads of Modern Portfolio Theory woven
by Markowitz, Sharpe, and Fama during the 1950s and 1960s
consumed the interests of theorists and academic journals, but
Wall Street paid no attention. However, all this changed in October
1974 with the culmination of the worst bear market since the Great
Depression.

Without question, the 1973–1974 bear market shook the
confidence of the old guard, the stock market establishment. The
financial damage was just too deep and widespread to wave off. Star
portfolio managers who rose to fame touting the "nifty-fifty" stocks
of the late 1960s disappeared, leaving behind the rubble that was
their portfolios. The self-inflicted wounds caused by years of senseless speculation were simply too grave to ignore.

"No one emerged unscathed," said Peter Bernstein, head of
Bernstein-Macaulay, a wealth management firm that personally
managed billions of dollars of individual and institutional portfolios, including numerous pension funds. According to Bernstein,
employees found the decline in their pension assets alarming.
Many wondered if they could afford to retire. This distress, which
reverberated throughout the world of finance, called for a change
in how professionals managed their clients' accounts.[38]

"The market disaster of 1974 convinced me that there had to
be a better way to manage investment portfolios," said Bernstein.
"Even if I could have convinced myself to turn my back on the theoretical structure that the academics were erecting, there was too
much of it coming from universities for me to accept the view of
my colleagues that it was a 'a lot of baloney.'" Peter Bernstein soon
became the founding editor of *The Journal of Portfolio Management*.

"My goal," he said, "was to build a bridge between gown and town: to foster a dialogue between the academics and the practitioners in language they could both understand and thereby to enrich the contributions of both."[39]

Thus for the first time in history, our financial destiny rested not on Wall Street or even in the hands of business-owners. As the financial industry moved forward in the late 1970s and into the early 1980s, the investment landscape would be defined by a group of university professors. From their ivory towers, they became the new High Priests of Modern Finance.

Although Bernstein's intention "to foster a dialogue between academia and the practitioners" was well meaning, the fact remained that the two schools of investing were speaking different languages. Modern Portfolio Theory was founded by academics, outside observers of the stock market who believed stock price volatility was the demon that must be defeated. Everything else, including portfolio management and its subsequent investment returns, is subservient to the quest. Conversely, business-driven investors are the insiders, the practitioners who owned businesses or at least think of stocks as business ownership. Their charge is not to defeat stock price volatility but to outwit it, so as to enhance their investment return. We can now say with certainty, business-driven investing is the philosophical antithesis of Modern Portfolio Theory.

But business-driven investing is not the antichrist. Business-driven investors did not cause the 1973–1974 bear market. No, that debacle lies at the feet of speculators who had masked themselves as investors. Glamming for the performance returns of the "nifty-fifty" stocks, these speculators had no idea what value they were receiving for the price being paid. It's been said "when you use the word 'value' and it means something besides 'price' you probably have to spell it out."[40] But the speculators who blew up the stock market in 1974 had no interest in hearing the message of value investing, much less trying to understand it.

Some observers thought the value camp would take back the reins from these reckless speculators and help drive the stock market back on the tracks. But their numbers were few and their attention was diverted. Into the breach, by default only, the High Priests of Modern Finance emerged. When Peter Bernstein said there was too much research to ignore, I don't think he fully appreciated how deep and wide the teachings of Modern Portfolio Theory had reached into academia. Dissertation committees at the major universities, including the University of Chicago, were yearly anointing new disciples (PhDs) who would soon become the new cardinals whose ultimate self-interests drove them to solicit more disciples. PhD dissertations circled Modern Portfolio Theory and became the fodder for a growing library of professional journals all spouting the same messaging.

Looking back, we can see that the tidal wave of academic research that was crashing down on Wall Street occurred at a fortuitous time. As the dust settled from the 1973–1974 bear market, a new bull market, one that would last a historic 18 years, was being planted. Investors, as they customarily do after enough time has lapsed, returned to the stock market in droves. "In the 1980s, the number of new investment advisors that were registered with the Securities and Exchange Commission tripled while the number of mutual funds quadrupled."[41]

Everything was now on the table. Investment objectives were being rewritten. Risk-tolerance questionnaires were invented. More than half of the questions asked how the investor felt about price volatility. The more risk averse the answers, the more conservative was the portfolio recommendation. Trading strategies were outlined, standards of performance were agreed upon and ratified with contracts signed by both advisors and clients.

Billions of dollars were soon flooding into the stock market. By 1989, nearly 100 investment firms had over $10 billion under management. The 10 largest asset managers had over $800 billion in assets out of an estimated institutional total of $5 trillion in stocks and bonds.[42] Investment firms were rapidly being organized. Modern Portfolio Theory was easily scalable, speeding up the takeover of the money management industry. A leviathan had been created, quietly at first but now unleashed, and it was preaching low price volatility, broadly diversified portfolios, and conservative returns. And before most fully recognized what was occurring, MPT had taken root, becoming the standard approach for investment management that has lasted to this day.

■ ■ ■

When Charlie asked his question—why the Berkshire model has not been widely copied and why has it not become the standard in investment management—he was speaking to the challenges outlined in a book written by Thomas S. Kuhn. Published in 1962, *The Structure of Scientific Revolutions* is considered one of the most, if not *the* most, influential philosophical works of the latter half of the twentieth century. It introduced the concept of paradigms and the now-familiar phrase "paradigm shift."

Thomas Kuhn's academic interests began in physics. He graduated from Harvard summa cum laude and immediately enrolled in the university's graduate program, earning both a master's degree and doctorate in physics, studying the application of quantum mechanics to solid state physics. He was elected to the prestigious Society of Fellows at Harvard. Soon thereafter, he began teaching a science class for undergraduate humanities students as part of the General Education in Science curriculum developed by Harvard's then-president, James B. Contant. Teaching the course led Kuhn to concentrate on the history of science, specifically examining the historical case studies of scientific revolutions.

In his landmark book, Kuhn challenged the conventional view that scientific progress moves in a pedestrian fashion as a series of accepted facts and theories. Although we might think that scientific discovery is a process of adding intellectual bricks to an already sturdy edifice, Kuhn showed that scientific progress sometimes occurs by crisis—tearing down the intellectual fabric of the prevailing model or paradigm and then reconstructing a brand-new model. In Kuhn's opinion there are times when advancement occurs only by revolution.

Under "normal science," he explains, puzzles are solved within the context of the dominant paradigm. As long as there is a general consensus about the paradigm, then normal science continues. But what happens when anomalies appear?

"I always found the word 'anomaly' interesting," said Warren. "Columbus was an anomaly, I suppose—at least for a while. What it means is something academicians can't explain. And rather than reexamining their theories, they simply discard any evidence of that sort as anomalous."[43] The High Priests of Modern Finance have been trying to discard the value investors who run high-active share, low-turnover portfolios for years, claiming they are an anomaly.

According to Kuhn, when an observed phenomenon is not adequately explained by the dominant paradigm, a new competing paradigm is born. Scientists left with an ineffectual model go to work on a new outline. Although you might think the transition from old paradigm to new is peacefully led by the collective who are in pursuit of the truth, Kuhn tells us just the opposite happens—hence the term "revolution."

Proponents of the dominant paradigm, when confronted with a new alternative, are left with two choices. They can jettison their long-held beliefs and divorce themselves from a lifelong intellectual and professional investment, or they can stand and fight. In the second case, we have what is known as a "paradigm collision," and the tactics for dealing with it are straightforward. First, proponents of the old paradigm seek to discredit the new one in any manner possible. Next they begin to repair the dominant paradigm so it better explains the environment. A perfect example: Fama's three forms of market efficiency seek to keep the efficient market hypothesis intact.

In the midst of a paradigm collision, the scientific community bifurcates, just as business-driven investors have bifurcated from the standard approach. The older group seeks to defend the primary paradigm (MPT) while others (Berkshirists) seek to institute a new paradigm. Business-driven is not so much a new paradigm—after all, it has been practiced by Warren by over 50 years—as it is a new willingness to promote business-driven investing as an alternative paradigm to the ineffectual approach outlined in Modern Portfolio Theory. Kuhn tells us once the paradigms collide, polarization occurs and "political recourse fails."

Although intense intellectual combat is the norm when two competing paradigms collide, there is another, more subtle way, which can ultimately settle the matter—time. It was Max Planck, German theoretical physicist and Noble laureate, who said, "A new scientific truth does not triumph by convincing its opponents and making them see the light, but rather because its opponents eventually die, and a new generation grows up that is familiar with it." Charlie, who also enjoys paraphrasing Planck, perhaps said it best: "Progress occurs one funeral at a time."

Historically, when paradigm shifts occur, they stretch out over many decades and involve multiple generations, which allows ample time to educate new proponents. When it can no longer be denied that the old paradigm has gone massively astray, there appears on the horizon an unstoppable force of new paradigm proponents—in this case, a legion of business-driven investors.

Modern Portfolio Theory and the efficient market hypothesis are still religiously taught in business schools, a fact that gives Warren no end of satisfaction. "Naturally, the disservice done students and gullible investment professionals who have swallowed EMT has been an extraordinary service to us and other followers of Graham," Buffett wryly observed. "In any sort of a contest—financial, mental, or physical—it's an enormous advantage to have opponents who have been taught it's useless to even try. From a selfish standpoint, we should probably endow chairs to ensure the perpetual teaching of EMT."[44]

Even so, until the paradigm shift is completed, the biggest challenge at the moment is how proponents of business-driven investing can survive in a world hostile to their success. With all the demerits that Modern Portfolio Theory has accrued over the years, you would think the stranglehold it has on the money management industry would loosen. But alas, more time is needed. Until then, business-driven investors will have to get comfortable living in a parallel universe.

To help with that, here is a summary of the major differences, or what we might call the rule set of the two competing investment paradigms.

The *standard approach to investing* accepts Modern Portfolio Theory as its guiding principle. It believes variance—price volatility—is almighty. Hence, all investment decisions, from an investor's long-term objectives to portfolio management, are driven by how a person emotionally handles the bounciness of stock prices. Portfolios are broadly diversified to minimize the variance of returns, while turnover ratios (how much buying and selling occurs) are elevated in an attempt to keep price variance in check. And not too far removed from high-turnover portfolios is an unrelenting goal to achieve short-term price performance. In the standard approach to investing, short-horizon arbitrage is the game.

In *business-driven investing* the guiding principle is the economic returns of stocks—i.e., the businesses you own. The long-term compounding growth of intrinsic value is almighty. Stock price volatility, the variance of returns, is an afterthought. Business-driven portfolios are focused, high active share, with low-turnover ratios in order to benefit from economic compounding. Short-term price performance is not considered useful as a meaningful gauge of progress. Instead, business-driven investors favor the long-term economic progress, the look-through earnings of the business they own. They frequently quote Ben Graham: "In the short run, the market is a voting machine but in the long run it is a weighing machine."[45]

In the standard approach, investors are in a constant frenetic chase for "votes." In the business-driven approach, investors are less anxious. Instead, they keep a careful eye on the economic "weights" of what they own, knowing full well the scales will eventually balance. In business-driven investing, long-horizon arbitrage is the game.

One last advantage business-driven investors have above all others, and it's critically important—a crystal-clear understanding of the differences between investment and speculation. They were taught by the best.

- Benjamin Graham spent his life writing about the issue of investing and speculation, particularly in the seminal textbook *Security Analysis*, Part 1, Chapter IV. "Distinctions

Between Investment and Speculation" and in *The Intelligent Investor*, Chapter 1, "Investment and Speculation: Results to Be Expected by the Intelligent Investor." The greatest danger investors face, he warned, is acquiring speculative habits without realizing they have done so. Investors end up with a speculator's return, thinking they were investing.

- In John Burr Williams' *The Theory of Investment Value*, Chapter III, Section 7, "Investors and Speculators," Williams writes "to gain by speculation, a speculator must be able to foresee price changes. Since price changes coincide with changes in marginal opinion, he must in the last analysis be able to foresee *changes in opinion* [italics his]."

- John Maynard Keynes wrote his last and most important book, *The General Theory of Employment, Interest, and Money*, in 1936. In Chapter 12, "The State of Long-Term Expectation," Section VI, he describes "the term *speculation* [as] the activity of forecasting the psychology of the market, and the term *enterprise* [as] the activity of forecasting the prospective yield of assets over their whole life."

- And of course Warren Buffett, who has spent his entire career counseling people on the need to understand the differences between investment and speculation. If you are not thinking about what the asset produces, he warns, you are leaning towards speculation. "If you focus on the prospective price change, what the next fellow will pay for it, you are speculating."[46]

If you are going to camp with the business-driven investors, know that our founding fathers have a pronounced, unaltered view on the topic of investing versus speculating. And we could argue that if you become a business-driven investor you would be less likely to speculate because the strategy of focusing on the economics of a business supersedes the worry over stock price changes. Business-driven investors act on market prices *after* they have occurred. Speculators act in anticipation of market prices.

Now, if you choose to camp with the standard approach to investing, you will look around helplessly for counsel on how to avoid speculation and embrace investment, but there is no counsel. The professional organizations, A to Z, that subscribe to the standard approach have abdicated their responsibility to define the differences between investment and speculation. Oh, they are very willing to have the debate but when it is time to codify what is investing and what is speculation, they shrink. Their paramount responsibility, which is to help investors make better decisions, somehow gets lost.

Long-term investing used to be a prudent course of action. Now when you tell someone you are a long-term investor, you are considered old-fashioned, out of step, clinging to a quaint idea for a time that has come and gone. The world is on the move, we are told. If you are not constantly buying and selling, you must be falling behind.

Being a business-driven investor operating in the Market Zone can sometimes feel like you are a round block trying to fit into a square hole. But we have been educated in the Investment Zone and we have learned how to thoughtfully measure our progress without having to rely on the Market Zone to tell us whether or not we are doing a good job. The question is not whether business-driven investors can be successful operating in the Market Zone, rife with all its challenges. It is a question of whether we have acquired the right temperament—studying lessons learned from the ultimate Money Mind.

When the market is speeding up and everyone is blindly, frantically racing for short-term performance, there invariably comes a point when the Money Mind simply slows down. And in doing so, sees everything.

6

The Money Mind:
Sportsman, Teacher, Artist

Remember the ingenious business and investing accomplishments that Warren achieved as a young boy, described in Chapter 1? Pretty amazing for someone so young, and a fascinating preview to the adult he would become. But one thing we didn't cover in that first chapter is his passion for playing games. At age six, Warren became a race promoter—marble races, that is. He would summon his sisters to the bathroom, where they would each line up a marble on the back edge of the bathtub filled with water. With the click of his stopwatch they all cheered for their marbles racing to the stopper, where Warren would declare the winner. Along with his childhood friend Bob Russell, Warren invented numerous games; one required recording license-plate numbers of passing cars and another involved counting how many times an individual letter of the alphabet would appear in that day's *Omaha World-Herald*. He also enjoyed playing Monopoly and Scrabble, and like all boys in Omaha, he loved baseball and Nebraska football. What connected all his childhood games together was competition. Warren loved to compete.

Today, as most people know, Warren is an enthusiastic bridge player. It has been said that his motivation for buying a computer was so he could play bridge online late into the night without having to leave home. "I always say I wouldn't mind going to jail if I had three cellmates who played bridge."[1] Many have noted the similarities between bridge and investing. Both are games of probabilities where confidence in decision-making is key. And the best part—both games keep dealing new hands. The puzzle-solving never stops. But make no mistake, Warren said, "Investing is the best game."[2]

You might also remember that Chapter 2 opens with the statement that investing is not a physical challenge, and that is true. But it is a game nonetheless, a thinking game. And like all games, investing is competition and those that play have a strong desire to win. That leads us to wonder whether the philosophy of sport has any important lessons for investors. The answer, it turns out, is yes—quite a lot.

■ ■ ■

The civilizations of ancient Greece, led by the greatest concentration of brilliant minds ever known, left many gifts to mankind. Chief among those gifts are sport, philosophy, and democracy, in that order. I am speaking in terms of chronology, not significance. You might be surprised to learn that the first Olympic game was held in 776 BC, 100 years before the introductions of philosophy and democracy. Plato considered sport a noble endeavor, because it served to identify people who possessed self-discipline, psychological endurance, and a civic dedication to the community, all the attributes necessary for a guardian-philosopher-king. In *The Republic* he wrote, "The same virtues that lead to success in athletics—for example, courage and endurance, also lead to success in philosophy, because the road to wisdom and virtue is, as Hesiod said, long and steep."[3]

In our world, sport is not often viewed in these lofty terms, for the simple reason most fans and athletes are focused singularly on the product of competition—the end result, the scoreboard tally. Attitudes are not much different in the investment world.

Sports psychologists divide athletes into two groups: product oriented or process oriented. The product-oriented athlete, as you might guess, is singularly focused on winning. They can think of nothing else. In contrast, the process-oriented athlete sees their sport on a much broader scale, finding multiple rewards in the activity itself, including "participation, striving for the team, personal excellence, aesthetic sensitivity, and rapport with competitors."[4]

John Gibson, author of *Performance versus Results: A Critique of the Values in Contemporary Sport,* wrote, "It is blindness to internal goods in sport that leads to the valuation of results over performance."[5] Michael Novak, philosopher, journalist, novelist, diplomat and author of over 40 books, was also a sports fan. He eloquently wrote, "There are priests who mumble through the Mass, teachers who detest students, and pedants who shrink from original ideas. So also, there are fans and sportswriters who never grasp the beauty or the treasure entrusted them."[6]

Investing is also a game of process and outcome. And like sports fans, those in the stock market rarely give much thought to process. And that's a shame because they will never grasp the "beauty" or the "internal goods" that come from the activity of thoughtful, involved investing. A business-owner operating in the Investment Zone understands all this.

Appreciating the process in sports or investing means acknowledging the journey, not just the results. "By process," says Douglas Hochstetler, professor of kinesiology at Penn State University, "I mean the journey of the sport experience—not only those end points in sport, crossing the finish line, but also those elements of sports that happen in-between, the stages or phases of the competitive project."[7] Michael Novak elegantly summarizes, "Most of an athletic career is prose, not poetry: boredom and discipline, not drama."[8]

Investing is much the same. Even so, there are highs and lows and a considerable amount of struggle. Certainly, Warren has had his fair share of struggles and he doesn't try to hide it. And like any world-class athlete, he has had to update the list from time to time.

The great investors understand and appreciate the long journey that is investing. They don't limit themselves to calculating short incremental returns, gains or losses, as the sole measuring stick of their investment ability. According to Hochstetler, "By viewing sport in terms of process, we begin to view the continuum of experience as an integral part of sport rather than relegated to tangential status. Viewing competition through the lens of process also provides meaning for the difficult moments."[9]

Investing too can be viewed as a "continuum of experience." That is a totally different perspective than just tallying wins and losses. You begin to appreciate there is deeper meaning behind all the individual moments. The love affair with investing, as with sport, comes from the activity, not just the results. Athletes refer to it as "the love of the game." They do it for the sake of something greater than one day's scoreboard. Those who respect the process take steps to uphold their sport, their approach to investing. We can say business-driven investors work hard to preserve both the "tests and the contests."[10]

What athletes have in common with investors is that both seek to achieve excellence. Athletes, like investors, are pragmatic, adaptive, and willing to change their habits and routines so as to improve their chances to win. In order to do so, athletes, like investors, are perpetually interested in gaining knowledge.

■ ■ ■

William James, the father of American pragmatism we met in Chapter 2, was also interested in how we gain knowledge. James' pragmatism is a form of Kantianism, which bridged the gap between rationalism and empiricism. It is referred to as "radical empiricism." The central idea is to connect our own experience with the collective experiences of others. In radical empiricism there are two types of knowledge—"knowledge of acquaintance" and "knowledge about."

Knowledge of acquaintance comes from the *experiencer*, the person who actually has had the experience of gaining the specific knowledge. In this case, we can say Warren is the experiencer. He made statements about investing by experiencing the act of buying and selling companies and stocks. In contrast, James' "knowledge about" is validated by a larger catalogue of knowledge, larger than any one person's life experience. It is what John Dewey, the American philosopher, psychologist, and educational reformer, in his 1938 book *Experience and Education* called *shared experience*. Dewey emphasized a social and interactive process of learning. He believed the best education involved learning by doing. However, he also believed that, to be effective, educational experience required interaction between the student and the environment. The student benefits by interacting with the shared experience, the greater catalogue of knowledge.

University of Berkshire Hathaway is a shared experience. It is also the title of a fine book by Daniel Pecaut and Corey Wren that highlights Berkshire's annual shareholder meetings from 1986 through 2015. Today, the Berkshire annual retreat is known as the Woodstock of Capitalism. It includes not only the Saturday shareholder meeting but many investment conferences before and after the meeting. Countless Berkshire students who come to Omaha each year gather in groups from early in the morning to late into the evening. At the shareholder meeting there is a solid library of books about all things Berkshire. The pinnacle is the Berkshire Hathaway Letters to Shareholders from 1965 to 2019: fifty-five years' worth of letters written by Warren, 874 pages in all.

What the University of Berkshire has accomplished is to combine the "knowledge of acquaintance" with "knowledge about." A financial journalist once asked Warren if he expected Berkshire to outperform the market over the next few years. The journalist posed the question as a hypothetical: might his own young son do just as well in a broad S&P fund? "I think your son will learn more," Warren the experiencer simply replied, "by being a shareholder of Berkshire."[11]

Today, virtual learning at the University of Berkshire is also available for those who live around the world. Berkshire students can watch videos of Warren and Charlie on Yahoo Finance. There is a Warren Buffett Archive on CNBC.com. It contains 26 full Berkshire Hathaway annual meetings going back to 1994, along with hours and hours of interviews with Warren, Charlie, and others. YouTube is also stocked full of videos of both Charlie and Warren, many including lectures and interviews. There is even a video of Warren's first-ever television interview in 1962, at the young age of 32.

That Warren became a teacher is not surprising. His father, his hero, was a teacher both in church and in government. Warren's mentor, Ben Graham, taught for 30 years at Columbia University. His partner, Charlie Munger, became a thought leader who expanded the concept of investing into far-reaching ideas across many disciplines. Warren himself taught his first class at Omaha University soon after returning from Columbia in 1951. He schooled his limited partners in the Buffett Partnership. And for the past 55 years he has been educating the Berkshire faithful.

William James was also a teacher. Shortly after publishing *The Principles of Psychology*, he conducted a series of lectures for Cambridge teachers in 1891 and1892. These lectures came to be known as "Talks to Teachers" and were published by Henry Holt and Company in 1899 under the title *Talks to Teachers on Psychology: And to Students on Some of Life's Ideals*. In his lectures, James asked the teachers to reconsider their position on education. "The old notion that book learning can be a panacea for the vices of society lies pretty well shattered today," he said. It was not that James thought books had no value; his concern was that students who relied solely on reading, without the benefit of teachers, would be left adrift. James believed in the holiness of teaching. He believed that "education would necessarily produce a stratum of men and women who, because of their sense of pride, ambition, rivalry, or inner strength, would rise to become the nation's leaders." In his mind, education was "nothing less than a battle for superiority."[12]

The best teachers, James believed, grounded their lessons in the idea of *association*. "Your pupils, whatever else they are, are at any rate little pieces of associating machinery. The 'nature,' the 'character' of an individual means really nothing but the habitual form of his association." In practical pedagogical terms, James explained, this meant teaching by comparing one thing to another. "An object not interesting in itself may become interesting through becoming associated with an object in which an interest already exists."[13]

What might seem an abstract notion of education theory has very real application in the world of investing. When Ben Graham said "Investing is most intelligent when it is most *businesslike*," he was teaching by association. When Warren said investors should think about stocks as ownership interests in a business, he too was teaching by association. Common stocks that were surreal for many investors suddenly made sense. The purpose of teaching, James wrote, is not to shock one's students but "to shape them towards optimistic and hygienic conclusions."[14] Business-driven investing, as outlined by Warren, is a grand example of William James' "healthy minds"—his characterization of those who have an attitude towards life that is open, engaged, and optimistic.

The Roman Stoic philosopher Seneca wrote "by teaching we learn." Proceedings of the National Academy of Sciences (PNAS) confirm Seneca's proposition. A PNAS study conducted in 2019 concluded that "giving advice improves academic outcomes for the advisor."[15] Any educator will tell you that teaching students makes you smarter about the material you are teaching. Warren has been teaching the Berkshire faithful and college students for decades. For years, Warren invited classrooms of students to Omaha where he would hold court, sharing his wisdom while answering endless questions on investing and the stock market as well as career advice and life lessons. No doubt the time he spent with students sharpened his thinking but there was much more to it than this.

CEOs, professional investors, and advisors are all teachers. They have a responsibility to educate their shareholders, institutional clients, and individual clients alike. Shareholders and clients, in turn, have the additional responsibility to share what they have learned with those closest to them.

Andrew Holowchak and Heather Reid, in their book *Aretism: An Ancient Sports Philosophy for the Modern Sports World*, argue that "in order for sport to be a good, it must be undertaken for the purpose of cultivating virtues that benefit not only the participant but also the greater community by producing more virtuous citizens."[16] I believe exactly the same goal holds for investing

How are we doing? Are we by our professional conduct producing more virtuous citizens? Is long-term investing virtuous? Is it held to high moral standards? In *The Republic* Plato recognizes four virtues: *prudence, justice, fortitude,* and *temperance.* They were called the cardinal virtues because Plato regarded them as the basic qualities required for leading a morally fit life, in addition to the theological virtues of *faith, hope,* and *charity.* Prudence is defined as acting with care for the future. Prudent investing is the cornerstone of investing. Those who believe in justice know how to recognize what is appropriate and well deserved, a skill critical for evaluating investment performance. Fortitude is defined as having courage in the face of adversity. We all know the importance of holding steadfast while managing a focus low-turnover portfolio. Lastly, Plato defined temperance as "*soundmindedness,*" which he believed was the most important of all virtues. Soundmindedness—that marvelous word may be the perfect descriptor for the Money Mind. Together, the four cardinal virtues are the linchpins for long-term investing and a critical part of the architecture that makes a Money Mind.

Those who have studied Warren Buffett's life can see a person who lives a virtuous life, not only in the game of investing but in the grander scheme of life. He demonstrates his faith in the goodness of the United States of America with hope defined as an expectation of receiving the gifts our country has bestowed upon its citizens for the last 244 years. And as we all know, Warren's charity is unmatched. He has pledged to give away 99% of his net worth to charitable organizations and foundations. In 2020, he donated $2.9 billion in Berkshire Hathaway "B" shares to the Bill and Melinda Gates Foundation, the Susan Thompson Buffett Foundation, the Sherwood Foundation, and the Howard G. Buffett Foundation and NoVo Foundation. It was the 15th straight year of annual giving. Thus far, Warren has donated $37 billion in Berkshire stock, measured by the value of the shares at the time they were donated. Today, Warren still owns shares in Berkshire worth around $67 billion, which means he will return over $100 billion in wealth to society. Nothing in history compares.

It has been said that "virtues have limited worth if they are confined to sport" and I would say also to investment.[17] If they are isolated to one activity then they are not genuine virtues. The Scottish philosopher Alasdair MacIntyre, in his book *After Virtue,* wrote, "Someone who genuinely possesses a virtue can be expected to manifest it in very different types of situations."[18] The virtue of investing is found not only in the minds of the practitioners, the teachers, but in the lessons learned by the students. "The beauty of virtue as the real prize of competition is that it benefits not just the victor but also the community at large."[19]

To the list of what it takes to develop a Money Mind we can add virtue. And a prerequisite for leading a virtuous life is a commitment to teach.

■ ■ ■

In his monograph "Talk to Students," William James included an essay titled "A Certain Blindness" in which he explored the meaning of life. "Whenever a process of life communicates an eagerness to him who lives it, there life becomes genuinely significant." This eagerness, he wrote, can appear in various activities: sports, art, writing, and reflective thought. But "wherever it is found, there is *zest*, the tingle, the excitement of reality."[20]

Zest is defined as having great enthusiasm and energy. For James "zest is the vibrant inside of human meaning."[21] John Kaag, philosophy professor at the University of Massachusetts and author of *American Philosophy: A Love Story*, adds, "Zest, the particular, peculiar thrill of experience, is the ultimate source of existential value."[22] When describing Warren, the word surely applies. Everyone who has made contact with Warren is instantly connected to his energy, optimism, humor, and boundless enthusiasm.

Twenty-five years ago, *The Warren Buffett Way* concluded with this final paragraph: "He is genuinely excited about coming to work every day. 'I have in life all I want right here,' he says. 'I love every day. I mean, I tap dance in here and work with nothing but people I like.'"[23] Twenty-five years later, nothing has changed. I guess you could say *Tap Dancing to Work* is a metaphor for "zest." It is also the title of a wonderful book by Carol Loomis, which catalogues 86 articles written about Warren Buffett over a span of 46 years, most of them by Carol herself. "When you finish this book," she wrote, "you will have seen the arc of Warren's business life."[24] And what a life it has been.

"I feel very good about my work," said Warren. "When I go into the office every morning, I feel like I'm going to the Sistine Chapel to paint. What could be more fun? It's like an unfinished painting. If I want to paint blue or red on the canvas, I can do it."[25] If Berkshire is a painting, then the pigment is the capital that the artist Warren Buffett applies with his brush.

The Sistine Chapel ceiling is one large fresco that depicts nine separate scenes from the Book of Genesis. The stunning fact about this majestic work, in addition to its sublime beauty, is that it was created by one person, working alone, under extremely difficult conditions. When Warren compares his own endeavors to Michelangelo, it is not from braggadocio; his personal humility is deeply held and widely known. I see it rather as a reflection of Warren's broad interests in many areas of human achievement. In that regard, considering Berkshire's history as one mammoth fresco is simply one more metaphor—a teaching tool that Warren particularly relishes.

The Berkshire fresco would depict many scenes, many challenges, many events. It would be difficult for anyone, even Warren, to single out the one scene in that fresco that is the most famous. It is even a challenge to tabulate the nine most important scenes that make up the Berkshire Hathaway financial masterpiece. So many people, companies, and investments large and small have all made an impact on Berkshire. But making sense of all those influences and "painting" the combined scene is the work of just one man. Johann Wolfgang von Goethe once said, "Without having seen the Sistine Chapel, one cannot form a truer picture of what one person is capable." In much the same way, we cannot really form an appreciation of Berkshire's story without seeing it as a piece of art from the hand of one individual. And once you have, you come away saying to yourself, "It is astonishing, it astonishes. One of us did that."[26]

Lance Esplund, who writes about art in *The Wall Street Journal,* tells us, "We forget in art, it is not the destination that matters and engages us, but the journey." The journey in art is the same as what is known as "the process" in sports and investing. It is said that looking at art requires a comfortable chair. Why a chair? Because to properly look at art we need to be comfortable, patient, and undistracted. "Then, like artists," said Esplund, "we might discover that we have moved beyond the art of looking, to the art of finding—the art of seeing."[27]

Art museums have discovered that the average visitor spends between 15 and 30 seconds with a piece of art.[28] They move quickly through the gallery, glancing at artwork, perhaps stopping only long enough to read a short description on a small card before moving on. It's the same with investing. People also move too fast through the stock market gallery. They spend a short minute reading an investment summary sheet, perhaps listening to a quick segment on a financial news network, or exchanging a few words with a friend who has a hot tip.

The decision to purchase a company is very much like an art appreciation class. An investor examines the qualities that classify all great works of business art: the products and services a company sells and its competitive position, the financial returns it generates, and management that decides how to allocate the capital. Investing, true investing, is an exploration of the art forms of a business. Compare this to people in the Market Zone who can see only ticker symbols and stock prices.

When investors *look* at a stock, they quickly tabulate the answers on a fact sheet without ever *seeing* the important question—how did this occur? And only by asking those questions do you have any real chance of truly understanding the answer and ultimately of achieving the insight about what the future answers may be. Just as a painting is too complex to be fully understood with a quick glance, so too is a company. No one can fully understand a company simply by tallying a few accounting factors, passing comments or flighty opinions.

■ ■ ■

William James said, "The greatest use of life is to spend it on something that will outlast it."[29] At the end of Steve Jordan's book, *The*

Oracle of Omaha, Warren says this about Berkshire: "I spent my lifetime working on it. I believe Berkshire's as permanent as you can come up with."[30] The original company, Berkshire Cotton Manufacturing, was incorporated in 1889. Warren took control of Berkshire in 1965. We can say the original Berkshire is 132 years old, although the modern version is a bit younger at 56, which is still very old compared to the average life span of most modern large companies.

Corporate longevity lies at the heart of understanding valuation as well as judging a company's long-term sustainable competitive advantage. The survival rate for most companies is not very long. Between 1965 and 2015, only half of the global companies with a market capitalization of at least of $250 million survived longer than 10 years. Those that survived and grew up to become members of the Fortune 5000 had a somewhat longer life span, but not by much. Today, the implied survival rate for the largest companies is, on average, only 16 years.[31]

The key to understanding corporate longevity is to recognize it is highly correlated to change, what Joseph Schumpeter called the "perennial gale of creative destruction." What we now know is short corporate lives are associated with rapid innovation. When the "rate of change is accelerating, corporate longevity is shrinking."[32]

Michelangelo's Sistine Chapel ceiling is 509 years old. Could Berkshire survive five centuries? Hard to imagine. On the other hand, maybe not such an outlandish thought when you consider that the process which has driven Berkshire for the last 56 years is compound interest—discovered by Jacob Bernoulli 338 years ago.

Now think about all the economic changes that have occurred over the last 300 years. The Industrial Revolution, discovery of penicillin, electricity, automobiles, airplanes and space travel. We have entered into a technological revolution with the invention of microchips, computers, and smartphones all connected to the World Wide Web. Despite Schumpeter's creative destruction, the one thing that has not been disrupted is the mathematical constant e—compound interest. So perhaps it is not out of bounds to imagine that Berkshire could last another 100 years, outliving every major large-cap company in the world.

Today, Berkshire is in transition. In 2018, Warren announced Ajit Jain, CEO of National Indemnity, would become vice chairman of insurance operations at Berkshire Hathaway and Greg Abel, CEO of Berkshire Hathaway Energy, would become vice chairman of the noninsurance operations. Todd Combs and Ted Wecshler, who joined Berkshire in 2011 and 2012 respectively, are now managing a portion of Berkshire's investment portfolio. Howard G. Buffett, Warren's oldest son, is positioned to assume the chairman's role when called upon. The necessary people are in place when the day comes that Warren is not answering shareholder questions at the annual meeting.

Even so, many question whether Berkshire will survive without Warren. "People say Warren is so special that Berkshire can't survive losing him," said Lawrence Cunningham, noted professor and author of several excellent books on Berkshire Hathaway and Warren Buffett. But "I say Berkshire is so special that it can survive even without him, thanks to the culture of permanence he cultivated for it."[33] Cunningham says the permanence of Berkshire resides in its culture. Susan Decker, a member of the Berkshire Hathaway board of directors, agrees. When asked if she thought Berkshire was sustainable after Warren, Decker replied in the affirmative saying, "It is about the culture." And longtime friend Carol Loomis, who has edited the Berkshire Hathaway annual reports for decades, echoed. "It's the people."[34]

With all that Warren Buffett has professionally achieved, arguably his greatest accomplishment is breathing life into a culture that became Berkshire Hathaway. At the heart of the company is a community of owner-partners, managers, and employees who above all else seek to rationally allocate capital. This primary objective is what fuels the engine that motors Berkshire. Why would anyone think this could not continue decades or more into the future? When asked whether his eventual exit will halt the five-plus decades of success, Warren simply replied, "The reputation belongs to Berkshire now."[35]

Epilogue

I first heard Warren Buffett say the words "Money Mind" on May 6, 2017. I started thinking about this book on May 7.

Not in any kind of organized, purposeful way—not at first. For a long time the notion of Money Mind was simply an idea sitting quietly in a corner of my brain, not causing any trouble but stubbornly refusing to relinquish its spot. Gradually, without conscious intent, I found myself visiting that idea more and more, and each time I discovered that it had gotten a little taller, a little more demanding. Until finally, one day in 2019, I knew I could ignore it no longer. I had to give that idea my full attention. It was time to start planning a new book.

I tasked myself to investigate fundamental questions. What exactly is a Money Mind? Where does it come from? What are its components? Can they be learned? And if so, how? Once I articulated the questions, I immediately knew the answer. Who better to teach us what it means to have a Money Mind than Warren Buffett himself, the splendid teacher and the ultimate Money Mind.

And so I started digging.

■ ■ ■

Ben Graham concludes *The Intelligent Investor* with this final, profound sentence: "To achieve *satisfactory* results is easier than most people realize; to achieve *superior results* is harder than it looks." Over the years, Warren Buffett, Graham's most famous pupil, has often repeated this phrase, although a bit more succinctly: "Investing is easier than you think but harder than it looks."

I thought I knew exactly what that meant. I was wrong.

When Warren said investing was "easier than you think," I took that to mean that in his view, all the difficult financial puzzles that others urged investors to undertake—forecasting the stock market, or determining how interest rates would change, or predicting the overall direction of the economy—were completely unnecessary. Things were easier for successful investors because they could simply skip all those annoying questions. And that is still the case.

It was the "harder than it looks" part that I got wrong. I thought it was a caution flag warning investors of all the work they would have to do, such as disentangle the income statement to determine a company's cash owner-earnings, analyze a balance sheet to tabulate returns on invested capital, and employ a discounted cash flow model to calculate a company's intrinsic value.

Collectively, I believed, all this calculation and analysis was harder than simply choosing stocks with low price-to-earnings ratios, low price-to-book-values, and high-dividend yields while avoiding all stocks with conversely high multiple factors. Wouldn't that be easier than all the laborious research and analysis of owner-earnings, ROIC, and DCF models? Maybe, but that's not what Graham and Warren meant by "harder than it looks."

The hard part is acquiring the right temperament, the temperament of a Money Mind. The objective of this book is to help us understand the building blocks that go into making this Money Mind so that we may begin to incorporate its principles in service to a life of value.

■ ■ ■

Our journey was chronological. We began with the first business book that 11-year-old Warren Buffett read, *One Thousand Way to Make $1000* by Frances Mary Cowan Minaker. She instructed young Warren that "the first step in starting a business of your own is to know something about it . . . so read everything published about the business you intend to start." As elementary as this sounds, and as simple as it is to do, the vast majority of investors read very little about the companies they own. Those who own index funds can be excused, as their bet is not on any one company but the investment class of common stocks.

But those that are making active bets on individual stocks should, at a minimum, take an interest in their companies' annual reports. It is surprising how few people even take the 10 minutes required to read the chairman's letter to shareholders. Make no mistake, if you don't understand the inner workings of a company, you will never reach the first level in what it means to have a Money Mind.

What other building blocks have we observed?

We must begin with the quality of *self-reliance*, which Roger Lowenstein once called "Buffett's trademark." It means relying on your own power and resources rather than others, and it is the start of a positive upward cycle in which self-reliance increases self-confidence, which promotes success, which further reinforces self-reliance. In a very real sense, self-reliance is the primary building block of the Money Mind, for everything else flows from the mental fortitude that it creates.

Self-reliance is what helps a Money Mind understand the intrinsic value of stocks owned, which in turn is critical for achieving the Stoic mindset investors need when interacting with Mr. Market. Whenever you look at Mr. Market and wonder whether he knows more than you, at that moment the jig is up. This does not mean you won't make mistakes. Warren has made mistakes and so have I and so will you. But the point when you begin thinking the market knows more than you is the moment when you have lost your self-reliance.

A Money Mind is strengthened by knowing that its understanding of investing is based on the concept of *rationality*, which combines the "shared experiences" of a wider body of knowledge with the insights of an "experiencer," someone with the direct business experience of what it means to own a company. Rational investors understand how markets work and can distinguish between the approaches that work and those that don't.

A Money Mind gains further strength by studying the mental models from other disciplines—what Charlie Munger calls "the art of achieving worldly wisdom." And a Money Mind is reinforced by examining the "psychology of misjudgments" in order to learn from mistakes.

A Money Mind understands that the world is constantly changing and the "challenge of change" requires *adaptation*. A Money

Mind rejects hiding behind outdated mental models and in its place embraces *pragmatism* as a way to "widen the field of search" for ideas that can help them become a better investor.

The Money Mind is also aware that meeting the challenge of change will take more than just technical skills, no matter how dazzling. In short, the Money Mind is an analytical competitive advantage that for most investors is the missing link. The key to investment success is acquiring the right *mindset*. Adding more math is not the answer.

The Money Mind is a *business-driven investor*. You don't have to own a business to acquire a Money Mind but you have to think like a business-owner and make the connection that the stock you own is a long-term partnership interest in a company, not a passing fancy that can be discarded on a whim. A Money Mind acknowledges the inviolable commandments of business ownership—never own a company that does not generate cash, never own a company that does not achieve returns above the cost of capital, and never buy a company without a margin of safety. A Money Mind has a keen insight to wealth creation that comes from owning companies that are able to compound shareholder value over time. And a Money Mind, like a business-owner, doesn't have to own every company in town, just the best businesses with favorable long-term prospects run by the most capable managers.

The Money Mind is comfortable operating with the lessons learned in the Investment Zone while chuckling at the folly being played in the Market Zone. The Money Mind is content observing the economic progress of their companies and does not need the market's daily price affirmation to tell them they are on the right track. If anything, the Money Mind recognizes the noise in the stock market while being better attuned to the value signals, knowing they will be justly weighed by the stock market in due course. In this way, the Money Mind is not reliant on short-term performance metrics to measure success, but rather plays the long game of achieving investment returns. And, crucially, a Money Mind is an investor, not a speculator. The Money Mind is focused on the asset—the company—and pays no mind to the beauty contest being waged by speculators.

A Money Mind is a sportsman, competitive and eager to win. But for the Money Mind there is more to the sport of investing than winning every race. A Money Mind appreciates the beauty of investing and its ultimate experience, and in doing so actually becomes a better investor by focusing first on process and only then on outcomes.

Like an artist, a Money Mind moves beyond "looking" at stocks for the answers, and engages in the art of "seeing" stocks to better understand how the company achieved its results. And a Money Mind appreciates that teaching is a sacred endeavor entrusted with educating others about investing so they, in turn, will rise to become the next teachers.

Lastly, the Money Mind is a virtuous mind. Strengthened by the cardinal virtues of prudent action, just rewards, and mental fortitude, they are then able to acquire the proper temperament to invest—the quality of *soundmindedness* that defines the Money Mind. Then with a faith in capital markets, and with the expectation of future financial returns, the Money Mind marches forward with generosity, help and devotion to partners, shareholders, and clients.

■ ■ ■

If we stop the journey here, the book has a nice ending. We fully understand the component parts that lead to the formation of a Money Mind. But understanding, without action, is not enough. What then is next? Once again Minaker's book gives us a push in the right direction. "The way to begin making money is to begin."

If you wake up tomorrow morning and decide you are going to adopt a Money Mind and become a business-driven investor, there are a few things you need to know. A business-driven investor in the stock market is a nonconformist. Ralph Waldo Emerson, you might remember, said that the nonconformist "must know how to estimate a sour face" while "the world whips you with displeasure."

Being a business-driven investor, bound to the principles learned in the Investment Zone, you will soon discover the Market Zone has its own ideas on how you should behave. The financial media are constantly grabbing for your attention with unsolicited advice about what you should do next. All around you, people will whisper that you should buy this or sell that. But a business-driven investor turns a deaf ear to the mosh-pit that is the stock market and instead becomes a vigilant overseer of the businesses they own.

A Money Mind steps back from the Market Zone. Instead of becoming a participant they become an observer. There will be no shortage of opinions hurled at them. But the Money Mind silently smiles, letting the "opinionator" drone on and on, then quietly turns away and does nothing.

I wish I could tell you that being a business-driven investor is as easy as taking the road less traveled, but the Money Mind's road is not for the faint of heart. Being a silent contrarian is not enough. More is required. William James reminds us that truth is discovered only by those who had the courage to act on their own beliefs. The greatest achievements of the great investors began with the courage of making a bold decision in the face of uncertainty.

When I wrote *The Warren Buffett Way* I made it plain I could not promise readers they would be able to achieve the same investment results as Warren. But I did promise them that if they applied the investment tenets outlined in the book, they would likely see improvement on their past results. In much the same way, *Inside the Ultimate Money Mind* does not guarantee you will achieve the same mental construct as Warren Buffett. But I have no doubt that if you are willing to spend time studying and thinking about the architecture of what it is to have a Money Mind, you will see a marked improvement in your temperamental balance when it comes to thinking about the stock market. This alone, I am convinced, will be worth the time spent reading this book.

■ ■ ■

But that is not all. Just as there is more to a rich life than your bank account, there are rewards that come from following the path of a Money Mind that go beyond investing. Someone who makes life decisions based on rationality rather than emotion, with this discipline alone moves to the top of the class. When thinking about how to solve a serious, troubling problem, why not take a pragmatic view instead of stubbornly hanging on to a bad idea? All of us, no matter our profession, will be well served by becoming a multi-disciplinary thinker. It is well recognized in education theory that someone who has a broad base of knowledge with general skills can much more easily achieve deeper knowledge and understanding in one specific area. And although we are geared to study success, the study of failure and misjudgment can be equally beneficial.

A Money Mind is a dynamic mind. And this is a good thing because the stock market is dynamic. It is a system in process that is constantly changing, learning, and adapting. For this reason, the Money Mind is a learning machine. Whatever fixed ideas you have about the stock market, rest assured they will need to be updated in the years ahead. And that means the Money Mind remains humble, conscious of its shortcomings, and not so naïve as to think that success will be the only outcome. But recognizing that the process is sound, a Money Mind is confident, knowing that failures, when they occur, will be few and fixable. And when all these forces come together, it inspires you to share what you have learned, not as a barnstormer or a pedant, but a quiet, calm, trusted adviser.

Most important, when the pieces of the Money Mind coalesce you begin to recognize that you are walking a new path. A path built on virtue, prudent behavior, a sense of justice, and fortitude in thought and action. I cannot promise that walking this path will make you rich. But I can promise you that your life will be enriched.

This is a book about investing. I am not qualified to counsel you on how to live your life, and even if I were, I would not presume. But I do know that when we move through the world with patience and charity, when we face problems rationally rather than with self-defeating emotion, when we enthusiastically embrace new ideas while cherishing deeply held values, life becomes easier, and more fulfilling. In all your roles—as a spouse, a parent, a colleague, a friend, a neighbor, a teacher, a citizen—your life will be richer. Of this, I am certain.

Acknowledgments

First and foremost, I want to express my deep appreciation to Warren Buffett—not only for his teachings but for allowing me to use his copyrighted material from the Berkshire Hathaway annual reports. It is next to impossible to improve upon what Warren has written. I have never hesitated to confess that the success of my books is a testament to him. Warren is, without question, the most successful investor in history and stands out as one of the most important role models any investor could select.

I would also like to thank Charlie Munger for his earliest words of support. Next to studying Warren, the journey of discovering the major mental models recommended by Charlie's "the art of achieving worldly wisdom" has been one of the most fulfilling accomplishments of my career. There is no doubt I am a better investor through being able to think in multidisciplinary terms. Charlie's motivation inspires me each and every day.

In developing my investment skills, no one has been more important in moving me from the theoretical to the practical than Bill Miller. He is a friend and intellectual coach. He introduced me to the Santa Fe Institute, the study of complex adaptive systems, and the deep well that is philosophical thought. Bill's intellectual generosity these past 37 years has meant more to me that I can say.

After I joined Bill Miller at Legg Mason Capital Management I later had the opportunity to study with Michael Mauboussin. An accomplished strategist, writer, and teacher, Michael is adjunct professor of the Security Analysis course at the Columbia Business School. You just get smarter hanging around a guy like Michael and I am grateful for the opportunity. A special thanks also goes to Paul Johnson, another insightful writer and adjunct professor at the

Columbia Business School, where he was responsible for launching the Value Investing course in the Executive MBA Program. Paul graciously agreed to read this book and served as a thoughtful sounding board. Thank you, Paul.

I have been fortunate to be included in a community of Berkshire writers and, as such, I am also a beneficiary of those that have studied Warren, Charlie, and Berkshire Hathaway. Special thanks goes to my friend Andy Kilpatrick; I consider him to be the official historian of Berkshire. I am indebted to Larry Cunningham for his masterful work of organizing Warren's writings and with his other insightful books. Let me also thank Bob Miles not only for his fine books but for his continued support to the study of all things Berkshire. And thanks to Carol Loomis, whose legacy of financial writing is unmatched. I have included a selected library of books on Berkshire in the appendix, along with a bibliography of titles on investing, psychology, and philosophy; deep thanks to all the authors who have contributed to my understanding.

Soon after *The Warren Buffett Way* was published I received a letter from Phil Fisher, then 87 years old. This led to a multiyear correspondence discussing different investment topics. Those early letters encouraged me that I was indeed on the right path. I will always be grateful for our friendship, although sadly it was all too brief.

Many others have been supportive and helpful in my years of studying Warren Buffett, Berkshire Hathaway and the art of investing. Let me begin with thanking Peter Lynch, Jack Bogle, Howard Marks, Peter Bernstein, Charles Ellis, Ed Thorp, John Rothschild, Bill Ruane, Lou Simpson, Ed Haldeman, and Ken Fisher.

I owe special thanks to Bob Coleman, who was the first of the Berkshire faithful to reach out to me while I was writing *The Warren Buffett Way*. Bob has an insatiable curiosity about investing and it has been a great benefit for me to be part of his conversations. Importantly, Bob introduced me to Tom Russo, who added to my understanding of global investing. Thank you, Tom. From there, the floodgates opened. I would also like to thank Chuck Akre, Wally Weitz, Mason Hawkins, Jamie Clark, Tom Gayner, Will

Thorndike, Amanda Agati, and Tren Griffin for their insights and counsel.

I am fortunate to be on a team of energetic and smart colleagues who are willing to think outside the investment box when needed. At EquityCompass Investment Management my thanks go to Richard Cripps, Chris Mutascio, Tom Mulroy, Mike Scherer, Bernie Kavanagh, Tim McCann, Larry Baker, Jim DeMasi, Kenya Overstreet, Bobby Thomas, Lauren Loughlin, Anthony Cersosimo, Sam Cripps, and Felicia Andrews.

My relationship with John Wiley & Sons these past 26 years has been a joy. They are dedicated custodians for *The Warren Buffett Way* and *The Warren Buffett Portfolio*, which I greatly appreciate. When I approached Kevin Harreld, senior acquisitions editor, about *Inside the Ultimate Money Mind* he greeted the project with enthusiasm and excitement, and has championed the book from inception to publication. Thank you, Kevin. I would also like to thank Susan Cerra, senior managing editor at John Wiley & Sons, for her support. And deep gratitude to the immensely talented Kevin West, whose stunning portrait of Warren makes the book cover glow.

In 1993, I was introduced to Myles Thompson, then publisher and editor at John Wiley & Sons, and told him about my idea of writing a book on Warren Buffett. It is my everlasting good fortune that he was willing to take a chance on a first-time writer with no impressive credentials. Had Myles turned me down, my life would have turned out much different, and not likely better. Thanks for everything, Myles.

I cannot adequately express my gratitude to Laurie Harper at Sebastian Literary Agency. Laurie is, in one word, special. She is incredibly smart, kind, and loyal. Okay, more than one word. Laurie navigates the publishing world with integrity, honesty, forthrightness, good humor, and grace. I could not be in better hands. Thank you, Laurie.

Last but certainly not least, I owe Maggie Stuckey, my editor and writing partner, more than I can express for her decades of help in turning a first-time writer into a decent author. This is the 10th book we have written together, and Maggie's special gifts have never shown brighter. The Pulitzer Prize–winning author Robert Caro recalls being told that if he ever wished to achieve something special as a writer he needed to "stop typing with his fingers and start typing with his mind." *Inside the Ultimate Money Mind* is definitely a thinking book and Maggie's ability to get inside my mind and help me connect the pieces is masterful. Although we are separated by a continent, I am always amazed at her ability to instantly and intimately connect to the material I have written. Maggie works tirelessly from one chapter to the next and back again. She is always searching for the best way to structure the material I have written and then articulate it in a clear and concise way. I as the writer and you as the reader are fortunate she chose to share her talents with us.

For all that is good and right about this book, you may thank the people I have mentioned above. For any errors or omissions, I alone am responsible.

Robert G. Hagstrom

Berkshire Hathaway Library

Arnold, Glen. *The Deals of Warren Buffett, Vol. 1: The First $100m.* Hampshire, Great Britain: Harriman House, 2017.

_____. *The Deals of Warren Buffett, Vol. 2: The Making of a Billionaire.* Hampshire, Great Britain: Harriman House, 2019.

Bevelin, Peter. *Seeking Wisdom: From Darwin to Munger.* Malmo, Sweden: Post Scriptum AB, 2003.

_____. *A Few Lessons for Investors and Managers: From Warren Buffett.* Marceline, MO: Wadsworth Publishing Co., 2012.

_____. *"All I Want To Know Is Where I'm Going To Die So I'll Never Go There": Buffett and Munger – A Study of Simplicity and Uncommon, Common Sense.* Marceline, MO: Wadsworth Publishing Co., 2016.

Bloch, Robert L. *My Warren Buffett Bible: A Short and Simple Guide to Rational Investing: 284 Quotes from the World's Most Successful Investor.* New York: Skyhorse Publishing, 2015.

Braem, Daniel. *Building the Next Berkshire.* Strategic Book Publishing Rights Agency, 2009.

Brodersen, Stig, and Preston Pysh. *Warren Buffett Accounting Book: Reading Financial Statements for Value Investing.* Pylon Publishing, 2014.

_____. *Back to School: Question & Answer Session with Business Students.* BN Publishing, 2008.

Buffett, Mary, and David Clark. *Buffettology: The Previously Unexplained Techniques That Have Made Warren Buffett the World's Most Famous Investor.* New York: Rawson Associates, 1997.

Buffett, Mary. *Warren Buffett and the Interpretation of Financial Statements.* New York: Scribner, 2008.

Buffett, Warren E. *Berkshire Hathaway Letters to Shareholders 1965–2019.*

Chan, Ronald W. *Behind the Berkshire Hathaway Curtain: Lessons from Warren Buffett to Business Leaders.* Hoboken, NJ: John Wiley & Sons, 2010.

Clark, David. *The Tao of Charlie Munger: A Compilation of Quotes from Berkshire Hathaway's Vice Chairman on Life, Business, and the Pursuit of Wealth.* New York: Scribner, 2017.

Connors, Richard J. *Warren Buffett on Business: Principles from the Sage of Omaha*. Hoboken, NJ: John Wiley & Sons, 2010.

Cunningham, Lawrence A. *The Essays of Warren Buffett: Lessons for Corporate America*. 5th ed. Lawrence A. Cunningham, 2019.

_____. *Buffett Essays Symposium: With Warren Buffett and Charlie Munger*. A 20th Anniversary Annotated Edition. The Cunningham Group & Harriman House, 2016.

_____. *Berkshire Beyond Buffett: The Enduring Value of Values*. New York: Columbia Business School Publishing, 2014.

_____. *How to Think Like Benjamin Graham and Invest Like Warren Buffett*. New York: McGraw-Hill, 2001.

Cunningham, Lawrence A., and Stephanie Cuba. *Margin of Trust: The Berkshire Business Model*. New York: Columbia Business School Publishing, 2020.

_____. *The Warren Buffett Shareholder: Stories from Inside the Berkshire Hathaway Annual Meeting*. Manhasset, NY: Cunningham Cuba & Harriman House, 2018.

Griffin, Tren. *Charlie Munger: The Complete Investor*. New York: Columbia University Press, 2015.

Hagstrom, Robert G. *The Warren Buffett Way*, 3rd Edition. Hoboken, NJ: John Wiley & Sons, 2014.

_____. *The Warren Buffett Portfolio: Mastering the Power of the Focus Investment Strategy*. New York: John Wiley & Sons, 1999.

Jain, Prem C. *Buffett Beyond Value: Why Warren Buffett Looks to Growth and Management When Investing*. Hoboken, NJ: John Wiley & Sons, 2010.

Janjigian, Vahan. *Even Buffett Isn't Perfect: What Can You Learn and Can't Learn from the World's Greatest Investor*. Portfolio, 2008.

Jordon, Steve. *The Oracle of Omaha: How Warren Buffett and His Hometown Shaped Each Other*. Marceline, MO: Wadsworth Publishing Co., 2013.

Keough, Donald R. *The Ten Commandments for Business Failure*. New York: Portfolio Penguin, 2011.

Kilpatrick, Andrew. *Of Permanent Value: The Story of Warren Buffett 2020 Elephant Edition*. Birmingham, AL: Andy Kilpatrick Publishing Empire, 2020.

_____. *Warren Buffett: The Good Guy of Wall Street*. New York: Donald I. Fine, 1992.

Kratter, Matthew R. *Invest Like Warren Buffett: Powerful Strategies for Building Wealth*. Independently published, 2016.

Light, Murray B. *From Butler to Buffett*. Amherst, NY: Prometheus Books, 2004.

Linder, Karen. *The Women of Berkshire Hathaway: Lessons from Warren Buffett's Female CEOs and Directors*. Hoboken, NJ: John Wiley & Sons, 2012.

Loomis, Carol J. *Tap Dancing to Work: Warren Buffett on Practically Everything, 1996–2012*. New York: Portfolio/Penguin, 2012.

Lowe, Janet. *Warren Buffett Speaks: Wit and Wisdom from the World's Greatest Investor*. Hoboken, NJ: John Wiley & Sons, 2007.

_____. *Damn Right! Behind the Scenes with Berkshire Hathaway Billionaire Charlie Munger*. New York: John Wiley & Sons, 2000.

Lowenstein, Roger. *Buffett: The Making of an American Capitalist*. New York: Random House, 1995.

Lu, Yefei. *Inside the Investments of Warren Buffett: Twenty Cases*. New York: Columbia Business School Publishing, 2016.

Matthews, Jeff. *Pilgrimage to Warren Buffett's Omaha: A Hedge Funds Manager's Dispatches from Inside the Berkshire Hathaway Annual Meeting*. New York: McGraw-Hill, 2008.

Mayhew, Ricard. *Manage Your Money Like Warren Buffett: How Warren Buffett Has Handled Some of the Financial Aspects of His Life*. CreateSpace Independent Publishing Platform, 2015.

Miles, Robert P. *The Warren Buffett CEO: Secrets from the Berkshire Hathaway Managers*. New York: John Wiley & Sons, 2002.

_____. *Warren Buffett Wealth: Principles and Practical Methods Used by the World's Greatest Investor*. Hoboken, NJ: John Wiley & Sons, 2004.

_____. *The World's Greatest Investment: 101 Reasons to Own Berkshire Hathaway*. Tampa, FL: Robert P. Miles, 1999.

Miller, Jeremy. *Warren Buffett's Ground Rules: Words of Wisdom from the Partnership Letters of the World's Greatest Investor*. London, UK: Profile Books, 2016.

Minaker, F. C. *One Thousand Ways to Make $1,000*. Austin, TX: Clinton T. Greenleaf, III, 2016.

Munger, Charles T., and Peter Kaufman, ed. *Poor Charlie's Almanack: The Wit and Wisdom of Charles T. Munger*. Marceline, MO: Wadsworth Publishing Co., 2005.

O'Loughlin, James. *The Real Warren Buffett: Managing Capital, Leading People*. London: Nicholas Brealey Publishing, 2002.

Pardoe, James. *How Warren Buffett Does It: 24 Simple Investing Strategies from the World's Greatest Value Investor*. New York: McGraw-Hill Education, 2005.

Pecaut, Daniel, and Corey Wrenn. *University of Berkshire Hathaway: 30 Years of Lessons Learned from Warren Buffet & Charlie Munger at the Annual Shareholders Meeting.* Sioux City, IA: Daniel Pecaut & Corey Wrenn, 2017.

Pick, Margaret Moos. *See's Famous Old-Time Candies.* San Francisco, CA: Chronicle Books, 2005.

Pysh, Preston G. *Warren Buffett's Three Favorite Books.* Pylon Publishing.

Rittenhouse, L .J. *Investing Between The Lines: How to Make Smarter Decisions by Decoding CEO Communications.* New York: McGraw-Hill, 2013.

_____. *Buffett Bites: The Essential Investor's Guide to Warren Buffett's Shareholder Letters.* New York: McGraw Hill, 2010.

_____. *Do Business with People You Can Trust: Balancing Profits and Principles.* L.J Rittenhouse, 2007.

Schroeder, Alice. *The Snowball: Warren Buffett and the Business of Life.* New York: Bantam Dell, 2008.

Swedore, Larry E. *Think and Invest Like Warren Buffett: A Winning Strategy to Help You Achieve Your Financial and Life Goals.* New York: McGraw-Hill, 2013.

Tavakoli, Janet. *Dear Mr. Buffett: What an Investor Learns 1,269 Miles from Wall Street.* Hoboken, NJ: John Wiley & Sons, 2009.

Train, John. *The Midas Touch: The Strategies That Have Made Warren Buffett America's Pre-eminent Investor.* New York: Harper & Row, 1987.

For Further Reading
INVESTING, PSYCHOLOGY, AND PHILOSOPHY

Investing

Anderson, Philip W., Kenneth Arrow, and David Pines. *The Economy as an Evolving Complex System.* New York: CRC Press, 1988.

Arthur, W. Brian. *Increasing Returns and Path Dependence in the Economy.* Ann Harbor, MI: The University of Michigan Press, 2008.

_____. *Complexity and the Economy.* New York: Oxford University Press, 2015.

Arthur, W. Brian, Steven N. Durlauf, and David A. Lane. *The Economy as an Evolving Complex System II.* Reading, MA: Addison-Wesley, 1997.

Baid, Gautam. *The Joys of Compounding: The Passionate Pursuit of Lifelong Learning.* Rev. ed. New York: Columbia Business School Publishing, 2020.

Bernstein, Peter L. *Capital Ideas: The Improbable Origins of Modern Wall Street.* New York: The Free Press, 1992.

_____. *Capital Ideas Evolving.* Hoboken, NJ: John Wiley & Sons, 2007.

_____. *Against the Gods: The Remarkable Story of Risk.* New York: John Wiley & Sons, 1996.

Biggs, Barton. *Hedge Hogging.* Hoboken, NJ: John Wiley & Sons, 2006.

Bogle, John C. *The Clash of Cultures: Investment vs. Speculation.* Hoboken, NJ: John Wiley & Sons, 2012.

_____. *Enough: True Measures of Money, Business, and Life.* Hoboken, NJ: John Wiley & Sons, 2009.

Calandro, Joseph Jr. *Applied Value Investing: The Practical Applications of Benjamin Graham's and Warren Buffett's Valuation Principles to Acquisitions, Catastrophe Pricing, and Business Execution.* New York: McGraw-Hill, 2009.

Carlen, Joe. *The Einstein of Money: The Life and Timeless Financial Wisdom of Benjamin Graham.* Amherst, NY: Prometheus Books, 2012.

Carret, Philip L. *The Art of Speculation.* Mansfield, CT: Martino, 2012.

Chancellor, Edward, ed. *Capital Returns: Investing Through the Capital Cycle. A Money Manager's Reports, 2002–2015.* London, UK: Palgrave, 2016.

Chatman, Seymour, ed. *Benjamin Graham: The Memoirs of the Dean of Wall Street.* New York: McGraw-Hill, 1996.

Cunningham, Lawrence A., Torkell, T. Eide, and Patrick Hargreaves. *Quality Investing: Owning the Best Companies for the Long Term.* Hampshire, Great Britain: Harriman House, 1988.

Ellis, Charles D., and James R. Vertin, eds. *Classics: An Investor's Anthology.* Dow Jones & Company, 1989.

_____. *Classics II: Another Investor's Anthology.* Homewood, IL: Business One Irwin, 1991.

Damodaran, Aswath. *Damodaran on Valuation: Security Analysis for Investment and Corporate Finance.* 2nd ed. Hoboken, NJ: John Wiley & Sons 2006.

Fisher, Philip A. *Common Stocks and Uncommon Profits: And Other Writings: Wiley Investment Classic.* Canada: John Wiley & Sons, 1996.

Furhan, William E., Jr. *Financial Strategy: Studies in the Creation, Transfer, and Destruction of Shareholder Value.* Homewood, IL: Richard D. Irwin, 1979.

Graham, Benjamin, and David Dodd. *Security Analysis: The Class of 1934 Edition.* New York: McGraw-Hill Book Company, 1934.

Graham, Benjamin. *Security Analysis,* 6th ed. New York: McGraw-Hill, 2009.

Graham, Benjamin, and Charles McGolrick. *Interpretation of Financial Statement.* New York: Harper & Row Publishers, 1964.

Graham, Benjamin. *The Intelligent Investor: A Book of Practical Counsel.* 4th rev. ed. New York: Harper & Row, 1973.

_____. *The Intelligent Investor: A Book of Practical Counsel.* Rev. ed., with updated commentary by Jason Zweig. New York: Harper Business Essentials, 2003.

Greenblatt, Joel. *You Can Be a Stock Market Genius (Even If You're Not Too Smart): Uncover the Secret Hiding Places of Stock Market Profits.* New York: Simon & Schuster, 1997.

Greenwald, Bruce C.N., Judd Kahn, Paul D. Sonkin, and Michael van Biema. *Value Investing: From Graham to Buffett and Beyond.* Hoboken, NJ: John Wiley & Sons, 2001.

Greenwald, Bruce, and Judd Kahn. *Competition Demystified: A Radically Simplified Approach to Business Strategy.* London, England: Penguin Books, 2005.

Hagstrom, Robert G. *Investing: The Last Liberal Art.* 2nd ed. New York: Columbia Business School Publishing, 2013.

Haskel, Jonathan, and Stian Westlake. *Capitalism without Capital: The Rise of the Intangible Economy.* Princeton, NJ: Princeton University Press, 2018.

Keynes, John Maynard. *The General Theory of Employment, Interest, and Money.* New York: Harcourt Brace & Company, 1964.

Knight, Frank H. *Risk, Uncertainty and Profit.* Washington, DC: Beard Books, 2002.

Koller, Tim, Mark Goedhart, and David Wessels. *Valuation: Measuring and Managing the Value of Companies.* Hoboken, NJ: John Wiley & Sons 2016.

_____. *The Four Cornerstones of Corporate Finance.* Hoboken, NJ: John Wiley & Sons 2011.

Lefèvre, Edwin. *Reminiscences of a Stock Operator.* New York: John Wiley & Sons, 1994.

Lo, Andrew W. *Adaptive Markets: Financial Evolution at the Speed of Thought.* Princeton, NJ: Princeton University Press, 2017.

Lo, Andrew W., and A. Craig MacKinelay. *A Non-Random Walk Down Wall Street.* Princeton, NJ: Princeton University Press, 1999.

Loeb, Gerald M. *The Battle of Investment Survival.* New York: John Wiley & Sons 1996.

Lowe, Janet. *Benjamin Graham on Value Investing: Lessons from the Dean of Wall Street.* Chicago, IL: Dearborn Financial, 1994.

_____. *The Rediscovered Benjamin Graham: Selected Writings of the Wall Street Legend.* New York: John Wiley & Sons, 1999.

_____. *The Man Who Beats the S&P: Investing with Bill Miller.* Canada: John Wiley & Sons, 2002.

Madden, Bartley J. *Valuation Creation Thinking.* Napersville, IL: Learning What Works, 2016.

Malkiel, Burton G. *A Random Walk Down Wall Street.* New York: W.W. Norton & Company, 1973.

Marks, Howard. *Mastering the Market Cycle: Getting the Odds on Your Side.* New York: Houghton Mifflin Harcourt, 2018.

_____. *The Most Important Thing: Uncommon Sense for the Thoughtful Investor.* Columbia Business School Publishing, 2011.

Mauboussin, Michael J. *More Than You Know: Finding Financial Wisdom in Unconventional Places.* New York: Columbia University Press, 2006.

_____. *Think Twice: Harnessing the Power of Counterintuition.* Boston: Harvard Business Press, 2009.

_____. *The Success Equation: Untangling Skill and Luck in Business, Sports, and Investing.* Boston: Harvard Business Review Press, 2012.

Perez, Carlota. *Technological Revolutions and Financial Capital: The Dynamics of Bubbles and Golden Ages.* Northampton, MA: Edward Elgar Publishing, 2002.

Poundstone, William. *Fortune's Formula: The Untold Story of the Scientific Betting System That Beat the Casinos and Wall Street.* New York: Hill and Wang, 2005.

Rappaport, Alfred. *Creating Shareholder Value: The New Standard for Business Performance.* New York: The Free Press, 1986.

_____. *Saving Capitalism from Short-Termism: How to Build Long-Term Value and Take Back Our Financial Future.* New York: McGraw-Hill, 2011.

Rappaport, Alfred, and Michael J. Mauboussin. *Expectations Investing: Reading Stock Prices for Better Returns.* Boston: Harvard Business School Press, 2001.

Rosenzweig, Phil, *The Halo Effect: And the Eight Other Business Delusions That Deceive Managers.* New York: Free Press, 2007.

Rubinstein, Mark. *A History of the Theory of Investments.* Hoboken, NJ: John Wiley & Sons, 2006.

Schwed, Jr. Fred. *Where Are the Customer's Yachts? Or A Good Hard Look at Wall Street.* Burlington, VT: Fraser Publishing Company, 1955.

Siegel, Jeremy J. *Stocks for the Long Run.* 2nd ed. New York: McGraw-Hill, 1998.

Smith, Adam. *The Money Game.* New York: Random House, 1968.

_____. *Supermoney.* Hoboken, NJ: John Wiley & Sons, 2006.

Smith, Edgar Lawrence. *Common Stocks as Long Term Investments.* New York: The MacMillan Company, 1928. Revised publication by Kessinger Publishing, LLC.

Sonkin, Paul D., and Paul Johnson. *Pitch the Perfect Investment: The Essential Guide to Winning on Wall Street.* Hoboken, NJ: John Wiley & Sons, 2017.

Spier, Guy. *The Education of a Value Investor: My Transformative Quest for Wealth, Wisdom, and Enlightenment.* New York: St. Martin's Press, 2014.

Thomas, Brian, ed. *Columbia Business School: A Century of Ideas.* New York: Columbia University Press, 2016.

Thorndike, William N., Jr. *The Outsiders: Eight Conventional CEOs and Their Radically Rational Blueprint for Success.* Boston: Harvard Business Review Press, 2012.

Thorp, Edward O. *A Man for All Markets: From Las Vegas to Wall Street, How I Beat the Dealer and the Market.* New York: Random House, 2019.

_____. *Beat The Dealer: A Winning Strategy for the Game of Twenty-One.* New York: Vintage Books, 1966.

Thorp, Edward O., and Sheen T. Kasssouf. *Beat the Market: A Scientific Stock Market System.* New York: Random House, 1967.

Towle, Margaret M., ed. *Masters of Finance: Interviews with Some of the Greatest Minds in Investing and Economics.* Greenwood Village, CO: IMCA, 2014.

Train, John. *The Money Masters: Nine Great Investors: Their Winning Strategies and How You Can Apply Them.* New York: Penguin Books, 1980.

Treynor, Jack L. *Treynor on Institutional Investing.* Hoboken, NJ: John Wiley & Sons, 2008.

Walsh, Justyn. *Keynes and the Market: How the World's Greatest Economist Overturned Conventional Wisdom and Made a Fortune on the Stock Market.* Hoboken, NJ: John Wiley & Sons, 2008.

Williams, John Burr. *The Theory of Investment Value.* Boston: Harvard University Press, 2002.

Psychology

Ainsle, George. *Breakdown of Will.* New York: Cambridge University Press, 2001.

Akerloff, George A., and Robert J. Shiller. *Animal Spirits: How Human Psychology Drives the Economy and Why It Matters for Global Capitalism.* Princeton, NJ: Princeton University Press, 2009.

Baron, Jonathan. *Thinking and Deciding.* New York: Cambridge University Press, 2008.

Belsky, Gary, and Thomas Gilovich. *Why Smart People Make Big Mistakes— And How to Correct Them.* New York: Simon & Schuster, 1999.

Cialdini, Robert B. *The Psychology of Persuasion.* New York: William Morrow, 1993.

_____. *Persuasion: A Revolutionary Way to Influence and Persuade.* New York: Simon & Schuster, 2016.

Duke, Annie. *Thinking in Bets: Making Smarter Decisions When You Don't Have All the Facts.* New York: Portfolio/Penguin, 2018.

Galbraith, John Kenneth. *A Short History of Financial Euphoria.* New York: Penguin Group, 1993.

Gawande, Atul. *The Checklist Manifesto: How to Get Things Right.* New York: Metropolitan Books, 2009.

Gennaioli, Nicola, and Andrei Shlefler. *A Crisis of Belief: Investor Psychology and Financial Fragility.* Princeton, NJ: Princeton University Press, 2018.

Gigerenzer, Gerd, Peter M. Todd, and the ABC Research Group. *Simple Heuristics That Make Us Smart.* New York: Oxford University Press, 1999.

Glovich, Thomas, Dale Griffin, and Daniel Kahneman, eds. *Heuristics and Biases: The Psychology of Intuitive Judgment.* New York: Cambridge University Press, 2002.

Hagstrom, Robert G. *The Detective and the Investor: Uncovering Investment Techniques from the Legendary Sleuths.* New York: Texere, 2002.

Halpern, Paul. *The Pursuit of Destiny: A History of Prediction.* Cambridge, MA: Perseus Publishing, 2000.

Kahneman, Daniel. *Thinking Fast and Slow.* New York: Farrar, Straus and Giroux, 2011.

Kahneman, Daniel, Paul Slovic, and Amos Tversky, eds. *Judgment under Uncertainty: Heuristics and Biases.* New York: Cambridge University Press, 1982.

Kindleberger, Charles P. *Manias, Panics, and Crashes: A History of Financial Crises.* New York: John Wiley & Sons, 1996.

Konnikova, Maria. *The Biggest Bluff: How I Learned to Pay Attention, Master Myself, and Win.* New York: Penguin, 2020.

Kurtz, Howard. *The Fortune Tellers: Inside Wall Street's Game of Money, Media, and Manipulation.* New York: Free Press, 2000.

Lakoff, George, and Mark Johnson. *Metaphors We Live By.* Chicago, IL: The University of Chicago Press, 1980.

Le Bon, Gustave. *The Crowd.* New York: Penguin Books, 1997.

Lewis, Michael. *The Undoing Project: A Friendship That Changed Our Minds.* New York: W.W. Norton & Company, 2017.

Mackay, Charles. *Extraordinary Popular Delusions and the Madness of Crowds.* New York: John Wiley & Sons, 1996.

Page, Scott. *The Model Thinker: What You Need to Know to Make Data Work for You.* New York: Basic Books, 2018.

Russo, J. Edward, and Paul J. H. Shoemaker. *Decision Traps: Ten Barriers to Brilliant Decision-Making and How to Overcome Them.* New York: Doubleday, 1989.

_____ *Winning Decisions: Getting It Right the First Time.* New York: Doubleday, 2002.

Sapolsky, Robert M. *Why Zebras Don't Get Ulcers: The Acclaimed Guide to Stress, Stress-Related Diseases, and Coping.* New York: Henry Holt & Company, 2004.

Shefrin, Hersh. *Beyond Greed and Fear: Understanding Behavioral Finance and the Psychology of Investing.* Boston, MA: Harvard Business School Press, 2000.

Sherden, William A. *The Fortune Sellers: The Big Business of Buying and Selling Predictions.* New York: John Wiley & Sons, 1998.

Shermer, Michael. *Why People Believe Weird Things: Pseudoscience, Superstition, and Other Confusions of Our Time.* New York: W. H. Freeman and Company, 1997.

_____. *How We Believe: The Search for God in an Age of Science.* New York: W. H. Freeman and Company, 2000.

Shiller, Robert J. *Market Volatility,* Boston, MA: MIT Press, 1997.

_____. *Irrational Exuberance.* Princeton, NJ: Princeton University Press, 2000.

_____. *Narrative Economics: How Stories Go Viral and Driven Major Economic Events.* Princeton, NJ: Princeton University Press, 2019.

Shleifer, Andrei. *Inefficient Markets: An Introduction to Behavioral Thought.* New York: Oxford University Press, 2000.

Statman, Meir. *Finance for Normal People: How Investors and Markets Behave.* New York: Oxford University Press, 2017.

Tavris, Carol, and Elliot Aronson. *Mistakes Were Made: But Not by Me.* New York: Houghton Mifflin Harcourt, 2007.

Thaler, Richard H. *Misbehaving: The Making of Behavioral Economics.* New York: W.W. Norton & Company, 2010.

_____. *The Winner's Curse: Paradoxes and Anomalies of Economic Life.* Princeton, NJ: Princeton University Press, 1992.

Thaler, Richard H., and Cass R. Sunstein. *Nudge: Improving Decisions about Health, Wealth, and Happiness.* New York: Penguin Books, 2009.

Tuckett, David. *Minding the Markets: An Emotional Finance View of Financial Instability.* London: Palgrave MacMillan, 2011.

Zeckhauser, Richard J., Ralph L. Keeney, and James K. Sebenius, eds. *Wise Choices: Decisions, Games, and Negotiations.* Boston, MA: Harvard Business School Press, 1996.

Zweig, Jason. *Your Money and Your Brain: How the New Science of Neuroeconomics Can Help Make You Rich.* New York: Simon & Schuster, 2007.

Philosophy

Abbott, Edwin A. *Flatland: A Romance of Many Dimensions.* New York: Barnes & Noble Books, 1963.

Audi, Robert. *The Architecture of Reason: The Structure and Substance of Rationality.* New York: Oxford University Press, 2001.

Buell, Lawrence. *Emerson*. Cambridge, MA: The Belknap Press of Harvard University Press, 2003.

Cottingham, John, ed. *Descartes: Meditations on First Philosophy with Selections from the Objections and Replies*. Cambridge, UK: Cambridge University Press, 2017.

Botton, Alain de. *The Consolations of Philosophy*. New York: Pantheon Books, 2000.

Dickstein, Morris, ed. *The Revival of Pragmatism: New Essays on Social Thought, Law, and Culture*. Durham, NC: Duke University Press, 1998.

Dörner, Dietrich. *The Logic of Failure: Recognizing and Avoiding Error in Complex Situations*. Reading, MA: Perseus Books, 1996.

Durant, Will. *The Story of Philosophy*. New York: A Touchstone Book, 1961.

Edman, Irwin *Emerson's Essays, Introduction*. New York: Harper & Row, 1951.

Elster, Jon. *Ulysses and the Sirens: Studies in Rationality and Irrationality*. New York: Cambridge University Press, 1990.

Epstein, David. *Range: Why Generalists Triumph in a Specialized World:* New York: Riverhead Books, 2019.

Esplund, Lance. *The Art of Looking: How to Read Modern and Contemporary Art*. New York: Basic Books, 2018.

Goetzmann, William H. *Beyond the Revolution: A History of American Thought from Paine to Pragmatism*. New York: Basic Books, 2009.

Grayling, A.C. *The History of Philosophy*. London: Viking, 2019.

Guyer, Paul, and Allen W. Wood, eds. *The Cambridge Edition of the Works of Immanuel Kant*. New York: Cambridge University Press, 2000.

Hadot, Pierre. *What Is Ancient Philosophy? (trans. Michael Chase)*. Cambridge, MA: The Belknap Press of Harvard University Press, 2002.

Hall, Edith. *Aristotle's Way: How Ancient Wisdom Can Change Your Life*. New York: Penguin Press, 2019.

Herman, Arthur. *How the Scots Invented the World: A True Story of How Western Europe's Poorest Nation Created Our World and Everything in It*. New York: Three Rivers Press, 2001.

Hyland, Drew A. *Philosophy of Sport*. St. Paul, MN: Paragon House, 1990.

James, William. *Pragmatism*. New York: Dover Publications, 1995.

Kaag, John. *Sick Souls, Healthy Minds: How William James Can Save Your Life*. Princeton, NJ: Princeton University Press, 2020.

_____. *American Philosophy: A Love Story*. New York: Farrar, Straus and Giroux, 2016.

Kant, Immanuel. *Critique of Pure Reason (Translated by Werner S. Pluhar)*. Indianapolis, IN: Hackett Publishing Company, 1996.

Kegan, Robert, and Lisa Laskow Lahey. *Immunity to Change: How to Overcome It and Unlock the Potential in Yourself and Your Organization.* Boston, MA: Harvard Business Press, 2009.

Klagge, James C., ed. *Wittgenstein Biography and Philosophy.* New York; Cambridge University Press, 2011.

Kripke, Saul A. *Wittgenstein on Rules and Private Language.* Cambridge, MA: Harvard University Press, 1982.

Kuhn, Thomas S. *The Structure of Scientific Revolutions.* Chicago, IL: University of Chicago Press, 1970.

Lally, Richard, Douglas Anderson, and John Kagg, eds. *Pragmatism and the Philosophy of Sport.* Lanham, MD: Lexington Books, 2013.

Menand, Louis. *The Metaphysical Club.* New York; Farrar, Straus and Giroux, 2001.

_____. *Pragmatism: A Reader.* New York: Vintage Books, 1997.

Mercier, Hugo, and Dan Sperber. *The Enigma of Reason.* Cambridge, MA: Harvard University Press, 2017.

Miller, William Ian. *The Mystery of Courage.* Cambridge, MA: Harvard University Press, 2000.

Monk, Ray. *Ludwig Wittgenstein: The Duty of Genius.* New York: Penguin Books, 1990.

Putnam, Ruth Anna, ed. *The Cambridge Companion to William James.* New York: Cambridge University Press, 1997.

Reid, Heather L., *Introduction to the Philosophy of Sport.* Lanham, MD: Rowman & Littlefield Publishers 2012.

Richardson, Robert D. *Emerson: The Mind on Fire.* Berkley, CA: University of California Press, 1995.

_____. *William James: In the Maelstrom of American Modernism.* Boston, MA: Houghton Mifflin Company, 2006.

Ridley, Matt. *The Rational Optimist: How Prosperity Evolves.* New York: Harper, 2010.

Ryall, Emily. *Philosophy of Sports.* New York: Bloomsbury Publishing, 2016.

Schjeldahl, Peter. *Hot, Cold, Heavy, Light: 100 Art Writings 1988–2018.* New York: Abrams Press, 2019.

_____. *Let's See: Writings on Art from The New Yorker.* New York: Thames & Hudson, 2008.

Shook, John R. *Dewey's Empirical Theory of Knowledge and Reality.* Nashville, TN: Vanderbilt University Press, 2000.

Simon, Herbert A. *Models of Bounded Rationality: Empirically Grounded Economic Reason.* Vol. 3. Cambridge, MA, MIT Press, 1997.

Simon, Linda. *Genuine Reality: A Life of William James.* New York: Harcourt Brace & Company, 1998.

Sluga, Hans, and David G. Stern, eds. *The Cambridge Companion to Wittgenstein.* New York: Cambridge University Press, 1996.

Smith, Justin E.H. *Irrationality: A History of the Dark Side of Reason.* Princeton, NJ: Princeton University Press, 2019.

_____. *The Philosopher: A History in 6 Types.* Princeton, NJ: Princeton University Press, 2016.

Stanovich, Keith E. *What Intelligence Tests Miss: The Psychology of Rational Thought.* New Haven, CT: Yale University Press, 2009.

_____. *Decision Making and Rationality in the Modern World.* New York: Oxford University Press, 2010.

_____. *Rationality and the Reflective Mind.* New York: Oxford University Press, 2011.

Stanovich, Keith E., Richard F. West, and Maggie E. Toplak. *The Rationality Quotient: Toward a Test of Rational Thinking.* Cambridge, MA: MIT Press, 2016.

Svendsen, Lars. *A Philosophy of Fear.* London, UK: Reaktion Books, 2008.

Whelan, Richard, ed. *Self-Reliance: The Wisdom of Ralph Waldo Emerson as Inspiration for Daily Living.* New York: Bell Tower, 1991.

White, Morton. *Pragmatism and the American Mind: Essays and Reviews in Philosophy and Intellectual History.* New York: Oxford University Press, 1973.

Whitehead, Alfred North. *Process and Reality.* New York: Free Press, 1978.

Wilson, Edward O. *Consilience: A Unity of Knowledge.* New York: Vintage Books, 1998.

Wittgenstein, Ludwig. *Culture and Value. (trans. Peter Winch).* Chicago, IL: University of Chicago Press, 1980.

Zilcosky, John, and Marlo A. Burks. *The Allure of Sports in Western Culture.* Toronto, Canada: University of Toronto Press, 2019.

Notes

Chapter 1: The Young Warren Buffett

1. F. C. Minaker, *One Thousand Ways to Make $1000: Practical Suggestions, Based on Actual Experience, for Starting a Business of Your Own and Making Money in Your Spare Time* (The Dartnell Corporation, 1936), p. 14.
2. Alice Schroeder, *The Snowball: Warren Buffett and the Business of Life* (New York: Bantam Dell, 2008), p. 64.
3. Minaker, *One Thousand Ways*, p. 15.
4. Ibid.
5. Ibid.
6. Ibid., p. 17.
7. Ibid.
8. Andrew Kilpatrick, *Of Permanent Value: The Story of Warren Buffett: 2015 Golden Anniversary Edition* (Birmingham, AL: AKPE Publishing, 2015), p. 39.
9. Ibid., p. 40.
10. Schroeder, *The Snowball*, p. 129.
11. Ibid., p. 130.
12. Ibid., p. 146.
13. Roger Lowenstein, *The Making of an American Capitalist* (New York: Random House, 2008), p. 46.
14. Jeremy C. Miller, *Warren Buffett's Ground Rules* (New York: HarperCollins, 2016), p. xii.
15. Lowenstein, *The Making of an American Capitalist*, p. 114.
16. John Train, *The Masters*, p. 12.
17. Miller, *Warren Buffett's Ground Rules*, p. 250.
18. Lowenstein, *The Making of an American Capitalist*, p. 120.
19. Berkshire Hathaway 2014 Annual Report, p. 25.
20. Ibid., p. 30.

Chapter 2: Developing an Investment Philosophy

1. John R. Minahan and Thusith I. Mahanama, "Investment Philosophy and Manager Evaluation, Again," *The Journal of Investing* (Spring 2017), 26–32.
2. Alice Schroeder, *The Snowball: Warren Buffett and the Business of Life* (New York: Bantam Dell, 2008), p. 643.
3. Roger Lowenstein, *The Making of an American Capitalist*, p. 5.

4. David McCullough, *The Pioneers: The Heroic Story of the Settlers Who Brought the American Ideal West* (New York: Simon & Schuster, 2019), p. 12.

5. Greg Ip, "The Era of Fed Power Is Over: Prepare for a More Perilous Road Ahead," *Wall Street Journal* (January 15, 2020).

6. Lowenstein, *The Making of an American Capitalist*, p. 11.

7. Steve Jordan, *The Oracle & Omaha* (Omaha World Herald, 2013), p. 19.

8. Michael Dirda, *Bound to Please: An Extraordinary One-Volume Literary Education* (W.W. Norton, 2004), p. 118.

9. Lowenstein, *The Making of an American Capitalist*, p. 36.

10. Jordan, *The Oracle & Omaha*, p. 33.

11. As told to me by Steve Jordan on September 25, 2019, who in turn had the conversation with Warren Buffett.

12. Lowenstein, *The Making of an American Capitalist*, p. 26.

13. *Becoming Warren Buffett*, HBO Documentary, February 11, 2017.

14. Andrew Kilpatrick, *Of Permanent Value*, p. 81.

15. Steve Jordan, September 25, 2019.

16. Irving Kahn and Robert Milne, *Benjamin Graham: The Father of Financial Analysis*, Occasional Paper Number 5, The Financial Analysts Research Foundation, 1977.

17. Benjamin Graham, *The Intelligent Investor: The Definitive Book on Value Investing, Revised Edition*, updated with new commentary by Jason Zweig (New York: Harper Business Essentials, 2003), p. xi.

18. Benjamin Graham, *The Intelligent Investor*, p. 287.

19. Joe Carlen, *The Einstein of Money*, p. 37.

20. Lowenstein, *The Making of an American Capitalist*, p. 36.

21. Ibid., p. 44.

22. Ibid., p. ix.

23. Jason Zweig, "When Your Neighbors Move Into Your Investment Portfolio," *Wall Street Journal* (December 7, 2018): B1.

24. Janet Lowe, *Benjamin Graham on Value Investing*, p. 12.

25. Graham, *Intelligent Investor*, p. 108.

26. Berkshire Hathaway 1987 Annual Report, p. 12.

27. Ibid.

28. The reference was made by Lou Simpson noted in Janet Lowe's book *Damn Right!* (New York: John Wiley & Sons, 2000), p. 77.

29. Robert Lenzner and Robert Dindiller, "The Not So Silent Partner," *Forbes* (January 22, 1996): 78.

30. See: Peter Bevelin, *Seeking Wisdom from Darwin To Munger* (Malmo, Sweden: Post Scriptum AB, 2003); Tren Griffin, *Charlie Munger: The Complete Investor* (New York: Columbia Business School Publishing, 2015); Janet Lowe, *Damn Right!*.

31. Robert Hagstrom, *Investing: The Last Liberal Art*, 2nd ed. (New York: Columbia Business School Publishing, 2015).

32. Dietrich Dörner, *The Logic of Failure: Recognizing and Avoiding Error in Complex Situations* (New York: Perseus Books, 1996), pp. 10.

33. Charles T. Munger, *Poor Charlie's Almanack: The Wit and Wisdom of Charles T. Munger* (Virginia Beach, VA: PCA Publications, 2005), pp. 393, 394.

34. Ibid., p. 398.

35. Munger, *Poor Charlie's Almanack*, pp. 430–433.

36. Dörner, *Logic of Failure*, pp. 186, 187.

37. Munger, *Poor Charlie's Almanack*, pp. 443, 444.

38. Lowenstein, *The Making of an American Capitalist*, p. xv.

39. Berkshire Hathaway 2015 Annual Meeting.

40. A. C. Grayling, *History of Philosophy* (London: Viking, 2019), p. 256.

41. Berkshire Hathaway 2014 Annual Report, p. 26.

42. Robert Lenzner, "Warren's Idea of Heaven," *Forbes* (October 18, 1993).

43. Griffin, *Charlie Munger*, p. 41.

44. Jason Zweig and Nicole Friedman, "Charlie Munger Unplugged," *Wall Street Journal*, May 3, 2019.

45. Remarks at Daily Journal Annual Conference, February 11, 2020; reported by Alex Griese in Whitney Tilson's blog

46. Griffin, *Charlie Munger*, p. 40.

47. Whitney Tilson blog.

48. Berkshire Hathaway 2010 Annual Meeting; author's personal notes. Also see: Daniel Pecaut and Corey Wrenn, *University of Berkshire Hathaway* (Sioux City, IA: Pecaut and Company, 2017), p. 215.

49. Charles S. Pierce, "How to Make Our Ideas Clear," *Popular Science Monthly* (January, 1878). Also in *Pragmatism: A Reader*, ed. Louis Menand (New York: Random House, 1997), p. 26.

50. John Kaag, *Sick Souls, Healthy Minds: How William James Can Save Your Life* (Princeton: Princeton University Press, 2020), p. 4.

51. Ibid., p. 7.

52. William James, "Pragmatism: Conception of Truth," Lecture 6. *Pragmatism* (New York: Dover Publications 1907, 1955), p. 24.

53. Ibid., p. 26.

54. Ibid., p. 31.

55. John Kaag, *American Philosophy: A Love Story* (New York: Farrar, Straus, and Giroux, 2016), p. 98.

56. Ibid.

57. Interview with Author, April 10, 2022.

Chapter 3: The Evolution of Value Investing

1. Brian Thomas, ed., *Columbia Business School: A Century of Ideas* (New York: Columbia University Press, 2016). The background information on Ben Graham's history at Columbia was referenced from this work.

2. Ibid, p. 32.

3. Ibid., p. 33.

4. Louis Rich, "Sagacity and Securities," *New York Times* (December 2, 1934), p. 13.

5. Benjamin Graham and David Dodd, *Security Analysis: The Classic 1934 Edition* (New York: McGraw-Hill, 1934), p. 14.
6. Ibid., p. 305.
7. Ibid., p. 23.
8. Janet Lowe, *Benjamin Graham on Value Investing: Lessons from the Dean of Wall Street* (Dearborn: Dearborn Financial Publishing, 1994). The background information on Ben Graham was referenced from this work.
9. Graham and Dodd, *Security Analysis*, p. 108.
10. Ibid., p. 303.
11. Ibid., pp. 612–613.
12. Berkshire Hathaway 1987 Annual Report.
13. Ibid.
14. As discussed with the author in London, UK on May 23, 2018. Confirmed in an email on March 22, 2020.
15. Andrew Kilpatrick, *Of Permanent Value: The Story of Warren Buffett: 2015 Golden Anniversary Edition* (Birmingham, AL: AKPE Publishing, 2015), p. 39.
16. Ibid., p. 40.
17. Berkshire Hathaway 1992 Annual Report.
18. Ibid.
19. Ibid.
20. Eugene F. Fama and Kenneth French, "The Cross-Section of Expected Returns," *Journal of Finance* XLVII, no. 2 (June 1992): 427–465; Fama and French, "Size and Book-to-Market Factors in Earnings and Returns," *Journal of Finance* (March 1995): 131–155.
21. Berkshire Hathaway 1990 Report.
22. Baruch Lev and Anup Srivastava, "Explaining the Demise of Value Investing." *SSRN Electronic Journal* ID3446895, September 4, 2019.
23. Ibid.
24. Eugene Fama and Kenneth French, "The Cross-Section of Expected Returns," *The Journal of Finance* 47, no. 2 (June 1992).
25. Amy Whyte, "Ken French: 'There Is No Way to Tell' If Value Premium Is Disappearing," *Institutional Investor* (January 29, 2020).
26. Michael Maubuossin and Daniel Callahan, "What Does a Price-Earnings Multiple Mean? An Analytical Bridge between P/Es and Solid Economics," Credit Suisse, January 29, 2014.
27. Ibid.
28. Ibid.
29. Berkshire Hathaway 1992 Annual Report.
30. Michael Mauboussin, "What Does an EV/EBITDA Multiple Mean?" *Blue Mountain Capital Management* (September 13, 2018).
31. Mauboussin and Callahan, "What Does a Price-Earnings Multiple Mean?"
32. Ibid.
33. Berkshire Hathaway 2000 Annual Meeting.
34. Ibid.
35. Ibid.
36. Berkshire Hathaway 2000 Annual Report.

37. Ibid.
38. Warren Buffett testimonial in Philip A. Fisher, *Common Stocks and Uncommon Profits: And Other Writings:* Wiley Investment Classic (New York: John Wiley & Sons, 1996).
39. As told by Ken Fisher in the Introduction of Robert G. Hagstrom, *The Warren Buffett Way*, 3rd ed. (Hoboken, NJ: John Wiley & Sons, 2014).
40. John Train, *The Money Masters: Nine Great Investors Their Winning Strategies and How You Can Apply Them* (New York: Penguin Books, 1980), p. 60.
41. Fisher, *Common Stocks and Uncommon Profits*, p. 19.
42. Philip Fisher, "Developing an Investment Philosophy," The Financial Analysts Research Foundation, Monograph Number 10, p. 29.
43. Fisher, *Common Stocks and Uncommon Profits*, pp. 16–18.
44. "The Money Men: How Omaha Beats Wall Street," *Forbes* (November 1, 1969): 82
45. Warren Buffett, "What We Can Learn From Philip Fisher," *Forbes* (October 19, 1987): 40.
46. John Burr Williams, "Fifty Years of Investment Analysis," The Financial Analysis Research Foundation.
47. John Burr Williams, *The Theory of Investment Value* (Fraser Publishing Company), Preface.
48. Berkshire Hathaway 1992 Annual Report.
49. Berkshire Hathaway 2000 Annual Meeting.
50. Berkshire Hathaway 1992 Annual Report.
51. John Burr Williams, pp. 167–169.
52. Berkshire Hathaway 2000 Annual Report.
53. Berkshire Hathaway 2010 Annual Report.
54. Bruce Greenwald, Judd Kahn, Paul Sonkin, and Michael van Biema, *Value Investing: From Graham to Buffett and Beyond* (New York: John Wiley & Sons, 2001), p. 159.
55. Robert G. Hagstrom, *The Detective and the Investor: Uncovering Investment Techniques from the Legendary Sleuths* (New York: Texere LLC, 2002).
56. Berkshire Hathaway 1989 Annual Report.
57. Robert G Hagstrom, *The Warren Buffett Way: Investment Strategies of the World's Greatest Investor* (New York: John Wiley & Sons, 1994), p. 291.
58. Tom Gayner, "Talks with Google," June 30, 2015.
59. Berkshire Hathaway 1997 Annual Meeting.
60. *Outstanding Investor Digest* (August 10, 1995): 21.
61. Christopher Freeman, "Schumpeter's Business Cycles and Techno-economic Paradigms," in *Techno-economic Paradigms: Essays in Honor of Carolta Perez*, edited by Wolfgang Dreschler, Erik Reinert, and Rainer Kattel (London: Anthem Press, 2009), p. 136.
62. Carolta Perez, *Technological Revolutions: The Dynamics of Bubbles and Golden Ages* (Cheltenham, UK: Edward Elgar, 2002), p. 11.
63. Ibid., pp. 14, 18.
64. Ibid., p. 30.
65. Ibid., p. 36.
66. Ibid.

67. Ibid., p .43.
68. W. Brian Arthur, "Increasing Returns and the New World of Business," *Financial Management* (July–August 1996).
69. Commonly referred to as "Arthur's Law."
70. Janet Lowe, *The Man Who Beats the S&P: Investing with Bill Miller* (John Wiley & Sons, Canada: 2002), p. 55. Also, interview with author.
71. Ibid., p., 56.
72. Ibid., p. 19.
73. Ibid.
74. Robert Hagstrom worked with Bill Miller at Legg Mason Capital Management from 1998 to 2012.
75. Lowe, *The Man Who Beats the S&P*, p. 63.
76. Ibid., p. 62.
77. William E. Fruhan, Jr., *Financial Strategy: Studies in the Creation, Transfer, and Destruction of Shareholder Value.* (Homewood, IL: Richard D. Irwin, 1979), pp. 65–66.
78. Bill Miller, Legg Mason Value Trust 2001 Annual Report.
79. Janet Lowe, *The Man Who Beats the S&P*, p. 66. Also, interview with author.
80. Brian McGuinness, *Wittgentein: A Young Life: Young Ludgwig 1889–1921*, University of California Press, 1988), p. 118.
81. Lowe, *The Man Who Beats the S&P*, p. 114.
82. Robert G. Hagstrom, *The Warren Buffett Portfolio: Mastering the Power of the Focus Investment Strategy* (New York: John Wiley & Sons, 1999), pp. 102–103.
83. Lowe, *The Man Who Beats the S&P*, p. 32.
84. Andrew Kilpatrick, *Of Permanent Value: The Story of Warren Buffett—2020 Elephant Edition* (Birmingham, AL: AKPE Publishing, 2020), p. 953.
85. Ibid.
86. Author's notes from the Berkshire Hathaway 2019 Annual Meeting.
87. Kilpatrick, *Of Permanent Value* (2020), p. 14.
88. Ibid.
89. Author Robert Hagstrom is the Senior Portfolio Manager for the EquityCompass Investment Management, LLC, Global Leaders Portfolio, which owns Apple, Inc.
90. Paul Johnson, "Seminar in Value Investing: EMBA," Apple: Case Study: 3A, May, 2020.
91. Ibid.
92. Kilpatrick, *Of Permanent Value* (2020), pp. 14–15.
93. *Columbia Business School: A Century of Ideas*, Brian Thomas, editor (New York: Columbia University Press, 2016).
94. Warren Buffett's speech to the Columbia Business School, "Superinvestors of Graham-and-Doddsville" appeared in the 1984 fall edition of *Hermes*.
95. Berkshire Hathaway 1992 Annual Report, p. 19.

Chapter 4: Business-Driven Investing

1. Benjamin Graham, *The Intelligent Investor* (New York: Harper & Row, 1973), p. 286.
2. Robert G. Hagstrom, *The Warren Buffett Way* (New York: John Wiley & Sons, 1995), p. 97.
3. Graham, *The Intelligent Investor*, p. 286.
4. Ibid., p. 102.
5. Ibid.
6. Ibid., p. 107.
7. Berkshire Hathaway 1987 Annual Report, p. 11.
8. Hagstrom, *The Warren Buffett Way*, p. 55.
9. A reference to Rodman Edward Serling; American screenwriter most famous for his science fiction TV series, *The Twilight Zone* (1959–1965).
10. Robert Lenzner, "Warren Buffett's Idea of Heaven: I Don't Have to Work with People I Don't Like," *Forbes* (October 18, 1993): 43.
11. Ibid.
12. Berkshire Hathaway 1987 Annual Report, p. 11.
13. Carol Loomis, "Inside Story of Warren Buffett," *Fortune* (April 11, 1988): 34.
14. *Fortune* (November 29, 1993): 11.
15. Berkshire Hathaway 1992 Annual Report, p. 15.
16. Berkshire Hathaway 1987 Annual Report, p. 7.
17. Berkshire Hathaway Letters to Shareholders (1977–1983), p. 51.
18. Andrew Kilpatrick, *Of Permanent Value: The Story of Warren Buffett* (Birmingham: AKPE Publishing, 2004), p. 1356.
19. Michael Mauboussin and Daniel Callahan, "Total Addressable Market: Methods to Estimate a Company's Potential Sales." Credit-Suisse Global Financial Strategies, September 1, 2015.
20. Berkshire Hathaway 1991 Annual Report, p. 8.
21. Lezner, "Warren Buffett's Idea of Heaven."
22. Berkshire Hathaway 1984 Annual Report, p. 15.
23. Berkshire Hathaway 1986 Annual Report, p. 25.
24. Empirical Research Partners, Stock Selection: Research and Results, "Free Cash Flow and the Stock Option Question," December, 2019.
25. Berkshire Hathaway Letters to Shareholders (1977–1983), p. 17.
26. Berkshire Hathaway 1987 Annual Report, p. 20
27. EquityCompass Investment Management, LLC., Tim McCann, Director of Research.
28. Berkshire Hathaway 1989 Annual Report, p. 5.
29. Paul Sonkin and Paul Johnson, *Pitch the Perfect Investment: The Essential Guide to Winning on Wall Street* (Hoboken, NJ: John Wiley & Sons, 2017), p. 69.
30. John Rasmussen, "Buffett Talks Strategy with Students," *Omaha-World Herald* (January 2, 1994): 26.

31. Sonkin and Johnson, *Pitch the Perfect Investment*, p. 69.
32. Ibid., pp. 63–64.
33. John C. Bogle, "The (Non) Lessons of History—and the (Real) Lessons of Returns and Costs." Remarks before The American Philosophical Society, Philadelphia, PA, November 10, 2012.
34. Sonkin and Johnson, *Pitch the Perfect Investment*, pp. 63–64.
35. Berkshire Hathaway 1994 Annual Report, p. 2.
36. Benjamin Graham and David Dodd, *Security Analysis* (1934), as quoted in Sonkin and Johnson, *Pitch the Perfect Investment*, p. 130.
37. Seth A. Klarman, *Margin of Safety: Risk Averse Value Investing Strategies for the Thoughtful Investor* (New York: Harper Collins, 1991), as quoted in Sonkin and Johnson, *Pitch the Perfect Investment*.
38. Berkshire Hathaway 1999 Annual Report, p. 5.
39. Andrew Kilpatrick, *Of Permanent Value: The Story of Warren Buffett* (Birmingham, AL: AKPE Publishing, 1998), p. 800.
40. A commonly quoted remark from Warren Buffett.
41. Berkshire Hathaway 1986 Annual Report, p. 5.
42. Berkshire Hathaway 1989 Annual Report, p. 22.
43. William N. Thorndike, Jr., *The Outsiders: Eight Unconventional CEOs and Their Radically Rational Blueprint for Success* (Boston: Harvard Business Review Press, 2012), p. 201.
44. Berkshire Hathaway 1994 Annual Report, p. 5.
45. Berkshire Hathaway 1983 Annual Report, p. 1.
46. Berkshire Hathaway 1980 Annual Report, p. 2.
47. Ibid.
48. Berkshire Hathaway 1982 Annual Report, p. 2.
49. Berkshire Hathaway 1991 Annual Report, p. 3.
50. Ibid.
51. Berkshire Hathaway 1993 Annual Report, p. 9.
52. Berkshire Hathaway 1991 Annual Report, p. 11.
53. Berkshire Hathaway 1997 Annual Report, p. 12.
54. Berkshire Hathaway 2019 Annual Report, p. 4.
55. Ibid.
56. Ibid.
57. Berkshire Hathaway 1983 Annual Report, p. 3.
58. Edgar Lawrence Smith, *Common Stocks as Long Term Investments* (New York: The Macmillan Company, 1928), p. 115.
59. Jack Treynor, *Treynor on Institutional Investing* (Hoboken, NJ: John Wiley & Sons, 2008), p. 425.
60. Ibid., p. 424.
61. Ibid.
62. Andrei Shleifer and Robert Vishny, "The New Theory of the Firm: Equilibrium Short Horizons of Investors and Firms," *American Economic Review: Papers and Proceedings*, 80, no. 2 (1990), 148–153.
63. Ibid.
64. Robert G. Hagstrom, *The Warren Buffett Way: The Third Edition* (Hoboken, NJ: John Wiley & Sons, 2014), p. 204.

Chapter 5: It's Not That Active Management Doesn't Work

1. Peter L. Bernstein, *Capital Ideas: The Improbable Origins of Wall Street* (New York: The Free Press, 1992), p. 44.
2. Ibid., p. 37.
3. Ibid., p. 46.
4. Ibid., p. 47.
5. Harry Markowitz, "Portfolio Selection," *The Journal of Finance* 7, no. 1 (March 1952): 77–91.
6. Ibid., p.77
7. Ibid., p. 89.
8. Berkshire Hathaway 1975 Annual Report, p. 3.
9. *Outstanding Investor Digest*, April 8, 1990, p. 18.
10. Berkshire Hathaway 1993 Annual Report, p. 13.
11. Ibid., p. 10.
12. Berkshire Hathaway 2014 Annual Report, p. 19.
13. Berkshire Hathaway 1993 Annual Report, p. 11.
14. Berkshire Hathaway 1996 Annual Report, p. 3.
15. Markowitz, p. 899.
16. Ibid.
17. Berkshire Hathaway 1993 Annual Report, p. 12.
18. Ibid., p. 11.
19. Ibid.
20. Robert G. Hagstrom, *The Warren Buffett Portfolio: Mastering the Power of the Focus Investment Strategy* (New York: John Wiley & Sons, 1999), p. 1.
21. *Outstanding Investor Digest* (August 8, 1996): 29.
22. K. J. Martijn Cremers and Antti Petajisto, "How Active Is Your Fund Manager? A New Measure That Predicts Performance," *Review of Financial Studies* 22, no. 9 (September 2009): 3329–3365.
23. Martign Cremers and Ankur Pareek, "Patient Capital Outperformance: The Investment Skill of High Active Share Managers Who Trade Infrequently," *Journal of Financial Economics* 122 (August 24, 2016): 288–305.
24. Ibid.
25. Martijn Cremers, "Active Share and the Three Pillars of Active Management: Skill, Conviction, and Opportunity," *Financial Analysts Journal* 73, no. 2 (2017): 61.
26. Ibid., p. 61.
27. Ibid., p. 63.
28. Ibid.
29. Amit Goyal and Sunil Wahal, "The Selection and Termination of Investment Management Firms by Plan Sponsors," *The Journal of Finance* 63, no. 4 (2008): 1805–1847.
30. Edward J. Russo and Paul J.H. Shoemaker, *Winning Decisions: Getting It Right the First Time* (New York: Doubleday, 2002).
31. Robert Rubin, *Harvard Commencement Address*, 2001.

32. Claude Shannon, "A Mathematical Theory of Communication," *The Bell Systems Technical Journal* (July, 1948): 379–423.
33. Fischer Black, quoted in Peter L. Bernstein, *Capital Ideas*, p. 124.
34. Berkshire Hathaway 1988 Annual Report, p. 17.
35. Ibid.
36. Jason Zweig, "From a Skeptic: A Lesson on Beating the Market," *Wall Street Journal* (December 22-23, 2018).
37. Ibid.
38. Bernstein, p. 3.
39. Bernstein, p. 14.
40. Peter Schjeldahl, *Let's See: Writing on Art from The New Yorker* (New York: Thomas & Hudson, 2008), p. 11.
41. Bernstein, p. 9.
42. Ibid.
43. *Outstanding Investor Digest*, September 24, 1998, p. 40.
44. Berkshire Hathaway 1998 Annual Report, p. 18.
45. Berkshire Hathaway 1987 Annual Report, p. 12.
46. Combined Quotes: Berkshire Hathaway 2000 Annual Report, p. 14, and Berkshire Hathaway 2013 Annual Report, p. 18.

Chapter 6: The Money Mind: Sportsman, Teacher, Artist

1. Andrew Kilpatrick, *Of Permanent Value: The Story of Warren Buffett: 2020 Elephant Edition* (Birmingham, AL: AKPE Publishing, 2020), p. 151.
2. *Warren Buffett Back to School: Question and Answer Session with Business Students* (BN Publishing: 2008), p. 9.
3. Heather Reid, *Introduction to the Philosophy of Sport* (Lanham, MD: Rowman & Littlefield Publishers, 2012), p. 12.
4. Arnold LeUnes and Jack Nation, *Sports Psychology: An Introduction* (Wadsworth, CA: Pacific Grove, 2002), as quoted in *Pragmatism and the Philosophy of Sport*, edited by Richard Lally, Douglas Anderson, and John Kagg (Lanham, MD: Lexington Books, 2013), p. 21.
5. John Gibson, *Performance versus Results: A Critique of the Values in Contemporary Sport* (Albany: State University of New York Press, 1993), p. 72.
6. Michael Novak, *The Joy of Sports: End Zones, Bases, Baskets, Bulls, and the Consecration of the American Spirit* (New York: Basic Books, 1976), p. 121.
7. Douglas R. Hochstetler, "Process and the Sport of Experience," in *Pragmatism and the Philosophy of Sport*, p. 18.
8. Novak, *Joy of Sports*, p. 159.
9. Hochstetler, "Process and the Sport of Experience," p. 29.
10. R. Scott Kretchmar, "From Test to Contest: An Analysis of Two Kinds of Counterpoint in Sport," *Journal of the Philosophy of Sport* 2 (1975): 23:30.
11. Robert Armstron, Eric Platt, Oliver Ralph, "Warren Buffett: I'm Having More Fun Than Any 88-Year-Old in the World," *Financial Times* (April 25, 2019).

12. Linda Simon, *Genuine Reality: A Life of William James* (New York: Harcourt Brace & Company, 1998), p. 264.
13. Robert D. Richardson, *William James: In the Maelstrom of American Modernism* (Boston: Houghton Mifflin Company, 2006), p. 342.
14. Simon, *Genuine Reality*, p. 267.
15. Lauren Eskreis-Winkler, Katherine Milkman, Dena M. Gromet, and Angela L. Duckworth, "A large-scale field experiment shows giving advice improves academic outcomes for the advisor," *PNAS* 116, no. 30 (July 23, 2019): 14808–14810.
16. Andrew M. Holowchak and Heather L. Reid, *Aretism: An Ancient Sports Philosophy for the Modern Sports World* (Lanham, MD: Lexington Books, 2011), p. 131.
17. Ibid., p. 128.
18. Reid, *Introduction to the Philosophy of Sport*, p. 129.
19. Ibid., p. 131.
20. John Kaag, *Sick Souls, Healthy Minds: How William James Can Save Your Life* (Princeton, NJ: Princeton University Press, 2020), p. 153.
21. Ibid., 155.
22. John Kaag, *American Philosophy: A Love Story* (New York: Farrar, Straus and Giroux, 2016), p. 245.
23. Robert G. Hagstrom, *The Warren Buffett Way: Investment Strategies of the World's Greatest Investor* (New York: John Wiley & Sons, 1994), p. 236.
24. Carol Loomis, *Tap Dancing to Work: Warren Buffett on Practically Everything, 1966–2012* (New York: Penguin, 2012), p. xviii.
25. Andrew Kilpatrick, *Of Permanent Value: The Story of Warren Buffett: 2015 Golden Anniversary Edition* (Birmingham, AL: AKPE Publishing, 2015), p. 3.
26. Peter Schjeldahl, *Hot Cold, Heavy, Light, 100 Art Writings, 1988–2016* (New York: Abrams Press, 2019), p. 32.
27. Lance Esplund, *The Art of Looking: How to Read Modern and Contemporary Art* (New York: Basic Books, 2018) p. 231.
28. Ibid.
29. Kaag, *Sick Souls, Healthy Minds*, p. 169.
30. Steve Jordan, *The Oracle of Omaha: How Warren Buffett and His Hometown Shaped Each Other* (Marceline, MO: Wadsworth, 2013), p. 211.
31. Michael Mauboussin and Dan Callahan, "Why Corporate Longevity Matters: What Index Turnover Tells Us About Corporate Results." Credit-Suisse: Global Financial Strategies (April 16, 2014).
32. Ibid.
33. Kilpatrick, *Of Permanent Value: 2015 Golden Anniversary Edition*, p. 1269.
34. Quotes from Sue Decker and Carol Loomis are attributed to the 2018 Berkshire Hathaway Shareholder Meeting.
35. Nicole Friedman, "Buffett Says Exit Won't Halt Successes," *Wall Street Journal* (May 5, 2018).

Index